Title: Exploring the Space Industry: Innovations, Challenges, and Future Trends

Copyright © [2024] by [Mustafa K. Al-Dori]

Published by [Self-Published]

Contact us:

mustafa.k.mustafa92@gmail.com

Dedication:
For my parents, whose love and guidance shaped my world.

About the Author

Dr. Mustafa Kamal Mustafa Al-Dori is a passionate scholar and practitioner in the field of business administration, specializing in marketing. He earned his doctorate from Ain Shams University, Faculty of Business, where he developed a deep understanding of the intricacies of marketing dynamics in today's ever-evolving business landscape.

Despite his academic credentials, Dr. Al-Dori's true passion lies in the practical application of management principles. He has played a pivotal role in numerous projects and has significantly contributed to small and medium-sized enterprises, where his insights and strategies have led to remarkable successes. His experience in the field has equipped him with a unique perspective, bridging the gap between theory and real-world application.

Dr. Al-Dori is also a distinguished speaker at various conferences, where he shares his expertise and innovative ideas. He has contributed to many training programs, empowering aspiring professionals with the knowledge and skills necessary for success in the competitive world of business.

His research work is widely recognized, with several publications in high-impact international journals. Dr. Al-Dori's commitment to advancing the field of marketing is evident in his contributions to academic discourse and his dedication to fostering the next generation of business leaders. Through his work, he continues to inspire others, demonstrating that the fusion of theory and practice is essential for achieving meaningful outcomes in the world of business.

About the book

"Exploring the Space Industry: Innovations, Challenges, and Future Trends" is a comprehensive book that delves deeply into the space industry, exploring how it has become one of the most innovative and challenging sectors in the modern era. The book aims to provide an in-depth overview of the history of space, technological advancements, key players, economic impact, challenges, and future opportunities.

Book Objectives:

This book is aimed at a wide audience, including:

- Technology and innovation enthusiasts

- Researchers in the space field

- Investors in the space industry

- Policy makers and legislators

- The general public interested in space exploration

Key Themes:

- **The History and Evolution of Space Exploration**: The book discusses how the industry has developed, from the early stages of space technology to the current era of commercial spaceflight. It reviews key historical milestones such as the Space Race, the establishment of national space agencies, and their impact on technological and scientific progress.

- **Diverse Space Industries**: The book explores various segments of the space industry, such as government space agencies, private companies, launch services, space tourism, satellite manufacturing, and scientific research.

- **Leading Technologies**: It covers the latest innovations in space technology, such as propulsion systems, robotics, and space mining, and how these technologies are applied in both current and future missions.

- **Practical Applications**: The book highlights how space technology is used in telecommunications, weather forecasting, global navigation systems, national security, and scientific research.

- **Key Players**: A detailed analysis of the major players in the space industry, including NASA, SpaceX, Blue Origin, and others. It also examines international collaborations and the growing competition between startups and established companies.

- **Economic Impact**: The book delves into the economic significance of the space industry, exploring market growth, regional contributions, and global investments, along with predictions for the future.

- **Regulatory and Ethical Frameworks**: It discusses legal, environmental, and ethical considerations surrounding space exploration, including international treaties and space governance.

- **Challenges and Opportunities**: The book focuses on the technical, economic, and societal challenges faced by the space industry, as well as opportunities for innovation and collaboration.

- **Future Trends**: The book looks ahead to the future of the space industry, examining topics like space colonization, artificial intelligence in space missions, and the role of space in sustainable development.

Importance of the Book:

This book serves as a crucial guide to understanding the complexities of the space industry and the future trends that may have an unprecedented impact on humanity. It aims to promote collaboration among stakeholders while encouraging innovation and strategic thinking.

Table of contents

Preface

The space industry has always captured the human imagination, from the earliest dreams of exploring the stars to the awe-inspiring technological feats of modern space missions. What was once considered science fiction has become a reality, with rockets regularly launching into orbit, satellites providing critical services across the globe, and the prospect of humans living on other planets no longer a distant fantasy.

This book, *Exploring the Space Industry: Innovations, Challenges, and Future Trends*, is a comprehensive examination of the dynamic and rapidly evolving field of space exploration. It seeks to provide readers with a deep understanding of the forces driving the industry, the key players involved, the technological advancements pushing the boundaries of what's possible, and the challenges that lie ahead. As the space industry becomes more integral to global economies and everyday life, its importance grows beyond the realm of engineers and scientists—it becomes a subject of interest for policymakers, investors, entrepreneurs, and the general public alike.

The structure of the book reflects this multifaceted nature. We begin by tracing the rich history of space exploration, looking at key milestones and how early advancements have shaped today's space sector. From there, we move to an exploration of the various types of space industries, from government agencies to private enterprises, and how they interact. The discussion extends to the technologies driving the industry, as well as the economic, regulatory, and ethical considerations shaping its future.

As the space industry continues to grow, its applications are increasingly diverse—ranging from telecommunications and earth observation to tourism and even the prospect of resource extraction from other celestial bodies. The opportunities are vast, but so are the challenges, whether they be technical, financial, or ethical. These are themes that we will explore in depth, particularly with an eye on future trends that could redefine the industry in the coming decades.

Ultimately, this book aims to provide a roadmap for understanding the space industry's past, present, and future. Whether you are a student, researcher, industry professional, or simply an enthusiast, I hope that this book will offer valuable insights into one of humanity's most ambitious endeavors. By fostering a better understanding of the innovations and challenges shaping the space industry, we can look ahead to a future where space exploration plays an increasingly central role in our lives.

Let us embark on this journey together, exploring not only the vastness of space but also the limitless potential of human innovation.

Introduction

In the grand tapestry of human achievement, the exploration of space stands out as one of the most remarkable endeavors of our time. From the moment humanity first gazed up at the stars, the desire to explore the unknown has driven countless innovations and inspired generations. The space industry has evolved from a mere aspiration into a thriving global enterprise, reshaping our understanding of the universe and our place within it.

Today, the space industry encompasses a wide array of activities, including scientific research, satellite communications, Earth observation, and even the burgeoning field of space tourism. With the advent of private companies like SpaceX, Blue Origin, and others, the landscape of space exploration has transformed dramatically, making it more accessible than ever before. These developments are not just technological marvels; they are gateways to a new era of discovery and opportunity.

As we delve into the chapters of this book, we will explore the intricate history of space exploration, tracing its origins from early technological breakthroughs to the modern-day missions that push the boundaries of human capability. We will examine the key players in the industry, both governmental and private, and highlight the collaborations that drive innovation forward.

We will also take a closer look at the technologies propelling the space sector, from advanced propulsion systems to artificial intelligence, and how they are revolutionizing our ability to explore beyond our planet. Additionally, the practical applications of space technology are vast, influencing everything from global communications to environmental monitoring, thus underscoring the industry's significance in our daily lives.

However, with these advancements come challenges. The regulatory frameworks governing space activities are still evolving, and ethical considerations regarding resource extraction, environmental impacts, and the commercialization of space are pressing issues that must be addressed.

The book aims to provide a balanced perspective on the opportunities and challenges facing the space industry today. We will explore growth trends, economic impacts, and the critical importance of collaboration among nations and private entities. Furthermore, we will look toward the future, contemplating innovations on the horizon and the potential for sustainable development in space.

As we embark on this journey through the cosmos, let us remember that the exploration of space is not just a quest for knowledge; it is a testament to human ingenuity, resilience, and the unyielding spirit of discovery. Whether you are an industry professional, a student, or a curious reader, this book invites you to engage with the stories, technologies, and challenges that define the space industry today and in the future. Together, let us explore the vastness of space and the infinite possibilities that lie beyond our Earth.

Chapter 1: History of Space Exploration

1. Early Developments in Space Technology
2. Key Milestones in Space Missions
3. The Space Race and Its Impact
4. Establishment of Space Agencies
5. Evolution of Commercial Spaceflight

Chapter 1

History of Space Exploration

Introduction

Space exploration stands as one of humanity's greatest achievements, marking a pivotal leap in our understanding of the universe and the mysteries that lie beyond our planet. This chapter delves into the fascinating journey of space exploration, beginning with the early technological advancements that paved the way for humanity's first steps into orbit and extending through the historic moments that reshaped global policies and scientific endeavors.

We will explore the early developments in space technology, highlighting the key innovations that made space missions possible. From the launch of "Sputnik," the world's first artificial satellite, to the groundbreaking "Apollo" missions that landed humans on the moon, this chapter will walk through the critical milestones that defined the space race. Additionally, we will examine the establishment of major space agencies, such as NASA and the European Space Agency, and their significant contributions to advancing space exploration.

Furthermore, the chapter will cover the evolution of commercial spaceflight, which has revolutionized the space industry by allowing private enterprises, like SpaceX, to participate in space missions and fundamentally change how we approach space exploration.

By understanding the history of space exploration, we gain insight into how far we have come and the foundation on which the future of the space industry is being built.

1. Early Developments in Space Technology

The dream of space exploration has captivated the human imagination for centuries, but it wasn't until the 20th century that advancements in technology made it a reality. The journey toward space began with key technological innovations in rocketry and aerodynamics. These innovations laid the groundwork for what would become an international race to conquer the stars, significantly impacting science, military strategy, and global collaboration. This section examines the earliest developments in space technology, from primitive rocketry experiments to the technological breakthroughs that enabled human spaceflight. We will explore the contributions of pioneers such as Konstantin Tsiolkovsky, Robert Goddard, and Wernher von Braun, whose work turned dreams of space travel into a scientific pursuit. Examples of early missions and projects that set the stage for modern space exploration will also be discussed.

1.1. Ancient Foundations of Rocketry

While modern space technology is rooted in 20th-century science, the basic principles of rocketry trace back centuries. The earliest recorded use of rocket-like devices occurred in China around the 13th century, where gunpowder was used in simple rockets for military purposes. These rudimentary rockets lacked guidance systems and were primarily used as weapons of war during battles, but they demonstrated a basic understanding of propulsion. Over time, other civilizations, such as those in the Middle East and Europe, experimented with early forms of rocket technology, but the understanding of how to control flight was still lacking.

The concept of using rockets to escape Earth's gravity and reach space, however, remained largely a dream until the modern era when scientific principles began to catch up with human imagination.

1.2. Konstantin Tsiolkovsky: The Father of Rocketry

Konstantin Tsiolkovsky, a Russian schoolteacher, is considered one of the founding figures of astronautics. In the late 19th century, Tsiolkovsky proposed theoretical models for space travel. Although he did not conduct physical experiments, his writings laid the mathematical and theoretical foundation for rocketry. One of his most significant contributions was the Tsiolkovsky rocket equation, which calculated the velocity a spacecraft must achieve to escape Earth's atmosphere.

Tsiolkovsky also envisioned the use of multi-stage rockets, a concept that would become essential for space travel. His visionary work, such as ideas for space stations and human colonization of space, was ahead of its time, but it inspired future scientists and engineers who turned his theories into practical designs.

Example: Tsiolkovsky's Influence on Modern Space Programs

Many of Tsiolkovsky's ideas, such as multi-stage rockets and the use of liquid fuel, were later incorporated into the design of rockets by Soviet and American space engineers. His work on the relationship between rocket speed and fuel consumption directly influenced the development of spacecraft like the Saturn V, which played a crucial role in the Apollo missions.

1.3. Robert Goddard: The Pioneer of Liquid-Fueled Rockets

While Tsiolkovsky provided the theoretical foundation, it was Robert H. Goddard, an American physicist, who translated those ideas into practical technology. Often referred to as the father of modern rocketry, Goddard was the first to successfully build and launch a liquid-fueled rocket, a major breakthrough in space technology. In 1926, Goddard launched the first liquid-fueled rocket in Auburn, Massachusetts, which flew for 2.5 seconds and reached an altitude of 41 feet.

Goddard's innovations included the development of gyroscopic stabilization, throttleable rocket engines, and fuel pumps. Despite facing skepticism from his peers and the public, his work was critical to the future of rocketry. Goddard's rockets were the first to demonstrate that controlled, powered flight beyond the atmosphere was feasible, paving the way for space exploration.

Example: Goddard's Legacy in Modern Rocketry

NASA and other space agencies honor Robert Goddard as one of the key pioneers in space technology. His experiments in the early 20th century directly influenced later developments in missile technology and space exploration, including the V-2 rocket developed by Wernher von Braun and his team during World War II.

1.4. The Development of the V-2 Rocket: Wernher von Braun's Contribution

Wernher von Braun, a German engineer, is perhaps best known for his work on the development of the V-2 rocket during World War II. The V-2 was the world's first long-range guided ballistic missile, and it marked a significant leap forward in rocket technology. Capable of reaching altitudes of over 100 kilometers, the V-2 was the first human-made object to travel into space.

Following World War II, von Braun and many of his colleagues were brought to the United States under Operation Paperclip, a secret program aimed at recruiting German scientists to aid in American technological development. In the United States, von Braun played a key role in developing rockets for NASA, including the Saturn V, which would later take astronauts to the moon.

Example: V-2 Rocket and Its Impact on Space Exploration

The V-2 rocket's design and technology directly influenced post-war space programs in both the United States and the Soviet Union. It was the first significant step in building rockets capable of reaching space, and its development paved the way for future space exploration missions. Without the V-2's technological advances, projects like Apollo might not have been possible as early as they were.

1.5. Sputnik and the Dawn of the Space Age

The Soviet Union's successful launch of *Sputnik 1* on October 4, 1957, marked the beginning of the space age and the start of the space race between the United States and the Soviet Union. *Sputnik 1* was the first artificial satellite to orbit the Earth, and its success stunned the world. At 58 centimeters in diameter and weighing 83.6 kilograms, *Sputnik 1* orbited the Earth in 96 minutes, sending back radio signals that could be detected by radios around the world.

The launch of *Sputnik 1* had a profound impact on the geopolitical landscape, intensifying Cold War tensions and sparking a fierce competition between the two superpowers for dominance in space. It also led to the creation of NASA in 1958, as the United States sought to catch up with Soviet advancements in space technology.

Example: The Global Impact of Sputnik

The launch of *Sputnik 1* not only demonstrated the Soviet Union's technological superiority at the time, but it also had a lasting impact on the world's perception of space exploration. It motivated the United States to invest heavily in space technology, eventually leading to the Apollo moon landings. In addition, *Sputnik* initiated discussions about international cooperation in space and the importance of space exploration for all humanity.

1.6. The Establishment of NASA and Early Space Programs

In response to the launch of *Sputnik*, the United States established the National Aeronautics and Space Administration (NASA) on October 1, 1958. NASA's primary goal was to ensure that America would not only catch up with but surpass the Soviet Union in space exploration. One of NASA's earliest programs was Project Mercury, which aimed to send the first Americans into space.

The program culminated in May 1961 with the launch of Alan Shepard aboard *Freedom 7*, making him the first American to travel into space. This success set the stage for the Apollo program, which aimed to land humans on the moon, an objective that was achieved on July 20, 1969, when Neil Armstrong and Buzz Aldrin stepped onto the lunar surface during the Apollo 11 mission.

Example: NASA's Role in the Space Race

NASA's early successes, such as the Mercury and Gemini programs, helped establish the United States as a dominant force in space exploration. These programs provided critical experience in human spaceflight and orbital mechanics, laying the groundwork for the Apollo moon landings and later missions to explore the solar system.

Conclusion

The early developments in space technology set the foundation for one of humanity's most remarkable achievements: the ability to explore space. From ancient rocketry to modern space agencies, the contributions of visionary scientists and engineers like Konstantin Tsiolkovsky, Robert Goddard, and Wernher von Braun were instrumental in transforming the dream of space exploration into a reality. The launch of *Sputnik* and the establishment of NASA marked the dawn of the space age, setting the stage for future missions that would expand our understanding of the universe.

2. Key Milestones in Space Missions

Space missions represent some of the greatest achievements in human history. Over the past six decades, humanity has made extraordinary strides in exploring the universe beyond our planet, from launching the first artificial satellite to landing astronauts on the moon and sending robotic probes to the farthest reaches of the solar system. Each mission has pushed the boundaries of what is possible, contributing to our understanding of space, advancing technology, and expanding our reach across the cosmos. This section delves into the key milestones in space missions, analyzing landmark events that have shaped the course of space exploration. We will explore early missions, human spaceflight achievements, lunar landings, interplanetary exploration, and the more recent missions aimed at understanding deep space.

2.1. The Launch of Sputnik 1 (1957)

On October 4, 1957, the Soviet Union launched *Sputnik 1*, the world's first artificial satellite, into Earth's orbit. This historic event marked the beginning of the space age and was a significant geopolitical achievement during the Cold War. *Sputnik 1* orbited the Earth in 96 minutes and sent back simple radio signals, which could be picked up by receivers around the world.

The launch of *Sputnik 1* had a profound impact, as it demonstrated the Soviet Union's capability to develop ballistic missile technology that could potentially deliver nuclear weapons over great distances. For the United States, it signaled that the Soviets were ahead in the space race, leading to increased funding for American space research and the eventual establishment of NASA in 1958.

Example: Global Reactions to *Sputnik 1*

The launch of *Sputnik 1* was met with awe and concern globally. In the United States, it led to a sense of urgency to match Soviet space achievements, which directly contributed to the acceleration of the American space program. It was also a psychological victory for the Soviet Union, as it demonstrated technological superiority in space.

2.2. Yuri Gagarin: The First Human in Space (1961)

On April 12, 1961, Soviet cosmonaut Yuri Gagarin became the first human to journey into outer space and orbit the Earth aboard the spacecraft *Vostok 1*. Gagarin's mission lasted just 108 minutes, but it was a monumental milestone in human space exploration. His successful flight made him an international hero and reinforced Soviet dominance in the early years of the space race.

This achievement demonstrated that humans could survive the rigors of space travel and marked a critical step toward more advanced human space missions, including landing on the moon. Gagarin's flight also prompted the United States to intensify its efforts, leading to President John F. Kennedy's famous speech in which he committed the nation to landing a man on the moon before the end of the 1960s.

Example: The Impact of Gagarin's Flight

Yuri Gagarin's flight was not only a significant achievement for the Soviet space program but also a turning point in the global perception of space exploration. It showed that human space travel was not just possible but also survivable, encouraging both the Soviet Union and the United States to invest heavily in manned spaceflight.

2.3. Apollo 11: The First Moon Landing (1969)

One of the most iconic milestones in space exploration occurred on July 20, 1969, when NASA's *Apollo 11* mission successfully landed humans on the moon. Astronauts Neil Armstrong and Buzz Aldrin became the first humans to set foot on the lunar surface, while Michael Collins orbited the moon in the command module. Armstrong's famous words, "That's one small step for man, one giant leap for mankind," echoed the enormity of the achievement.

The successful landing of *Apollo 11* fulfilled President Kennedy's goal and marked the United States' victory in the space race. It also demonstrated the technological prowess of NASA, showcasing the capability to safely send astronauts to the moon and return them to Earth. The mission was a defining moment not only for the space program but also for human history, representing the potential for human exploration beyond Earth.

Example: The Legacy of Apollo 11

The Apollo 11 mission had a lasting impact on space exploration, sparking a new era of interest in the possibilities of lunar and interplanetary exploration. It also reinforced the idea that humans could go beyond Earth and achieve seemingly impossible feats through scientific and engineering innovation.

2.4. The Mars Rovers: Exploring the Red Planet (1997–Present)

Mars has long been a target of space exploration, and the successful landing of NASA's *Pathfinder* rover in 1997 marked a significant milestone in exploring another planet. The rover sent back images and data that transformed our understanding of Mars' surface and atmosphere. Following this success, NASA sent a series of more advanced rovers, including *Spirit* and *Opportunity* in 2004, and *Curiosity* in 2012. These missions provided invaluable insights into the geology, climate, and potential habitability of Mars.

One of the most recent milestones was the landing of NASA's *Perseverance* rover in 2021. Equipped with cutting-edge technology, including a helicopter drone (*Ingenuity*), *Perseverance* is tasked with searching for signs of past life and collecting samples for future return to Earth. These missions have laid the groundwork for future human exploration of Mars and continue to push the boundaries of what robotic technology can achieve in space.

Example: The Scientific Achievements of the Mars Rovers

The data gathered by the Mars rovers has revolutionized our understanding of the planet's history, particularly the evidence that liquid water once existed on its surface. This discovery has profound implications for the possibility of life beyond Earth and has guided the objectives of future Mars exploration missions.

2.5. The Voyager Missions: Reaching the Edge of the Solar System (1977–Present)

Launched in 1977, NASA's twin Voyager probes— *Voyager 1* and *Voyager 2*—were designed to explore the outer planets of the solar system. *Voyager 1* flew by Jupiter and Saturn, while *Voyager 2* provided the first and only close-up images of Uranus and Neptune. After completing their primary missions, the Voyager spacecraft continued their journey toward the outer edges of the solar system.

In 2012, *Voyager 1* became the first human-made object to enter interstellar space, followed by *Voyager 2* in 2018. The Voyager missions are among the most successful in the history of space exploration, as they have provided a wealth of data about the outer planets and continue to send back information from beyond the solar system.

Example: The Ongoing Impact of the Voyager Missions

The Voyager spacecraft have provided humanity with its most distant exploration of the solar system, offering unprecedented insights into the outer planets and the environment beyond the influence of the Sun. Their longevity and continued operation decades after launch demonstrate the resilience of space technology and its potential for long-term scientific discovery.

2.6. The International Space Station (ISS): A Model for International Collaboration (1998–Present)

The construction and operation of the International Space Station (ISS) is a landmark in space exploration, representing one of the most complex engineering projects in history. Launched in 1998, the ISS is a collaborative effort between NASA, Roscosmos (Russia), ESA (Europe), JAXA (Japan), and CSA (Canada). It serves as a platform for scientific research in microgravity and a proving ground for future missions to the moon, Mars, and beyond.

The ISS is also a model for international collaboration in space, with astronauts from various countries living and working together aboard the station. It has enabled a wide range of experiments in fields such as biology, physics, and materials science, significantly advancing our understanding of space environments and their effects on living organisms.

Example: The Scientific and Diplomatic Achievements of the ISS

The ISS has fostered unprecedented international cooperation in space exploration, bringing together nations with different interests and capabilities to work toward common goals. Scientifically, it has produced thousands of research studies and continues to serve as a critical platform for learning how humans can live and work in space for extended periods.

2.7. SpaceX and the Era of Commercial Spaceflight (2008–Present)

One of the most significant recent milestones in space exploration has been the rise of private companies in space missions, led by SpaceX. Founded by Elon Musk, SpaceX has revolutionized space travel by significantly reducing the cost of launching payloads into space through the development of reusable rockets. In 2008, SpaceX's *Falcon 1* became the first privately developed liquid-fueled rocket to reach orbit. This achievement was followed by more ambitious missions, including the *Falcon 9* and *Dragon* spacecraft, which began delivering cargo to the ISS.

In 2020, SpaceX's *Crew Dragon* successfully carried NASA astronauts to the ISS, marking the first time a private company launched humans into space. The company's ongoing development of the *Starship* spacecraft aims to make interplanetary travel, including missions to Mars, a reality in the near future.

Example: SpaceX and the Future of Space Travel

SpaceX's innovations have disrupted the traditional model of government-led space exploration, opening up new possibilities for commercial ventures in space. The successful launch and recovery of reusable rockets have drastically reduced the cost of space access, making space exploration more sustainable and paving the way for future missions to the moon, Mars, and beyond.

Conclusion

The milestones in space missions have not only expanded our understanding of the universe but also demonstrated the resilience, ingenuity, and collaborative spirit of humanity. From the launch of *Sputnik 1* to the ongoing work aboard the ISS and the commercial ventures led by companies like SpaceX, each achievement has built upon the last, opening new frontiers for exploration. As we look to the future, the lessons learned from these missions will undoubtedly shape the next era of space exploration, pushing us closer to answering some of the most profound questions about our place in the cosmos.

3. The Space Race and Its Impact

The Space Race was a pivotal period during the Cold War in which the United States and the Soviet Union competed for supremacy in space exploration. This competition was not merely about technological advancement; it had deep political, military, and ideological implications. The Space Race, which spanned from the late 1950s to the 1970s, saw groundbreaking achievements such as the launch of the first artificial satellite, the first human spaceflight, and the historic landing of humans on the Moon. These events catalyzed rapid advancements in science and technology, significantly impacting geopolitics, education, and global perceptions of power. This chapter explores the key events of the Space Race, the motivations driving both superpowers, and the lasting legacy of this intense period of human exploration.

3.1. Origins of the Space Race

The origins of the Space Race can be traced back to the Cold War rivalry between the United States and the Soviet Union. Following World War II, both nations emerged as superpowers with vastly different ideologies: the United States championed capitalism and democracy, while the Soviet Union promoted communism and a centrally planned economy. This ideological divide led to intense competition in various arenas, including military power, influence in developing nations, and technological dominance.

One of the key drivers of the Space Race was the development of intercontinental ballistic missiles (ICBMs). Both superpowers understood that dominance in space could translate to military superiority on Earth, as the same technology used to launch satellites and spacecraft could be adapted to deliver nuclear weapons over vast distances. The first major step in the Space Race came when the Soviet Union successfully launched *Sputnik 1* in 1957, shocking the world and signaling the beginning of a new era in space exploration.

Example: The Launch of *Sputnik 1* and Its Global Impact

The Soviet Union's launch of *Sputnik 1* on October 4, 1957, marked the world's first successful satellite mission. This event had a profound impact, especially in the United States, where it sparked fears of Soviet technological superiority and the possibility that the USSR could launch a nuclear attack from space. In response, the United States accelerated its own space program, leading to the creation of NASA in 1958.

3.2. Soviet Achievements in the Early Space Race

The Soviet Union scored several early victories in the Space Race, starting with the launch of *Sputnik 1*. Following this success, the USSR launched *Sputnik 2* on November 3, 1957, carrying *Laika*, the first living creature to orbit the Earth. Although *Laika* did not survive the mission, it demonstrated the Soviet Union's ability to send living beings into space.

Perhaps the most significant Soviet achievement came on April 12, 1961, when cosmonaut Yuri Gagarin became the first human to orbit the Earth aboard *Vostok 1*. Gagarin's mission, which lasted just 108 minutes, was a monumental milestone in human spaceflight and cemented the Soviet Union's dominance in the early years of the Space Race. Gagarin became an international hero, and his mission put immense pressure on the United States to catch up.

Example: Yuri Gagarin's Legacy

Yuri Gagarin's successful mission not only boosted Soviet prestige but also had a profound psychological impact on the United States. It led to a renewed commitment by the U.S. government to win the Space Race, culminating in President John F. Kennedy's pledge to land a man on the Moon by the end of the decade.

3.3. The American Response: Project Mercury and Gemini

In response to Soviet successes, the United States embarked on an ambitious space program designed to match and eventually surpass the achievements of the USSR. NASA's first manned spaceflight program, Project Mercury, aimed to send an American astronaut into orbit. On May 5, 1961, astronaut Alan Shepard became the first American in space during a suborbital flight aboard *Freedom 7*. While Shepard's flight did not achieve orbit, it marked a crucial step forward for the U.S. space program.

The next phase of American space efforts came with the Gemini program, which ran from 1961 to 1966. The Gemini missions were designed to test key technologies and techniques necessary for a lunar landing, including space rendezvous, docking, and extravehicular activity (spacewalking). These missions played a vital role in preparing NASA for its ultimate goal: landing a man on the Moon.

Example: Gemini 4 and America's First Spacewalk

On June 3, 1965, astronaut Ed White performed the first American spacewalk during the Gemini 4 mission. White's 23-minute spacewalk demonstrated that humans could work outside a spacecraft in the vacuum of space, a critical skill for future lunar missions.

3.4. The Race to the Moon

The pinnacle of the Space Race was the competition to land humans on the Moon. Following Yuri Gagarin's successful mission, President John F. Kennedy made a bold commitment: the United States would land a man on the Moon and return him safely to Earth before the end of the decade. This challenge was embodied in the Apollo program, which became the central focus of NASA's efforts throughout the 1960s.

The Soviet Union, too, had aspirations of reaching the Moon, and it developed its own lunar program. However, the Soviets encountered significant setbacks, including the failure of their N1 rocket, which was designed to carry cosmonauts to the Moon. In contrast, NASA's Apollo program made steady progress, culminating in the successful launch of *Apollo 11* on July 16, 1969. Four days later, on July 20, 1969, astronaut Neil Armstrong became the first human to walk on the Moon, followed by Buzz Aldrin. This achievement marked the United States' victory in the Space Race and fulfilled Kennedy's ambitious goal.

Example: The Cultural and Political Impact of *Apollo 11*

The successful landing of *Apollo 11* had a profound cultural and political impact around the world. It was a unifying moment for the United States, showcasing the nation's technological prowess and reaffirming its status as a global superpower. The mission also inspired generations of scientists, engineers, and explorers to pursue careers in space and science.

3.5. The Decline of the Space Race

By the early 1970s, the intense competition between the United States and the Soviet Union in space began to wane. The successful landing of *Apollo 11* had essentially won the Space Race for the United States, and public interest in further lunar missions began to decline. NASA completed six successful lunar landings between 1969 and 1972, but after *Apollo 17* in 1972, the program was discontinued due to budget constraints and shifting priorities.

Meanwhile, the Soviet Union continued to focus on developing space stations, leading to the launch of *Salyut*

1 in 1971, the world's first space station. While the USSR never successfully landed cosmonauts on the Moon, its focus shifted toward long-duration missions and establishing a permanent human presence in space.

Example: The Shift Toward Space Cooperation

The end of the Space Race gave way to a new era of cooperation between the United States and the Soviet Union in space exploration. In 1975, the two nations collaborated on the *Apollo-Soyuz Test Project*, the first international human spaceflight mission. This marked the beginning of a new chapter in space exploration, where collaboration replaced competition.

3.6. The Long-Term Impact of the Space Race

The Space Race left a lasting legacy that continues to shape space exploration today. One of the most significant impacts was the rapid advancement of technology. The innovations developed during the Space Race, including advancements in rocketry, telecommunications, and computer technology, had far-reaching applications beyond space exploration.

The Space Race also led to increased investment in education, particularly in the fields of science, technology, engineering, and mathematics (STEM). In the United States, the launch of *Sputnik 1* spurred significant government investment in education, resulting in the establishment of programs to encourage young people to pursue careers in science and technology.

Additionally, the Space Race fundamentally altered the way humanity views its place in the universe. The iconic images of Earth taken from space, such as the *Earthrise* photo captured during the *Apollo 8* mission, helped foster a sense of global interconnectedness and environmental awareness.

Example: The Role of STEM Education in the Space Race Legacy

One of the most enduring impacts of the Space Race was its role in promoting STEM education. In response to the Soviet Union's early successes, the U.S. government established programs like the National Defense Education Act, which aimed to improve education in science and mathematics. This emphasis on STEM education continues to influence the development of new generations of scientists and engineers.

Conclusion

The Space Race was a defining chapter in the Cold War, driven by political, military, and ideological motivations. From the launch of *Sputnik 1* to the landing of *Apollo 11* on the Moon, the Space Race saw unprecedented achievements in space exploration that forever changed our understanding of the universe. While the competition between the United States and the Soviet Union was fierce, it ultimately led to collaboration and laid the foundation for future space missions. The technological advancements, scientific discoveries, and cultural shifts that emerged from the Space Race continue to shape the trajectory of space exploration in the 21st century.

4. Establishment of Space Agencies

The establishment of space agencies was a direct response to the rapid advancements in space exploration during the mid-20th century. With the launch of Sputnik 1 in 1957 and the ensuing Space Race between the United States and the Soviet Union, both superpowers recognized the need for dedicated organizations to manage, coordinate, and advance their space programs. As space exploration expanded globally, other countries followed suit, creating their own national space agencies to promote scientific research, technological development, and international collaboration. This chapter explores the origins, purposes, and achievements of major space agencies, including NASA, Roscosmos, the European Space Agency (ESA), and other prominent national space agencies. The establishment of these agencies has profoundly shaped the direction and scope of space exploration, from early missions to modern initiatives aimed at exploring distant planets and advancing human spaceflight.

4.1. NASA: The Birth of the U.S. Space Program

4.1.1. Origins of NASA

The National Aeronautics and Space Administration (NASA) was established on July 29, 1958, following the United States' realization that it was lagging behind the Soviet Union in space exploration. The launch of Sputnik 1 by the Soviets in 1957 sent shockwaves through the U.S. government and public, leading to the creation of NASA as a civilian space agency. NASA was tasked with coordinating all American space exploration activities, including manned spaceflight, planetary exploration, and scientific research.

4.1.2. NASA's Early Achievements

In its early years, NASA focused on catching up with the Soviet Union, culminating in the Mercury and Gemini programs. These programs laid the groundwork for the Apollo missions, which aimed to land humans on the Moon. On July 20, 1969, NASA achieved one of the most iconic moments in human history when Apollo 11 successfully landed on the Moon, and astronaut Neil Armstrong took his first steps on the lunar surface.

Example: Apollo 11 and NASA's Role in Shaping Global Perceptions

Apollo 11 not only represented a victory for NASA but also cemented the United States' position as a leader in space exploration. The mission demonstrated the technological prowess of NASA and showcased its ability to undertake complex, high-stakes missions. The event was broadcast globally, inspiring millions and positioning NASA as a symbol of innovation and ambition.

4.2. Roscosmos: The Soviet (and Russian) Space Agency

4.2.1. Formation and Early Successes

The Soviet Union established its space program under military leadership, with significant advancements being made under the guidance of Sergei Korolev, the chief architect of Soviet space achievements. Roscosmos, the successor to the Soviet space program, was officially founded in 1992 following the dissolution of the Soviet Union. However, the Soviet Union had already achieved numerous milestones, including the launch of Sputnik 1, the first human in space (Yuri Gagarin in 1961), and the first spacewalk (Alexei Leonov in 1965).

4.2.2. Roscosmos in the Post-Soviet Era

In the post-Soviet era, Roscosmos shifted its focus towards collaboration with international space agencies, particularly NASA. One of the most significant achievements of Roscosmos in the modern era is its ongoing contributions to the International Space Station (ISS), where Russian cosmonauts play a vital role. The Soyuz spacecraft, developed during the Soviet era, remains a reliable vehicle for transporting astronauts to and from the ISS.

Example: Soyuz's Role in International Space Collaboration

The Soyuz spacecraft has been instrumental in maintaining human presence in space since the end of the Space Shuttle program in 2011. Its reliability and affordability have made it a critical component of international space missions, and it continues to be used for manned spaceflights to the ISS, solidifying Roscosmos' role in global space exploration.

4.3. The European Space Agency (ESA)

4.3.1. Formation of ESA

The European Space Agency (ESA) was established in 1975 as a collaborative effort among European nations to pool resources and expertise in space exploration. ESA's goal was to establish a unified European presence in space and to develop cutting-edge technologies and scientific missions that would rival those of the United States and the Soviet Union. The agency was formed by merging two pre-existing organizations: the European Space Research Organization (ESRO) and the European Launcher Development Organisation (ELDO).

4.3.2. Key ESA Missions and Achievements

ESA has since become one of the world's leading space agencies, with numerous successful missions under its belt. Notable achievements include the launch of the *Ariane* series of rockets, which have become a reliable vehicle for launching satellites, and the *Rosetta* mission, which successfully landed a probe on a comet in 2014. ESA also plays a key role in the ISS, contributing technology, funding, and astronauts.

Example: The *Rosetta* Mission and Its Impact

The *Rosetta* mission, which culminated in the first-ever landing of a probe on a comet, showcased ESA's capabilities and scientific ambitions. The mission provided invaluable data on the composition of comets and contributed to our understanding of the early solar system. *Rosetta* was hailed as a major scientific achievement and underscored ESA's role as a leader in space exploration.

4.4. China's Space Program: The Rise of CNSA

4.4.1. Formation of the China National Space Administration (CNSA)

China's space ambitions began in earnest in the 1950s, but the China National Space Administration (CNSA) was officially established in 1993. Since then, China has made significant strides in space exploration, particularly in the 21st century, as it seeks to establish itself as a global leader in space technology. CNSA's focus includes manned spaceflight, lunar exploration, and the development of advanced satellite systems.

4.4.2. Key Achievements of CNSA

In recent years, CNSA has achieved several important milestones, including the launch of *Shenzhou* manned missions, the deployment of *Tiangong* space laboratories, and the landing of the *Chang'e* missions on the Moon. In 2019, China became the first country to land a rover on the far side of the Moon, marking a major achievement in lunar exploration.

Example: The *Chang'e 4* Mission and Its Importance

The *Chang'e 4* mission, which successfully landed on the far side of the Moon in January 2019, demonstrated China's growing capabilities in space exploration. This mission not only provided critical scientific data but also highlighted China's ambitions to explore deep space, with plans to send missions to Mars and beyond.

4.5. India's Space Program: ISRO's Achievements

4.5.1. Formation of ISRO

The Indian Space Research Organisation (ISRO) was founded in 1969, with the goal of developing space technology for India's socioeconomic development. ISRO has since become one of the world's most cost-effective and efficient space agencies, known for its innovative approach to satellite technology and space exploration.

4.5.2. Major ISRO Milestones

ISRO has achieved several significant milestones, including the successful launch of the Mars Orbiter Mission (Mangalyaan) in 2014, which made India the first country to reach Mars on its first attempt. ISRO has also developed a robust satellite program, including communication, weather, and navigation satellites, that supports India's infrastructure and development.

Example: Mangalyaan's Historic Mission

Mangalyaan, or the Mars Orbiter Mission, was a landmark achievement for ISRO, demonstrating India's ability to undertake complex interplanetary missions at a fraction of the cost typically associated with such endeavors. This success placed ISRO in the global spotlight and showcased its potential as a major player in space exploration.

4.6. The Role of Private Space Agencies

4.6.1. The Rise of Commercial Space Exploration

In recent years, private space agencies such as SpaceX, Blue Origin, and Virgin Galactic have emerged as major players in the space industry. These companies, driven by visionary entrepreneurs like Elon Musk and Jeff Bezos, have accelerated the pace of innovation and reduced the cost of space access, challenging traditional government-run space agencies.

4.6.2. Collaboration Between Public and Private Sectors

Governments and space agencies are increasingly collaborating with private companies to achieve ambitious space exploration goals. NASA, for example, has partnered with SpaceX to transport astronauts to the ISS, while Blue Origin is working on lunar landers for future Moon missions.

Example: SpaceX's Role in Redefining Space Access

SpaceX has revolutionized space exploration by developing reusable rockets, such as the Falcon 9, that significantly reduce the cost of launching payloads into space. Its achievements, including the successful crewed launch of *Dragon* spacecraft to the ISS, have positioned SpaceX as a leader in the future of space travel.

4.7. The Role of International Space Collaboration

4.7.1. The International Space Station (ISS)

The ISS is a symbol of international cooperation in space exploration. Built and operated by space agencies from the United States (NASA), Russia (Roscosmos), Europe (ESA), Japan (JAXA), and Canada (CSA), the ISS serves as a laboratory for scientific research and a hub for collaboration between countries.

4.7.2. Future International Space Projects

Looking forward, international collaboration will continue to play a crucial role in space exploration. Projects like the Lunar Gateway, a planned space station in lunar orbit, and the Artemis program, which aims to return humans to the Moon, involve multiple countries working together to achieve common goals.

Example: The ISS as a Model for Future Collaboration

The ISS has been operational for over two decades, hosting astronauts from around the world and facilitating thousands of scientific experiments. Its success demonstrates the importance of international partnerships in achieving long-term space exploration goals.

Conclusion

The establishment of space agencies around the world has been a defining feature of space exploration since the mid-20th century. These agencies, whether operating independently or in collaboration, have pushed the boundaries of human knowledge and technological achievement. From NASA's Apollo missions to Roscosmos' contributions to the ISS, and from ESA's cutting-edge scientific missions to the rise of CNSA and ISRO, space agencies have played a pivotal role in advancing our understanding of the universe. As private space companies join the effort, the future of space exploration promises to be even more dynamic and collaborative.

5. Evolution of Commercial Spaceflight

The evolution of commercial spaceflight marks a significant shift in the landscape of space exploration, transitioning from government-dominated ventures to a vibrant marketplace driven by private enterprise. This transformation began in earnest in the late 20th century, fueled by advancements in technology, changing economic paradigms, and a growing interest in space from non-governmental entities. The commercialization of space has led to increased competition, innovation, and cost reductions, opening up new possibilities for scientific research, satellite deployment, space tourism, and even interplanetary exploration. This chapter examines the journey of commercial spaceflight, highlighting key players, technological advancements, and the impact of regulatory frameworks on the growth of the industry. Through various examples, it will illustrate how commercial entities are reshaping our understanding of what is possible in space.

5.1. Historical Background of Commercial Spaceflight

5.1.1. Early Days of Space Exploration

The early years of space exploration were predominantly led by government agencies, with the United States and the Soviet Union at the forefront. Initiatives like NASA's Apollo program and the Soviet Union's Vostok missions captured the world's attention and demonstrated the potential of human spaceflight. However, the high costs and risks associated with these programs limited the involvement of private companies in space activities.

5.1.2. The Shift Towards Commercialization

In the 1980s and 1990s, the U.S. government began to recognize the potential benefits of involving private companies in space exploration. Legislative measures, such as the Commercial Space Launch Act of 1984, aimed to encourage private investment in the space sector. This shift laid the groundwork for commercial entities to enter the space market and provide launch services, satellite deployment, and other capabilities.

Example: The Formation of Companies like SpaceX

SpaceX, founded by Elon Musk in 2002, exemplifies the shift towards commercial spaceflight. With the goal of reducing space transportation costs and enabling the colonization of Mars, SpaceX has developed the Falcon 1, Falcon 9, and Falcon Heavy rockets. The company's innovative approach and successful missions have positioned it as a leader in the commercial space sector, attracting partnerships with NASA and other organizations.

5.2. The Rise of Private Space Companies

5.2.1. Key Players in the Industry

Numerous private companies have emerged in the commercial spaceflight arena, each contributing unique capabilities and services. Key players include:

- **SpaceX**: Pioneering reusable rocket technology and offering a range of launch services.

- **Blue Origin**: Founded by Jeff Bezos, focusing on suborbital and orbital flight with its New Shepard and New Glenn rockets.

- **Virgin Galactic**: Aiming to provide space tourism experiences with its SpaceShipTwo vehicle.

- **Northrop Grumman**: Previously Orbital ATK, providing launch services and spacecraft for cargo delivery to the ISS.

5.2.2. Innovations in Launch Technology

The development of reusable launch systems has been a game-changer for the commercial spaceflight industry. SpaceX's Falcon 9 rocket, which can land vertically after delivering payloads to orbit, has dramatically reduced the cost of space access. Other companies, such as Blue Origin, are also exploring reusability in their launch systems, contributing to a more sustainable approach to space travel.

Example: SpaceX's Falcon 9 Launches

SpaceX's Falcon 9 rocket has successfully completed numerous missions, including crewed flights to the ISS. The rocket's ability to land and be refurbished for multiple flights has not only lowered costs but also increased the frequency of launches, demonstrating the viability of commercial spaceflight as a competitive alternative to traditional government programs.

5.3. Regulatory Framework for Commercial Spaceflight

5.3.1. Government Involvement and Oversight

The growth of the commercial spaceflight industry has necessitated the development of regulatory frameworks to ensure safety, liability, and sustainability. In the United States, the Federal Aviation Administration (FAA) is responsible for regulating commercial space launches and reentries. The FAA's Office of Commercial Space Transportation (AST) oversees licensing and safety requirements for private space companies.

5.3.2. International Regulations and Cooperation

As commercial spaceflight expands globally, international regulations and cooperation have become increasingly important. Organizations such as the United Nations Office for Outer Space Affairs (UNOOSA) facilitate discussions on space law and promote collaboration between countries in space exploration efforts. The establishment of international agreements is essential for addressing challenges related to liability, space debris, and the use of outer space resources.

Example: The Outer Space Treaty of 1967

The Outer Space Treaty, signed by over 100 countries, lays the groundwork for international space law. It emphasizes the peaceful use of outer space and establishes principles for cooperation in space activities. As commercial entities increasingly operate in space, adherence to these principles will be crucial for maintaining a collaborative and safe environment.

5.4. Commercial Spaceflight and Scientific Research

5.4.1. Opportunities for Scientific Discovery

Commercial spaceflight has opened new avenues for scientific research, enabling private companies to conduct experiments in microgravity and develop innovative technologies. Partnerships between commercial entities and research institutions have led to groundbreaking discoveries in fields such as medicine, materials science, and Earth observation.

5.4.2. The Role of Space Habitats and Laboratories

Commercial space stations, such as Axiom Space and Bigelow Aerospace, are being developed to provide platforms for research and habitation in low Earth orbit. These habitats will enable long-term scientific investigations and serve as testbeds for technologies needed for future exploration missions to the Moon and Mars.

Example: The ISS as a Platform for Commercial Research

The International Space Station (ISS) has been utilized by various private companies to conduct scientific research. For instance, companies like NanoRacks and Boeing have established programs that allow researchers to send experiments to the ISS, leveraging its unique microgravity environment. This collaboration exemplifies the potential of commercial spaceflight to advance scientific knowledge.

5.5. Space Tourism: A New Frontier

5.5.1. The Emergence of Space Tourism

Space tourism has gained significant attention in recent years, driven by the ambitions of private companies to offer suborbital and orbital flights to civilians. Pioneering efforts in this sector are led by companies such as Virgin Galactic and Blue Origin, which aim to provide extraordinary experiences for space tourists.

5.5.2. Future Prospects for Space Tourism

As technology advances and the costs of space travel decrease, space tourism is expected to become a more accessible and mainstream industry. This evolution could lead to new economic opportunities, tourism markets, and increased public interest in space exploration.

Example: Virgin Galactic's SpaceShipTwo

Virgin Galactic's SpaceShipTwo is designed to carry tourists to the edge of space, providing a few minutes of weightlessness and stunning views of Earth. The company has conducted successful test flights and aims to begin commercial operations, making it one of the first companies to offer space tourism experiences to the public.

5.6. The Future of Commercial Spaceflight

5.6.1. Expanding Horizons: Mars and Beyond

The future of commercial spaceflight is poised to include ambitious missions to Mars and beyond. Companies like SpaceX are actively working on technologies to enable crewed missions to the Red Planet, aiming to establish a human presence on Mars within the coming decades.

5.6.2. International Collaboration and Innovation

The ongoing collaboration between government agencies and commercial entities will play a crucial role in shaping the future of space exploration. By pooling resources and expertise, stakeholders can tackle complex challenges and advance scientific goals in ways that were previously unimaginable.

Example: NASA's Artemis Program and Commercial Partnerships

NASA's Artemis program, which aims to return humans to the Moon and establish a sustainable presence by the end of the decade, relies on partnerships with commercial companies for transportation, lander development, and scientific research. This collaboration highlights the importance of the commercial space sector in achieving ambitious exploration goals.

Conclusion

The evolution of commercial spaceflight represents a transformative era in space exploration, characterized by innovation, competition, and collaboration. The growth of private companies has diversified the space industry, allowing for increased access to space, advancements in technology, and the realization of new opportunities for scientific research and tourism. As we look to the future, the interplay between commercial and governmental efforts will shape the next chapter of human space exploration, with the potential to unlock unprecedented discoveries and inspire generations to come.

Chapter 2: Types of Space Industries

1. Government Space Agencies vs. Private Enterprises
2. Launch Services and Vehicle Development
3. Satellite Manufacturing and Deployment
4. Space Tourism: Opportunities and Challenges
5. Scientific Research and Exploration

Chapter 2

Types of Space Industries

Introduction

The space industry has evolved into a multifaceted sector, driven by both government agencies and private enterprises. While historically dominated by national governments and space agencies like NASA, the European Space Agency (ESA), and Roscosmos, the landscape has dramatically shifted with the rise of private companies. These private entities, such as SpaceX, Blue Origin, and others, have introduced new competition, innovation, and commercial opportunities in space exploration and technology development.

This chapter explores the various segments of the space industry, including the critical role of launch services, satellite manufacturing, and deployment. It also delves into emerging sectors like space tourism and highlights the importance of scientific research in shaping the future of space exploration. By examining the differences between government-led missions and private ventures, this chapter provides a detailed look at the evolving space ecosystem and the collaborative dynamics that are driving its expansion.

1. Government Space Agencies vs. Private Enterprises

Space exploration has long been a domain dominated by government agencies. For decades, organizations like NASA (National Aeronautics and Space Administration) in the United States, ESA (European Space Agency), and Roscosmos (Russian Federal Space Agency) spearheaded humanity's journey into space. However, in recent years, the rise of private enterprises such as SpaceX, Blue Origin, and Rocket Lab has transformed the space industry. These private players have not only contributed to the innovation and commercialization of space exploration but have also presented new models of collaboration, competition, and ambition.

This section explores the differences and synergies between government space agencies and private enterprises, looking into their distinct roles, missions, funding mechanisms, and contributions to the global space ecosystem. By examining their strengths and weaknesses, we can understand how the relationship between government and private entities is reshaping the future of space exploration.

1.1 Government Space Agencies: History, Role, and Scope

Government space agencies have historically played a central role in space exploration. Agencies like NASA, ESA, and Roscosmos were founded in the mid-20th century, primarily during the Cold War, when space was seen as the next frontier in geopolitical rivalry between the United States and the Soviet Union. This period, known as the "Space Race," led to significant advancements in space technology, culminating in milestones such as the Apollo 11 moon landing in 1969.

1.1.1 Funding and Budgeting

One of the defining characteristics of government space agencies is their funding model. These agencies rely primarily on taxpayer funding, and their budgets are allocated by national governments. NASA's annual budget, for instance, is determined by the U.S. Congress, which allocates funds based on the nation's scientific, military, and diplomatic priorities. ESA's budget comes from contributions by member states, and similar arrangements exist for agencies like Roscosmos and ISRO (Indian Space Research Organisation).

Despite the significant financial resources at their disposal, government space agencies often face budget constraints and political pressure. Funding levels can fluctuate depending on the political climate and public interest in space exploration. For example, NASA's budget as a percentage of U.S. GDP peaked at 4.41% during the Apollo program but has since decreased to around 0.5%. This shift has impacted the scope and scale of many government-led space missions.

1.1.2 Key Missions and Achievements

Government space agencies are responsible for many of the most iconic achievements in space exploration. Notable examples include NASA's Apollo missions, the

Space Shuttle program, the Hubble Space Telescope, and the Mars rovers. ESA has contributed to several collaborative missions, including the Rosetta mission to land on a comet and the development of the Ariane family of launch vehicles.

These agencies tend to focus on large-scale, high-risk missions that require long-term investment and coordination. Deep space exploration, planetary science, and human spaceflight are areas where government agencies continue to lead. NASA's Artemis program, aimed at returning humans to the Moon and establishing a sustainable presence there, exemplifies the scale of such undertakings.

1.2 Private Enterprises: The New Space Pioneers

In contrast to the centralized and bureaucratic nature of government space agencies, private enterprises operate with a more entrepreneurial approach. Over the past two decades, companies like SpaceX, Blue Origin, and Rocket Lab have redefined what is possible in space exploration by introducing cost-effective, innovative solutions to traditional space challenges.

1.2.1 Funding and Business Models

Private enterprises in the space industry are largely funded by a combination of private investment, commercial contracts, and government contracts. SpaceX, for instance, is privately held and financed through a mix of private equity, customer contracts, and government funding. The company has successfully raised billions in venture capital and private investment, which has allowed it to develop revolutionary technologies like the reusable Falcon 9 rocket.

These companies also rely on revenue from commercial customers. For instance, SpaceX provides launch services for telecommunications satellites and cargo delivery to the International Space Station (ISS) under contract with NASA. Companies like Planet Labs and Maxar Technologies sell Earth observation data to businesses and governments, demonstrating the growing commercialization of space-related services.

1.2.2 Key Achievements and Contributions

Private enterprises have contributed significantly to reducing the cost of space access. SpaceX, in particular, has pioneered reusable rocket technology, significantly lowering the price per kilogram of launching payloads into orbit. Before SpaceX, the average cost to launch a satellite into low-Earth orbit was around $18,500 per kilogram. SpaceX's Falcon 9 rocket has reduced this to approximately $2,700 per kilogram, making space more accessible to a broader range of actors.

Other private companies are following suit. Blue Origin, founded by Amazon's Jeff Bezos, is developing the New Glenn and New Shepard rockets, both of which are intended to lower the cost of launching humans and cargo into space. Rocket Lab, a New Zealand-based company, focuses on launching small satellites, an increasingly important part of the commercial space sector.

Moreover, private enterprises have demonstrated remarkable agility in terms of innovation. While government agencies tend to operate on longer timelines due to bureaucratic processes and public accountability, private companies like SpaceX have shown they can quickly iterate on designs, test new technologies, and achieve rapid advancements. This agility was demonstrated when SpaceX became the first private company to send astronauts to the ISS in 2020 under NASA's Commercial Crew Program.

1.3 Collaborative Models: Public-Private Partnerships

While government space agencies and private enterprises have historically operated in separate domains, there has been a growing trend toward collaboration. Public-private partnerships (PPPs) have become a cornerstone of modern space exploration, blending the resources and expertise of both sectors.

1.3.1 NASA's Commercial Crew Program

One of the most notable examples of collaboration between government agencies and private companies is NASA's Commercial Crew Program. This initiative was designed to reduce the cost of transporting astronauts to and from the ISS by contracting with private companies to provide launch services. SpaceX and Boeing were selected to develop spacecraft capable of carrying crew to the ISS, and in 2020, SpaceX's Crew Dragon successfully completed its first manned mission.

The program represents a shift in NASA's role, from being the sole operator of human spaceflight missions to acting as a customer of services provided by private companies. This model allows NASA to focus on deep space exploration while leveraging private sector innovation for lower-cost missions in low-Earth orbit.

1.3.2 International Space Station (ISS) Commercialization

The ISS, a symbol of international cooperation in space, has also become a platform for private sector involvement. In 2019, NASA announced plans to open the ISS to private companies for manufacturing, research, and tourism. Companies like Axiom Space are developing plans to build private modules attached to the ISS, eventually leading to the establishment of independent commercial space stations.

This collaborative approach allows private companies to access the infrastructure and expertise developed by government agencies, while the agencies benefit from the efficiency and innovation that the private sector brings.

1.4 Distinct Challenges Faced by Government and Private Entities

Despite their successes, both government space agencies and private enterprises face unique challenges.

1.4.1 Government Challenges

Government space agencies often struggle with bureaucratic inertia and fluctuating political priorities. Large-scale programs like NASA's Artemis or ESA's Galileo navigation system require long-term funding commitments, which can be threatened by political changes. The slow pace of decision-making in government agencies can hinder innovation and delay mission timelines.

1.4.2 Private Sector Challenges

Private companies, on the other hand, face different hurdles. While they can innovate rapidly, they are often constrained by the need to secure continuous investment and maintain profitability. Space exploration is an inherently risky and capital-intensive industry, and the financial viability of long-term projects, like space tourism or asteroid mining, remains uncertain.

Moreover, private enterprises face regulatory challenges. National and international regulations governing space activities, such as the Outer Space Treaty of 1967, were designed with government actors in mind and may not always align with the ambitions of private companies. As the industry grows, regulatory frameworks will need to adapt to ensure that space remains a sustainable and accessible domain for all.

1.5 The Future of Space Exploration: A Hybrid Model?

Looking forward, the line between government space agencies and private enterprises is likely to blur further. Governments will continue to play a crucial role in regulating space activities, conducting scientific missions, and ensuring national security in space. At the same time, private companies will increasingly take on commercial, tourism, and even human spaceflight missions.

The success of this hybrid model depends on cooperation, innovation, and the establishment of clear regulatory frameworks. As both sectors continue to evolve, the partnership between government agencies and private companies will be crucial for advancing humanity's presence in space.

2. Launch Services and Vehicle Development

The development of launch services and vehicles is one of the most fundamental and rapidly evolving sectors within the space industry. Over the decades, advancements in rocket technology and the increased demand for launching payloads into orbit have led to significant innovations. Historically, launching a spacecraft was a complex and expensive endeavor dominated by national space agencies like NASA and Roscosmos. However, the emergence of private enterprises such as SpaceX, Blue Origin, and Rocket Lab has revolutionized the launch industry. Today, reusable rockets, miniaturized payloads, and cost-effective launch solutions are becoming more prevalent, making space more accessible than ever.

In this section, we will explore the evolution of launch services, the technological developments behind modern rockets, and the diverse range of vehicles used to carry payloads into space. We'll also look at how both government and private entities are pushing the boundaries of innovation in this critical area of space exploration, using specific examples to highlight the achievements and ongoing challenges in launch services and vehicle development.

2.1 Evolution of Launch Services

2.1.1 The Early Years: From V-2 Rockets to the Space Race

The foundation of modern launch services can be traced back to the development of rocket technology during World War II, with the German V-2 rocket being the first ballistic missile capable of reaching the edge of space. Following the war, this technology formed the basis for the first space launch vehicles, leading to the beginning of the Space Race between the United States and the Soviet Union in the 1950s and 1960s.

The Soviet Union achieved several key milestones, including launching Sputnik, the first artificial satellite, in 1957 and sending the first human, Yuri Gagarin, into space in 1961. In response, the United States developed the Redstone and Atlas rockets, which culminated in the Saturn V rocket used in the Apollo moon landings. These early launch services were government-controlled and had a singular focus on achieving strategic and scientific superiority in space.

2.1.2 The Rise of Commercial Launch Services

In the decades following the Apollo program, the focus shifted toward more practical applications of space technology, such as launching satellites for communication, navigation, and Earth observation. The commercial demand for satellite launches gave rise to companies providing launch services outside of government agencies.

A key moment in the commercialization of space came in 1984 when the U.S. government passed the Commercial Space Launch Act, allowing private companies to offer launch services. This law paved the way for companies like Arianespace, the world's first commercial satellite launch provider, to establish themselves. Arianespace, a European company, introduced the Ariane family of rockets, which became highly successful in launching commercial satellites.

The demand for commercial launches grew steadily throughout the 1990s and early 2000s, leading to increased competition. However, the high cost of launches and the technical challenges of developing reliable rockets meant that only a few companies could compete in this arena. This situation changed dramatically with the arrival of companies like SpaceX, which would revolutionize launch services.

2.2 Technological Advancements in Vehicle Development

2.2.1 The Role of Reusability in Reducing Costs

One of the most significant breakthroughs in vehicle development has been the introduction of reusable rockets. Traditional expendable launch vehicles (ELVs) were designed for single use, which made launching payloads into space an expensive endeavor. For example, NASA's Space Shuttle program aimed to reduce costs through partial reusability, but the complexity and high refurbishment costs limited its economic viability.

SpaceX, founded by Elon Musk in 2002, sought to change this by developing fully reusable rockets. The Falcon 9, first launched in 2010, was designed with a reusable first stage. In 2015, SpaceX successfully landed the first stage of the Falcon 9 after a mission, marking the beginning of a new era in rocket reusability. By reusing rockets, SpaceX was able to dramatically lower the cost of launches, making space more accessible for both commercial and government customers.

Blue Origin, led by Amazon's Jeff Bezos, has also made significant strides in reusable rocket technology. The company's New Shepard rocket, designed for suborbital space tourism, has successfully flown and landed multiple times. Blue Origin is also developing the New Glenn rocket, which will feature a reusable first stage for orbital launches.

2.2.2 Miniaturization and Small Satellite Launch Vehicles

As satellite technology has evolved, satellites have become smaller, lighter, and more capable. This shift has led to the development of small satellite launch vehicles (SSLVs), which are designed specifically to carry smaller payloads into orbit. SSLVs offer lower launch costs and greater flexibility for satellite operators who do not require the large payload capacities of traditional rockets.

One of the pioneers in this field is Rocket Lab, a U.S.-New Zealand company that developed the Electron rocket, a dedicated small satellite launch vehicle. Electron has been highly successful in launching small satellites for commercial and government customers. The rocket's ability to deliver payloads into orbit at a fraction of the cost of larger launch vehicles has made it a key player in the growing market for small satellite launches.

Rocket Lab is also innovating with its Photon spacecraft platform, which is designed to provide satellite operators with an integrated spacecraft solution, further simplifying the process of deploying small satellites into space.

2.2.3 Heavy-Lift Vehicles and Deep Space Missions

While small satellite launch vehicles are gaining prominence, the need for heavy-lift launch vehicles (HLVs) remains critical for deep space exploration and large payloads. NASA's Space Launch System (SLS) is a prime example of a heavy-lift vehicle designed for missions beyond low-Earth orbit (LEO). The SLS is intended to carry astronauts to the Moon as part of the Artemis program and eventually to Mars.

SpaceX's Starship, currently in development, is another heavy-lift vehicle that promises to transform space exploration. Starship is designed to be fully reusable and capable of carrying large payloads to the Moon, Mars, and beyond. With a payload capacity far exceeding that of any existing rocket, Starship could enable a new era of deep space missions and interplanetary colonization.

2.3 Key Players in the Launch Services Market

2.3.1 SpaceX: The Pioneer of Reusable Rockets

SpaceX is the most prominent example of how private enterprises have revolutionized the launch services market. The company's Falcon 9 and Falcon Heavy rockets have become the go-to launch vehicles for a wide range of missions, from commercial satellite deployments to crewed missions for NASA. Falcon Heavy, first launched in 2018, is currently the most powerful operational rocket in the world.

The reusability of SpaceX's rockets has allowed the company to offer significantly lower launch prices than its competitors, leading to a major shift in the market. The company's rapid development timeline and ambitious goals—such as the colonization of Mars—have positioned it as a leader in the global space industry.

2.3.2 Blue Origin: Competing with Innovation

Blue Origin, although not as far along in the commercial launch market as SpaceX, is rapidly developing its capabilities. The company's New Shepard suborbital rocket has been a significant milestone in reusable rocket technology, and its New Glenn rocket promises to compete with SpaceX for orbital launches. Blue Origin's long-term vision includes space tourism and large-scale space infrastructure projects, such as space stations and lunar bases.

2.3.3 Rocket Lab: Leader in Small Satellite Launches

Rocket Lab has carved out a niche in the market for small satellite launches. Its Electron rocket, which specializes in delivering smaller payloads to orbit, has been a critical player in the growing small satellite industry. With the introduction of its Photon platform, Rocket Lab is positioning itself as a full-service provider for small satellite operators, from launch to in-orbit operations.

2.4 Global Market Dynamics and Competition

2.4.1 The Role of International Players

While U.S.-based companies like SpaceX and Blue Origin dominate headlines, international players continue to play a significant role in the launch services market. Arianespace, based in Europe, has a long history of launching commercial satellites and government payloads. Its Ariane 5 rocket has been a workhorse of the European space program, and the upcoming Ariane 6 is designed to compete in the modern launch market by offering greater flexibility and lower costs.

Russia's Roscosmos, with its Soyuz rocket, remains a key player in human spaceflight and satellite launches. Soyuz is one of the most reliable rockets in history and has been used to transport astronauts to the International Space Station (ISS) for decades. However, competition from private companies like SpaceX has started to erode Russia's dominance in this area.

China has also emerged as a major player in the launch services market. The China National Space Administration (CNSA) has developed a range of launch vehicles, including the Long March series, which are used for both domestic and international launches. China's ambitious space exploration plans, including missions to the Moon and Mars, demonstrate its growing influence in the global space industry.

2.4.2 The Competitive Landscape

The launch services market is becoming increasingly competitive as more private companies and national space agencies enter the fray. SpaceX's dominance in terms of pricing and reliability has forced other companies to innovate or risk being left behind. Blue Origin, Rocket Lab, and Arianespace are all working to develop new technologies and reduce costs to remain competitive in this fast-changing industry.

In addition to traditional launch services, new business models are emerging. Companies like SpaceX are offering rideshare missions, where multiple small satellites share a single launch, further reducing costs for customers. This has opened up space access to a wider range of organizations, including universities, startups, and non-profit organizations.

2.5 Future Trends in Launch Vehicle Development

2.5.1 Fully Reusable Rockets and Single-Stage-to-Orbit (SSTO)

The ultimate goal of many companies is to develop fully reusable rockets capable of reaching orbit without discarding any stages. SpaceX's Starship and Blue Origin's New Glenn are steps in this direction, but the development of single-stage-to-orbit (SSTO) vehicles remains a significant engineering challenge. SSTO vehicles would dramatically reduce launch costs and make space access even more routine.

2.5.2 Hypersonic and Air-Breathing Propulsion

Another area of development is hypersonic and air-breathing propulsion systems, which could revolutionize how payloads are launched into space. These systems would enable vehicles to achieve much higher speeds and altitudes without relying on traditional rocket engines. Companies like Reaction Engines in the UK are working on air-breathing engines that could one day be used for space launches.

2.5.3 Space-Based Launch Systems

Looking further into the future, space-based launch systems, such as space elevators or launch platforms in orbit, are being explored as potential game-changers for space access. Although these concepts remain speculative, they represent the kind of long-term thinking that could redefine how we access space in the decades to come.

Conclusion

Launch services and vehicle development have undergone a dramatic transformation over the past two decades, thanks to technological innovations and the rise of private enterprises. The competition between traditional space agencies and new entrants like SpaceX and Blue Origin has led to reduced launch costs, increased access to space, and the development of reusable rockets. As the industry continues to evolve, the next generation of launch vehicles promises to push the boundaries of what is possible, from fully reusable rockets to interplanetary travel.

3. Satellite Manufacturing and Deployment

Satellite manufacturing and deployment play a central role in the space industry, enabling a wide range of services including communication, Earth observation, navigation, scientific research, and national security. As satellite technology has evolved, the industry has seen tremendous growth, driven by innovations in miniaturization, propulsion systems, and advancements in launch capabilities. What was once the domain of large government agencies has now expanded to include commercial companies, universities, and even non-profit organizations.

This section delves into the process of manufacturing satellites, from design and assembly to testing and integration with launch vehicles. It also covers the various methods of deploying satellites into space, such as rideshare missions and dedicated launches, and highlights the increasing importance of small satellites and constellations. Additionally, we will explore how advancements in satellite technology are revolutionizing industries and changing how we interact with space-based assets. Real-world examples of companies like Boeing, Lockheed Martin, and SpaceX will provide context for understanding the evolving landscape of satellite manufacturing and deployment.

3.1 The Satellite Manufacturing Process

3.1.1 Design and Engineering

The manufacturing of satellites begins with the design and engineering phase, which involves creating a satellite that can meet specific mission requirements. The design phase is highly dependent on the intended use of the satellite, whether it be for communication, remote sensing, navigation, or scientific purposes. During this stage, engineers focus on factors such as payload capacity, power systems, propulsion, thermal control, and structural integrity.

For instance, communication satellites are designed to carry transponders and antennas to relay data across vast distances, while Earth observation satellites are equipped with high-resolution cameras and sensors to capture detailed images of the Earth's surface. The Hubble Space Telescope, for example, required precise design considerations to ensure its mirror could capture distant celestial objects without interference from Earth's atmosphere.

With the advent of small satellites, particularly CubeSats, the design and engineering process has become more accessible to a wider range of organizations, including universities and startups. CubeSats are small, modular satellites that can be customized for a variety of missions at a fraction of the cost of traditional large satellites.

3.1.2 Assembly and Integration

Once the design is finalized, the satellite enters the assembly and integration phase. This involves assembling various subsystems, such as power units, communication equipment, propulsion systems, and scientific instruments, into a compact, functional unit. The assembly process requires precision, as even the smallest flaw can jeopardize the mission.

Satellite manufacturers like Boeing and Lockheed Martin have state-of-the-art facilities for assembling and integrating large satellites. Boeing, for example, has produced some of the most advanced communication satellites, including the Wideband Global SATCOM (WGS) system, which provides secure communications for military forces around the world. Lockheed Martin, on the other hand, is known for building weather satellites, such as the GOES-R series, which provides real-time data for weather forecasting and environmental monitoring.

For small satellites, the assembly process is simpler, but it still requires precision. Companies like Planet Labs, which operates a constellation of small Earth observation satellites, have pioneered the mass production of small satellites, allowing them to quickly scale their operations and deploy large constellations in low Earth orbit (LEO).

3.1.3 Testing and Validation

Before a satellite is launched into space, it must undergo rigorous testing to ensure it can withstand the harsh conditions of space. This includes thermal vacuum testing, vibration testing, and electromagnetic interference testing. Thermal vacuum testing simulates the extreme temperatures and vacuum of space, while vibration testing ensures the satellite can survive the forces experienced during launch.

Testing is especially critical for satellites that are intended to operate for long periods in space, such as geostationary communication satellites, which remain in orbit for 15 years or more. Any failure during this phase can result in costly delays or even mission failure. For instance, the James Webb Space Telescope (JWST) underwent extensive testing to ensure its instruments would function properly in the cold, dark environment of space, far from the Earth.

3.2 Types of Satellites

3.2.1 Communication Satellites

Communication satellites are among the most well-known types of satellites, providing the backbone for global telecommunications, broadcasting, and internet services. These satellites are typically placed in geostationary orbit (GEO), where they remain fixed over a particular point on the Earth's surface, allowing for continuous communication coverage.

Intelsat, one of the largest operators of communication satellites, operates a fleet of GEO satellites that provide connectivity services to businesses, governments, and media companies around the world. These satellites relay signals for television broadcasts, internet services, and secure government communications.

3.2.2 Earth Observation Satellites

Earth observation satellites play a critical role in monitoring the planet's environment, natural resources, and weather patterns. These satellites are equipped with high-resolution cameras and sensors that capture detailed images of the Earth's surface, which are used for applications ranging from agriculture and urban planning to disaster response and climate change monitoring.

The Landsat program, operated by NASA and the U.S. Geological Survey (USGS), is one of the longest-running Earth observation programs, providing over four decades of continuous imagery of the Earth's surface. More recently, private companies like Planet Labs have launched large constellations of small Earth observation satellites, allowing for near-real-time monitoring of the entire planet.

3.2.3 Navigation Satellites

Navigation satellites form the backbone of the Global Positioning System (GPS) and other global navigation satellite systems (GNSS), providing precise location and timing information to users around the world. GPS, operated by the U.S. Air Force, is widely used for navigation in aviation, shipping, and everyday applications such as smartphone navigation.

Other countries have developed their own navigation satellite systems, such as Russia's GLONASS, the European Union's Galileo, and China's BeiDou system. These systems provide redundancy and improved accuracy, especially in regions where GPS signals may be weak or unavailable.

3.2.4 Scientific and Research Satellites

Scientific and research satellites are designed to study the universe, the Earth, and other celestial bodies. These satellites carry specialized instruments to gather data on everything from the composition of distant stars to the behavior of Earth's magnetic field.

NASA's Hubble Space Telescope, for example, has provided stunning images of distant galaxies and nebulae, revolutionizing our understanding of the universe.

Meanwhile, the European Space Agency's (ESA) Gaia satellite is mapping the positions and movements of over a billion stars in the Milky Way, providing invaluable data for astrophysicists.

3.2.5 Military and Defense Satellites

Military and defense satellites are used for a variety of purposes, including reconnaissance, surveillance, communication, and missile detection. These satellites play a crucial role in national security by providing real-time intelligence to military forces and government agencies.

The United States operates a range of defense satellites, including the Defense Support Program (DSP) satellites, which are designed to detect missile launches around the world. In addition, the National Reconnaissance Office (NRO) operates a fleet of spy satellites that provide imagery and signals intelligence.

3.3 Satellite Constellations and Mega-Constellations

3.3.1 Low Earth Orbit (LEO) Constellations

In recent years, there has been a surge in the deployment of satellite constellations in low Earth orbit (LEO). These constellations consist of multiple small satellites working together to provide continuous coverage over large areas of the Earth. LEO constellations are particularly popular for communication and Earth observation applications due to their lower latency and improved resolution compared to satellites in higher orbits.

One of the most prominent examples of a LEO constellation is SpaceX's Starlink project, which aims to provide global broadband internet coverage using thousands of small satellites. As of 2024, Starlink has deployed over 4,000 satellites, making it the largest satellite constellation in operation. Other companies, such as Amazon's Project Kuiper and OneWeb, are also developing their own LEO constellations to provide global internet coverage.

3.3.2 Challenges of Mega-Constellations

While satellite constellations offer numerous advantages, they also present significant challenges, particularly in terms of space debris and orbital congestion. With thousands of satellites being launched into LEO, the risk of collisions and the creation of space debris increases. SpaceX and other companies have implemented collision-avoidance systems and satellite deorbiting procedures to mitigate these risks, but concerns remain about the long-term sustainability of mega-constellations.

Regulatory agencies, such as the U.S. Federal Communications Commission (FCC) and the International Telecommunication Union (ITU), are working to establish guidelines for the safe deployment and operation of large satellite constellations.

3.4 Satellite Deployment Strategies

3.4.1 Dedicated Launches

Dedicated launches involve sending a single satellite or a specific group of satellites into space using a launch vehicle that is tailored to the mission's requirements. This approach is typically used for large, expensive satellites that require specific orbital insertion and mission-critical parameters.

For example, NASA's James Webb Space Telescope (JWST) was launched on a dedicated Ariane 5 rocket in 2021 due to the telescope's size and complexity. The precision and reliability of a dedicated launch were crucial to ensuring the success of the mission.

3.4.2 Rideshare Launches

Rideshare launches, on the other hand, involve multiple satellites sharing the same launch vehicle, which helps reduce costs for satellite operators. This approach is particularly popular for small satellites and CubeSats, which do not require the full payload capacity of a large rocket.

Companies like SpaceX offer rideshare services through their Falcon 9 rocket, allowing customers to share the cost of a launch. In 2021, SpaceX conducted the Transporter-1 mission, which set a record by launching 143 small satellites on a single Falcon 9 rocket.

3.4.3 Deploying Satellites from the International Space Station (ISS)

In addition to traditional launch vehicles, satellites can also be deployed from the International Space Station (ISS). This method is often used for small satellites, such as CubeSats, which can be launched using deployers attached to the ISS. The advantage of deploying satellites from the ISS is that it allows for more frequent and flexible launch opportunities.

For example, the NanoRacks CubeSat Deployer (NRCSD) is a device used to launch small satellites from the ISS. This method has been used by numerous academic institutions and research organizations to deploy their CubeSats into orbit.

3.5 Future Trends in Satellite Manufacturing and Deployment

3.5.1 Mass Production of Small Satellites

The mass production of small satellites is a trend that is reshaping the satellite manufacturing industry. Companies like Planet Labs and OneWeb are pioneering the production of small satellites in large quantities, allowing for rapid deployment of constellations and lowering the cost of access to space.

3.5.2 On-Orbit Servicing and Satellite Refueling

On-orbit servicing and satellite refueling are emerging technologies that could extend the lifespan of satellites and reduce the need for costly replacements. Companies like Northrop Grumman and Astroscale are developing systems that can rendezvous with satellites in orbit to perform repairs, refuel them, or deorbit them at the end of their mission.

3.5.3 Advanced Propulsion Systems for Satellites

Advanced propulsion systems, such as electric propulsion and solar sails, are being developed to improve the efficiency and capabilities of satellites. Electric propulsion systems, in particular, are becoming more common in commercial satellites, as they allow for longer mission durations and more precise orbital adjustments.

Conclusion

Satellite manufacturing and deployment have evolved rapidly in recent years, thanks to technological innovations and the increasing involvement of private companies. The rise of small satellites, constellations, and mega-constellations is reshaping the industry, making space more accessible and affordable than ever before. As the demand for satellite-based services continues to grow, the future of satellite manufacturing and deployment promises to bring even more advancements, from on-orbit servicing to advanced propulsion systems.

4. Space Tourism: Opportunities and Challenges

Space tourism, once a concept confined to the realm of science fiction, has become a tangible and rapidly evolving sector of the space industry. As private companies such as SpaceX, Blue Origin, and Virgin Galactic continue to make significant strides in space technology, the prospect of commercial space travel for non-professional astronauts is increasingly within reach. This emerging industry promises to open up space to individuals beyond government-sponsored astronauts and offer a range of experiences, from suborbital flights to potential lunar excursions.

However, alongside these exciting opportunities come numerous challenges. These include the high cost of entry, safety concerns, regulatory hurdles, and the environmental impact of space travel. Furthermore, the broader implications of space tourism, such as its role in promoting scientific research, inspiring future generations, and contributing to the space economy, need to be considered. This chapter will explore the opportunities and challenges of space tourism, with examples from leading companies and an analysis of the future trajectory of this nascent industry.

4.1 The Evolution of Space Tourism

4.1.1 Early Attempts and Milestones

The idea of space tourism has been around for decades, but it wasn't until the early 2000s that the first real steps toward making it a reality were taken. In 2001, American businessman Dennis Tito became the world's first space tourist, paying an estimated $20 million to fly to the International Space Station (ISS) aboard a Russian Soyuz spacecraft. Tito's flight marked a pivotal moment in the history of space tourism, demonstrating that private individuals could, with the right resources, reach space.

Following Tito, a handful of other wealthy individuals, such as South African entrepreneur Mark Shuttleworth and American engineer Gregory Olsen, followed suit, also traveling to the ISS aboard Soyuz spacecraft. These early missions paved the way for the development of commercial space tourism, but the costs were prohibitively high, limiting access to only the extremely wealthy.

In recent years, the landscape has shifted dramatically, with companies like SpaceX, Virgin Galactic, and Blue Origin developing spacecraft specifically designed for commercial space tourism. These companies aim to significantly reduce the cost of space travel and make it more accessible to a broader segment of the population, though prices still remain in the millions of dollars for more ambitious flights.

4.1.2 Key Players in Space Tourism

Several private companies are at the forefront of the space tourism industry, each with a unique approach to providing space travel experiences.

- **Virgin Galactic**: Founded by billionaire Richard Branson, Virgin Galactic is one of the most well-known space tourism companies. It focuses on offering suborbital flights aboard its SpaceShipTwo vehicle, which is launched from a carrier aircraft. Virgin Galactic completed its first fully crewed flight in July 2021, with Branson himself aboard, marking a significant milestone for the company. The experience allows passengers to experience a few minutes of weightlessness and witness the curvature of the Earth from the edge of space.

- **Blue Origin**: Founded by Amazon CEO Jeff Bezos, Blue Origin's space tourism program is centered around its New Shepard vehicle, a reusable rocket designed for suborbital flights. Like Virgin Galactic, Blue Origin offers passengers the opportunity to experience weightlessness and observe Earth from space. Blue Origin's first crewed flight in July 2021 included Bezos, his brother, and the oldest and youngest people to ever travel to space, showcasing the potential of space tourism for a broad audience.

- **SpaceX**: SpaceX, led by Elon Musk, has taken a more ambitious approach to space tourism by focusing on orbital and even lunar missions. In 2021, SpaceX successfully launched the Inspiration4 mission, the first all-civilian crew to orbit Earth. The company is also planning to send tourists around the Moon with its Starship vehicle in the coming years. SpaceX's emphasis on orbital and deep space tourism differentiates it from other players in the industry and points to the potential for long-duration space travel for non-professionals.

4.2 Opportunities in Space Tourism

4.2.1 Economic Opportunities

One of the primary opportunities presented by space tourism is its potential to contribute to the global economy. The space tourism market is projected to grow significantly in the coming decades, with estimates suggesting it could become a multi-billion-dollar industry. This growth is expected to drive investment in space infrastructure, job creation, and technological innovation, as companies work to develop more affordable and efficient ways to access space.

Space tourism also has the potential to spur economic activity in related sectors, such as aerospace manufacturing, spaceport development, and hospitality. Spaceports, in particular, represent a new area of economic opportunity, as regions around the world compete to attract space tourism companies and capitalize on the influx of tourists.

4.2.2 Scientific Research and Innovation

In addition to its economic potential, space tourism offers unique opportunities for scientific research. Commercial space flights could provide researchers with greater access to microgravity environments, enabling experiments in fields such as biology, medicine, and materials science. Space tourism vehicles, particularly those designed for suborbital flights, can serve as platforms for conducting short-duration experiments that would otherwise require government-sponsored missions.

Moreover, the development of space tourism technology, such as reusable rockets and spacecraft, has the potential to drive innovation across the broader space industry. Advances made in the context of space tourism could lead to improvements in space transportation, space habitats, and even long-term human space exploration.

4.2.3 Inspiration and Public Engagement

One of the less tangible but equally important opportunities associated with space tourism is its potential to inspire future generations and increase public engagement with space exploration. By making space more accessible to private individuals, space tourism can help demystify space travel and generate excitement about the possibilities of human exploration beyond Earth.

The visibility of high-profile space tourism flights, such as those undertaken by Bezos and Branson, has already sparked renewed interest in space exploration, with millions of people following these missions in real time. Space tourism could play a crucial role in building public support for space programs and inspiring young people to pursue careers in science, technology, engineering, and mathematics (STEM) fields.

4.3 Challenges Facing Space Tourism

4.3.1 High Costs and Accessibility

One of the most significant challenges facing space tourism is the high cost of entry. Current space tourism experiences are priced in the hundreds of thousands to millions of dollars, making them accessible only to a small, affluent demographic. While companies like SpaceX, Blue Origin, and Virgin Galactic aim to reduce the cost of space travel over time, it remains unclear how long it will take for prices to drop to levels that are affordable for a broader segment of the population.

Moreover, space tourism's exclusivity raises questions about the social equity of access to space. Critics argue that space tourism, in its current form, caters primarily to the ultra-wealthy and diverts resources and attention away from more pressing issues on Earth, such as poverty, climate change, and public health.

4.3.2 Safety Concerns

The inherent risks associated with space travel represent another major challenge for the space tourism industry. While companies have made significant advancements in spacecraft design and safety protocols, spaceflight remains a risky endeavor. The 2014 crash of Virgin Galactic's SpaceShipTwo during a test flight, which resulted in the death of one pilot, underscores the dangers involved.

To mitigate these risks, space tourism companies must continue to prioritize safety in the design, testing, and operation of their vehicles. Regulatory agencies, such as the Federal Aviation Administration (FAA) in the United States, also play a critical role in overseeing safety standards for commercial space travel. However, given the nascent nature of the industry, it is likely that safety regulations will continue to evolve as more space tourism flights are conducted.

4.3.3 Regulatory and Legal Hurdles

The regulatory environment for space tourism presents another set of challenges. Space travel operates in a complex legal framework, governed by both national laws and international treaties, such as the Outer Space Treaty of 1967. As space tourism becomes more common, governments and regulatory bodies will need to address issues such as liability for accidents, property rights in space, and the environmental impact of space travel.

In the United States, the FAA is responsible for licensing commercial space launches and ensuring public safety. However, the agency currently operates under a "learning period," during which it is limited in its ability to impose new regulations on space tourism companies. This period is set to expire in the near future, and there is ongoing debate about the appropriate level of regulation for the space tourism industry.

4.3.4 Environmental Impact

The environmental impact of space tourism is another area of concern. Rocket launches release significant amounts of carbon dioxide and other pollutants into the atmosphere, contributing to climate change. While the space tourism industry is still in its early stages, the environmental effects of frequent space tourism flights could become more pronounced as the industry grows.

Additionally, the increasing number of rocket launches raises concerns about the long-term sustainability of space activities. Space debris, or "space junk," is already a significant issue in low Earth orbit (LEO), and the introduction of space tourism vehicles could exacerbate the problem. Companies and regulatory bodies will need to develop strategies to minimize the environmental footprint of space tourism and ensure that space remains a viable domain for future generations.

4.4 The Future of Space Tourism

4.4.1 Suborbital vs. Orbital Space Tourism

As the space tourism industry evolves, there will likely be a distinction between suborbital and orbital space tourism experiences. Suborbital flights, such as those offered by Virgin Galactic and Blue Origin, provide a relatively short, affordable introduction to space travel. These flights allow passengers to experience weightlessness and see the curvature of the Earth, but they do not enter orbit.

Orbital space tourism, on the other hand, offers a more immersive experience, with passengers spending several days in space and potentially visiting destinations such as the ISS or private space stations. While orbital space tourism is currently much more expensive than suborbital flights, companies like SpaceX are working to lower the cost and make longer-duration space travel accessible to more people.

4.4.2 Space Hotels and Private Space Stations

Looking further into the future, space tourism could extend beyond short-duration flights to include longer stays in space hotels or private space stations. Companies like Axiom Space and Bigelow Aerospace are already developing plans for commercial space habitats that could accommodate tourists, researchers, and even business travelers. These space stations could serve as destinations for extended stays in space, offering amenities and activities similar to those found in luxury resorts on Earth.

Conclusion

Space tourism represents a new frontier in the commercialization of space, offering exciting opportunities for economic growth, scientific research, and public engagement. However, the industry also faces significant challenges, including high costs, safety concerns, regulatory hurdles, and environmental impact. As space tourism continues to develop, companies and governments will need to work together to address these challenges and ensure that space travel is safe, sustainable, and accessible to a broader segment of the population.

The future of space tourism holds great promise, with the potential for orbital flights, space hotels, and even lunar excursions becoming a reality in the coming decades. If successful, space tourism could play a key role in shaping the future of human space exploration and opening up the cosmos to all.

5. Scientific Research and Exploration

Scientific research and exploration have been at the core of space missions since the dawn of space exploration. These activities are driven by humanity's desire to understand the universe, study celestial bodies, and improve our technological capabilities. From the initial missions of sending probes and satellites to orbit the Earth, to the ambitious efforts to explore planets like Mars, space exploration has consistently expanded our knowledge of the cosmos and fostered scientific breakthroughs.

Today, space exploration goes beyond mere curiosity, serving as a catalyst for developing new technologies, conducting experiments in microgravity, and even seeking solutions to global challenges like climate change. The involvement of both government space agencies, such as NASA and ESA, and private companies, like SpaceX and Blue Origin, has significantly increased the scope and pace of scientific endeavors in space. This chapter will discuss the various aspects of scientific research and exploration, examining its past achievements, present developments, and future potential, alongside the opportunities and challenges it faces.

5.1 The Early Days of Scientific Research in Space

5.1.1 The Role of Satellites in Space Research

The use of satellites marked the first major leap in scientific research in space. The launch of Sputnik 1 by the Soviet Union in 1957, which became the first artificial satellite to orbit Earth, revolutionized science by providing a new platform for observing the Earth, studying atmospheric conditions, and conducting telecommunications experiments. In the years that followed, various satellites were launched by different countries, contributing to fields like Earth observation, astronomy, and environmental science.

- **Explorer 1**: In 1958, the United States launched Explorer 1, which discovered the Van Allen radiation belts, zones of charged particles trapped by Earth's magnetic field. This finding provided a crucial understanding of how the Earth's magnetosphere interacts with solar winds, protecting the planet from harmful radiation.

- **Hubble Space Telescope**: Launched in 1990, the Hubble Space Telescope has been instrumental in advancing our understanding of the universe. By observing distant galaxies, black holes, and supernovas, it has transformed our knowledge of cosmology, providing images and data that have led to numerous scientific discoveries.

5.1.2 Lunar and Planetary Exploration

The 1960s and 1970s witnessed humanity's first steps in exploring other celestial bodies. NASA's Apollo program, which culminated in the successful landing of astronauts on the Moon in 1969, remains one of the most iconic achievements in space exploration. The scientific experiments conducted by Apollo astronauts, such as collecting lunar rocks and deploying seismic sensors, provided invaluable data about the Moon's composition and geology.

- **Apollo Program**: Beyond the famous Moon landings, Apollo missions contributed to our understanding of lunar science by studying the Moon's surface and environmental conditions. Experiments such as the Solar Wind Composition Experiment and the Passive Seismic Experiment offered insights into the lunar environment and its interaction with solar radiation.

- **Mars Missions**: NASA's Viking missions in the 1970s became the first successful attempts to land on Mars and conduct scientific experiments on the planet's surface. These missions provided groundbreaking data on Mars' atmosphere and soil composition, setting the stage for future missions aimed at discovering whether life ever existed on the planet.

5.2 Present-Day Scientific Research in Space

5.2.1 International Space Station (ISS) as a Scientific Platform

The ISS serves as one of the most important platforms for conducting scientific research in space. Orbiting the Earth at an altitude of approximately 400 km, the ISS provides a unique environment for studying the effects of microgravity, cosmic radiation, and other space-related phenomena. A collaboration between space agencies such as NASA, Roscosmos, ESA, JAXA, and CSA, the ISS hosts a wide array of scientific experiments, many of which are impossible to conduct on Earth.

- **Microgravity Research**: The microgravity environment of the ISS allows researchers to study physical and biological processes that are obscured by Earth's gravity. This includes research in fluid dynamics, combustion, material science, and crystallography. For example, experiments conducted on the ISS have contributed to advancements in drug development by allowing scientists to grow protein crystals more efficiently in microgravity.

- **Human Health and Space Medicine**: The ISS also plays a vital role in understanding the effects of long-term space travel on human health. Studies on bone density loss, muscle atrophy, and the impacts of cosmic radiation are crucial for preparing future missions to Mars and other deep-space destinations. NASA's Twins Study, which compared the health data of astronaut Scott Kelly, who spent a year in space, with that of his twin brother on Earth, provided insights into how the human body adapts to long-duration spaceflights.

5.2.2 Robotic Space Missions

In addition to crewed missions, robotic spacecraft have become a fundamental tool in scientific research and exploration. These unmanned missions allow for the exploration of distant planets, moons, and asteroids that are beyond the reach of human astronauts.

- **Mars Rovers**: NASA's Mars rovers, including Spirit, Opportunity, Curiosity, and Perseverance, have played a pivotal role in exploring the Martian surface. Equipped with a suite of scientific instruments, these rovers have analyzed rock samples, captured images, and searched for signs of past water activity on Mars. The Perseverance rover, launched in 2020, is currently conducting a detailed search for biosignatures—evidence of past microbial life—on the red planet.

- **Juno Mission**: NASA's Juno mission to Jupiter has provided stunning new data on the planet's atmosphere, magnetic field, and composition. Juno's findings have offered a deeper understanding of the gas giant's weather patterns and interior structure, helping scientists refine their models of planet formation.

5.2.3 Space Telescopes and Observatories

Space-based telescopes and observatories have expanded our ability to study the universe without interference from Earth's atmosphere. These instruments are essential for investigating phenomena such as black holes, dark matter, and exoplanets.

- **James Webb Space Telescope (JWST)**: Scheduled for launch in December 2021, the James Webb Space Telescope is expected to revolutionize our understanding of the universe. Designed to observe infrared light, JWST will provide unprecedented views of distant galaxies, star formation, and planetary systems, offering insights into the early stages of the universe.

- **Chandra X-ray Observatory**: The Chandra X-ray Observatory, launched in 1999, has been instrumental in studying high-energy phenomena such as supernovae, black holes, and neutron stars. Its X-ray observations have revealed the energetic processes occurring in the centers of galaxies and provided evidence for the existence of dark matter.

5.3 The Role of Private Companies in Scientific Research

In recent years, private companies have become increasingly involved in scientific research and exploration, leveraging their technological expertise and commercial resources to contribute to space science.

5.3.1 SpaceX and Commercial Science Missions

SpaceX, one of the leading private space companies, has played a significant role in facilitating scientific research through its launch services. The company's Falcon 9 rocket has become a reliable vehicle for launching scientific payloads into space, including satellites, space probes, and ISS resupply missions.

- **Dragon Laboratory**: SpaceX's Dragon spacecraft is designed to transport cargo to and from the ISS. In addition to delivering supplies for astronauts, Dragon is used to carry scientific experiments that can be conducted aboard the ISS. For instance, Dragon has transported biological research projects, materials science experiments, and technology demonstrations to the space station.

5.3.2 Blue Origin and New Shepard's Scientific Payloads

Blue Origin, founded by Jeff Bezos, is another private company contributing to space research. Its New Shepard vehicle, designed for suborbital space tourism, also carries scientific payloads on its test flights. These missions provide researchers with access to a brief microgravity environment, enabling experiments in fields such as fluid dynamics, material science, and astrophysics.

5.4 Challenges in Scientific Research and Exploration

5.4.1 Funding and Budget Constraints

One of the most significant challenges facing scientific research in space is the high cost of conducting missions. Government space agencies often face budget constraints, which can limit the scope of their scientific missions. For instance, NASA's budget is subject to fluctuations based on political priorities, which can affect the agency's ability to fund long-term exploration programs.

5.4.2 Technical Limitations

Space exploration involves overcoming numerous technical challenges, from developing reliable propulsion systems to designing spacecraft that can withstand the harsh conditions of space. These technical hurdles often result in delays and cost overruns, which can impede scientific progress.

5.5 Future Directions for Scientific Research and Exploration

5.5.1 Human Missions to Mars

One of the most ambitious goals for the future of space exploration is sending humans to Mars. NASA's Artemis program aims to return humans to the Moon by 2024, with the long-term goal of using the Moon as a stepping-stone for missions to Mars. Scientific research on Mars, including the search for signs of past life and the study of the planet's geology, will be a key focus of these missions.

5.5.2 Astrobiology and the Search for Life

The search for extraterrestrial life continues to be one of the most exciting areas of scientific research in space. Missions like NASA's Europa Clipper, set to launch in the 2020s, will investigate the possibility of life on Jupiter's moon Europa, which is believed to harbor a subsurface ocean beneath its icy crust.

Conclusion

Scientific research and exploration remain central to humanity's efforts to understand the universe and push the boundaries of knowledge. From early satellite missions to current explorations of distant planets, space research has provided groundbreaking insights into our world and the cosmos. As private companies join the scientific community, the future of space exploration looks more promising than ever.

The collaborative efforts between governmental organizations and private enterprises have led to a surge in innovative technologies and mission concepts that were once considered unattainable. With advancements in robotics, artificial intelligence, and propulsion systems, the scope of scientific inquiries expands daily, allowing researchers to tackle complex questions about our solar system and beyond.

The upcoming missions to Mars and the ongoing studies of celestial bodies such as Europa and Titan hold the potential for significant discoveries, including the possibility of extraterrestrial life. As we prepare for human exploration of Mars, understanding the impacts of long-duration space travel on human health will be paramount. The insights gained from these missions will not only enhance our scientific knowledge but may also lead to developments that benefit life on Earth, such as advancements in health care and sustainability.

Moreover, the involvement of private space companies has introduced new paradigms in funding and conducting research. These entities are not only launching scientific payloads but also developing new platforms for research that were previously unattainable, such as commercial space stations and lunar bases. The future of space tourism, coupled with scientific research, will also encourage public interest and investment in space endeavors, making the cosmos more accessible to a broader audience.

In conclusion, as we look toward the stars, the intersection of scientific research, technological innovation, and collaborative efforts between the public and private sectors will undoubtedly play a pivotal role in shaping the future of space exploration. The challenges we face, including funding, technological barriers, and ethical considerations, must be addressed to unlock the full potential of our quest for knowledge beyond Earth. The journey of discovery is far from over, and the next chapters of space exploration promise to be as groundbreaking as those that have come before.

Chapter 3: Technologies Driving the Space Industry

1. Propulsion Systems and Their Advancements
2. Satellite Technology and Communications
3. Robotics and Automation in Space Missions
4. Earth Observation Technologies
5. Emerging Technologies: Space Mining and Habitats

Chapter 3

Technologies Driving the Space Industry

Introduction

The rapid advancements in technology have been pivotal in shaping the modern space industry, making once-distant possibilities a reality. From launching spacecraft to monitoring distant galaxies, innovations in engineering and science have enabled humanity to explore beyond the confines of Earth. This chapter delves into the core technologies driving the space sector, examining how propulsion systems, satellite communications, and robotics have transformed space exploration and commercialization.

We will explore the cutting-edge tools and systems that have become essential to space missions, from advancements in propulsion technologies that push the boundaries of travel to satellite innovations that connect the globe. Moreover, we'll discuss the increasingly critical role of automation and robotics in navigating space environments, the technologies used in Earth observation, and the emergence of revolutionary concepts like space mining and space habitats. These technologies not only enable the expansion of space exploration but also offer new opportunities for sustainable development and future colonization efforts.

1. Propulsion Systems and Their Advancements

Propulsion systems form the backbone of space exploration, enabling spacecraft to escape Earth's gravitational pull and traverse the vastness of space. Over the decades, significant advancements have been made in this field, allowing for greater efficiency, reduced costs, and the possibility of longer and more complex missions. From the early days of chemical rockets to the emerging concepts of ion propulsion and nuclear engines, propulsion technologies have evolved dramatically, reflecting the growing ambitions of both government space agencies and private enterprises.

This section provides an in-depth exploration of the different types of propulsion systems that have been developed and the advancements that have made them more efficient, powerful, and capable of supporting humanity's future space endeavors. By understanding how propulsion systems work and how they have improved over time, we can appreciate their pivotal role in enabling space exploration, satellite deployment, and interplanetary travel.

1.1 Early Propulsion Systems: Chemical Rockets

Chemical propulsion systems, which are still widely used today, were the first to be developed for space travel. These systems work by burning propellants, typically a combination of fuel and an oxidizer, to create a high-pressure gas that is expelled from the engine, generating thrust.

One of the earliest and most famous chemical propulsion systems is the **Saturn V** rocket, which was used during the Apollo missions to send astronauts to the Moon. The Saturn V, developed by NASA, was a multistage liquid-fuel rocket that relied on kerosene and liquid oxygen in its first stage, with the subsequent stages using liquid hydrogen and liquid oxygen for greater efficiency in space. The Saturn V stood as a symbol of human ingenuity, with its powerful engines capable of producing 34.5 million newtons of thrust.

In recent decades, chemical propulsion systems have been optimized for cost and reusability. For example, **SpaceX's Falcon 9** rocket employs a modified chemical propulsion system that not only delivers payloads to orbit but also returns to Earth for reuse. This represents a breakthrough in cost-effectiveness for space exploration, paving the way for affordable space missions.

1.2 Solid vs. Liquid Propellant Systems

Chemical rockets can generally be classified into two types based on the propellant used: **solid propellant systems** and **liquid propellant systems**.

- **Solid Propellant Rockets**: These systems are simpler in design and more reliable, as they store both the fuel and oxidizer in a solid state, ready for ignition. Once ignited, they burn until all the fuel is expended. Solid propellant rockets are often used in military applications and as boosters in large space missions. An example is the **Solid Rocket Boosters (SRBs)** used in the **Space Shuttle** program.

- **Liquid Propellant Rockets**: These systems provide greater control over thrust and efficiency by using liquid fuel and oxidizer stored in separate tanks, which are combined in the combustion chamber. Liquid-fueled rockets can be shut down or restarted mid-flight, offering more flexibility in mission design. The **Raptor engines** of SpaceX's **Starship** are a recent example of highly efficient, reusable liquid propulsion systems that use methane and liquid oxygen.

While both solid and liquid propulsion systems have their advantages, liquid systems have become more common in modern space exploration due to their superior efficiency and versatility.

1.3 Electric Propulsion Systems: Ion Thrusters and Hall Effect Thrusters

One of the most revolutionary advancements in propulsion technology is the development of **electric propulsion systems**. Unlike chemical rockets, electric propulsion systems use electricity to accelerate ions to extremely high velocities, creating a stream of charged particles that produce thrust. Although they generate less thrust than chemical propulsion systems, they are far more efficient, consuming less fuel over longer durations.

- **Ion Thrusters**: Ion propulsion systems, such as the **Xenon Ion Thruster** used on NASA's **Dawn** spacecraft, work by ionizing a neutral gas (typically xenon) and accelerating the ions through an electric field. These systems are incredibly efficient and capable of running for years with minimal fuel consumption. Dawn's mission to the asteroid belt demonstrated the effectiveness of ion propulsion for long-duration, deep-space missions.

- **Hall Effect Thrusters**: Another type of electric propulsion, the Hall Effect Thruster, uses a magnetic field to trap electrons, which then ionize the propellant. This technology is being used in spacecraft such as **ESA's BepiColombo**, which is on its way to explore Mercury. Hall thrusters offer a balance between efficiency and thrust, making them suitable for missions requiring long-term stability and low fuel consumption.

1.4 Nuclear Thermal Propulsion

Another promising area of propulsion technology is **nuclear thermal propulsion (NTP)**, which involves using a nuclear reactor to heat a propellant, typically hydrogen, and then expelling the superheated gas through a nozzle to generate thrust. NTP offers the potential for greater efficiency than chemical rockets, with the possibility of significantly reducing the travel time for missions to Mars or beyond.

NASA and private companies have been actively researching NTP systems, envisioning their use for crewed missions to Mars. By halving the time needed to reach Mars, NTP could reduce the health risks to astronauts associated with long-duration space travel.

1.5 Solar Sails and Light Propulsion

In the realm of truly futuristic propulsion technologies, **solar sails** represent an exciting concept. Solar sails use the pressure exerted by sunlight to propel spacecraft. As photons from the Sun collide with the sail, they transfer momentum to the spacecraft, propelling it forward. Although the acceleration is slow, it requires no fuel, making it ideal for long-term space missions.

The **IKAROS spacecraft** launched by the Japan Aerospace Exploration Agency (JAXA) is a notable example of a solar sail mission. This technology holds the potential for long-term, interstellar travel where fuel efficiency is paramount.

1.6 Hybrid Propulsion Systems

Hybrid propulsion systems combine the strengths of different propulsion technologies to achieve greater efficiency and versatility. For instance, a spacecraft might use chemical rockets for the initial launch and ion propulsion for deep-space maneuvers. Hybrid systems are especially appealing for missions requiring varied propulsion capabilities across different stages of flight.

An example of hybrid propulsion is the proposed missions to Mars, where chemical rockets will be used for launch and landing, while ion or nuclear propulsion systems could handle interplanetary travel.

1.7 Future Advancements and Experimental Technologies

Looking to the future, several experimental propulsion technologies are being explored, each with the potential to revolutionize space travel. Among these are **fusion propulsion systems**, which aim to harness the energy produced by nuclear fusion reactions to create an extremely efficient and powerful propulsion system. Though still in its early stages, fusion propulsion could drastically reduce travel times within the solar system and make interstellar travel a realistic possibility.

Another area of interest is **antimatter propulsion**, which, while still theoretical, could offer incredible energy efficiency by using the annihilation of matter and antimatter to produce thrust. Although current technology is far from realizing antimatter propulsion, ongoing research in particle physics may one day make this a reality.

Conclusion

Propulsion systems are fundamental to the future of space exploration. As we continue to push the boundaries of space travel, the development of more advanced and efficient propulsion systems will be critical to our success. From the chemical rockets that launched humanity into space to the electric and nuclear propulsion systems that promise interplanetary travel, each advancement in propulsion technology brings us closer to exploring the farthest reaches of our universe.

2. Satellite Technology and Communications

Satellites play a crucial role in modern society, serving as the backbone of global communications, navigation systems, weather forecasting, and Earth observation. These space-based systems have transformed industries and contributed significantly to scientific research, national security, and global connectivity. Over the past several decades, advancements in satellite technology have enabled faster, more efficient data transmission, wider coverage, and greater resilience in space environments.

In this section, we explore the key components of satellite technology, including their design, types, and functions. We also delve into the critical role they play in telecommunications, data transmission, and scientific research. Furthermore, we examine the technological innovations that have pushed the boundaries of satellite performance, making them more versatile and powerful. Examples of real-world satellite applications, such as global positioning systems (GPS), telecommunications, and Earth observation, will illustrate how this technology has become an indispensable part of everyday life.

2.1 Early Satellite Development and Milestones

The history of satellite technology began with the launch of **Sputnik 1** by the Soviet Union in 1957, marking the dawn of the space age. This was the first artificial satellite to orbit the Earth, and although its functions were limited to transmitting radio pulses, it laid the groundwork for the development of more sophisticated satellites.

Shortly after Sputnik, the United States launched **Explorer 1** in 1958, which discovered the Van Allen radiation belts around Earth. This early phase of satellite technology focused primarily on scientific research and national prestige, driven by the geopolitical competition of the Cold War.

A major milestone came in 1962 with the launch of **Telstar 1**, the first active communications satellite. Telstar transmitted live television signals between the United States and Europe, revolutionizing global communications. Since then, the satellite industry has grown exponentially, supporting an ever-expanding array of applications.

2.2 Types of Satellites

Satellites can be classified into various categories based on their function, orbit, and design. The most common types include:

- **Communication Satellites (COMSATs)**: These satellites are used for transmitting television, radio, and internet signals across vast distances. Modern communication satellites, such as **Inmarsat** and **Intelsat**, facilitate high-speed broadband and mobile communications across the globe. They often operate in geostationary orbits, remaining fixed relative to a specific point on Earth.

- **Weather Satellites**: Designed to monitor atmospheric conditions and provide data for weather forecasting, these satellites use sophisticated sensors to capture detailed images and track weather patterns in real-time. The **GOES (Geostationary Operational Environmental Satellite)** series by NASA and NOAA has been instrumental in tracking hurricanes and other natural disasters.

- **Navigation Satellites**: These satellites provide positioning and timing services for GPS (Global Positioning System), GLONASS, Galileo, and other regional navigation systems. They are critical for aviation, shipping, land transport, and even personal navigation through smartphones. The **GPS constellation** developed by the United States Department of Defense is one of the most widely used satellite systems for navigation.

- **Earth Observation Satellites**: These are used for monitoring environmental changes, land usage, deforestation, and agricultural practices. **Landsat** and **Sentinel satellites** are some of the most prominent Earth observation satellites, providing high-resolution imagery used in scientific research, urban planning, and environmental conservation.

- **Scientific Satellites**: Dedicated to research and exploration, these satellites collect data on space weather, cosmic radiation, and distant celestial bodies. NASA's **Hubble Space Telescope** and the European Space Agency's **Gaia** mission are examples of scientific satellites that have provided groundbreaking insights into the universe.

Each type of satellite is optimized for its specific role, but the development of multifunctional satellites is becoming increasingly common, allowing them to serve multiple purposes simultaneously.

2.3 Satellite Orbits: LEO, MEO, GEO, and Beyond

The orbit in which a satellite is placed plays a critical role in its functionality and the services it can provide. There are three main types of satellite orbits:

- **Low Earth Orbit (LEO)**: Satellites in LEO operate between 160 and 2,000 kilometers above the Earth's surface. They are commonly used for Earth observation, imaging, and certain communication functions. **Starlink**, a satellite constellation launched by SpaceX, operates in LEO to provide high-speed internet services. LEO satellites have shorter orbital periods, meaning they circle the Earth more frequently, but their coverage area is smaller, requiring constellations of multiple satellites for global coverage.

- **Medium Earth Orbit (MEO)**: MEO satellites operate between 2,000 and 35,786 kilometers above Earth. The **GPS** system operates in MEO, offering a compromise between the wide coverage of GEO satellites and the rapid orbit of LEO satellites. These satellites are often used for navigation and timing services.

- **Geostationary Orbit (GEO)**: GEO satellites orbit at around 35,786 kilometers and match the Earth's rotation, meaning they remain fixed above a specific location. These satellites are ideal for communication and broadcasting services, as they provide consistent coverage to large areas. Most television and internet satellites, such as those used by **Dish Network** and **DirecTV**, operate in GEO.

- **Highly Elliptical Orbit (HEO)**: These orbits allow satellites to spend extended periods over specific areas of the Earth, particularly in high-latitude regions. Satellites in HEO are often used for communication in the polar regions and for scientific missions that require long observation times over a particular area.

Satellites in different orbits serve different purposes, and the selection of orbit depends on the satellite's mission requirements.

2.4 Satellite Communications: How It Works

Satellite communication systems consist of three main components:

- **The Satellite**: This acts as a relay station, receiving signals from Earth-based transmitters and sending them to receivers in different parts of the world. The satellite itself contains transponders, antennas, and power systems, which ensure that signals are properly received, processed, and transmitted.

- **Ground Stations**: These are located on Earth and serve as the link between the satellite and terrestrial networks. Ground stations send data to the satellite (uplink) and receive data from the satellite (downlink). Large antennas are often used to communicate with satellites in geostationary orbit, while smaller, mobile antennas are common for LEO satellites.

- **User Devices**: These are the devices that ultimately receive or send data through the satellite system. These range from television receivers to mobile phones and GPS units. The signals from satellites are often distributed through terrestrial networks, enabling seamless integration with mobile and internet services.

An example of how this system works is the **Iridium satellite network**, which provides global satellite phone services. The Iridium satellites operate in LEO, relaying signals between ground stations and mobile devices, allowing for communication even in remote areas where traditional cell networks are unavailable.

2.5 Innovations in Satellite Technology

In recent years, several key innovations have enhanced satellite performance, making them more powerful, efficient, and versatile:

- **Miniaturization and CubeSats**: One of the most significant advancements in satellite technology is the miniaturization of components, which has led to the development of **CubeSats** and **nanosatellites**. These small, cost-effective satellites are typically used for scientific research, Earth observation, and communication. Despite their size, they offer many of the capabilities of larger satellites. Universities and startups often deploy CubeSats for research missions at a fraction of the cost of traditional satellites.

- **Phased Array Antennas**: These antennas allow satellites to beam signals in specific directions without physically moving the antenna. Phased array technology is used in systems like **OneWeb**, which aims to provide global broadband services by using a large constellation of LEO satellites. This technology improves signal quality and increases the bandwidth available for communication.

- **High-Throughput Satellites (HTS)**: HTS technology has greatly increased the capacity of communication satellites. These satellites are designed to deliver high data rates, making them suitable for applications such as video streaming and high-speed internet. **ViaSat-3** is an example of an HTS system that provides significantly higher bandwidth compared to traditional communication satellites.

- **Autonomous Satellite Operations**: With advancements in artificial intelligence and machine learning, satellites are becoming more autonomous. Autonomous satellites can make real-time decisions, adjust their orbits, and manage power consumption without requiring constant control from Earth. This is particularly useful for deep-space missions where communication delays make manual control challenging.

2.6 Satellite Applications in Telecommunications and Internet Services

Satellites are a critical component of global telecommunications and internet services. They provide broadband to rural and remote areas, connect ships and aircraft, and ensure continuity of service during natural disasters.

One prominent example is **Starlink**, a satellite internet constellation launched by SpaceX. Starlink aims to provide high-speed internet access to underserved regions using thousands of small satellites in LEO. The use of LEO satellites allows for lower latency and higher speeds compared to traditional GEO satellites.

Another example is **SES**, which operates a fleet of GEO satellites to provide television, internet, and communication services to millions of users worldwide. These satellites ensure that people in remote or underdeveloped areas have access to critical communication infrastructure.

2.7 Challenges and Future Trends in Satellite Technology

While satellite technology has made tremendous strides, it faces several challenges, including:

- **Space Debris**: The increasing number of satellites in orbit has led to a growing concern about space debris. Collisions between satellites and debris can create more fragments, posing a risk to active satellites. Efforts are underway to develop debris mitigation technologies, including active debris removal systems and improved satellite disposal methods.

- **Spectrum Allocation**: As more satellites are launched, the demand for radio frequencies has increased. Efficient spectrum management is essential to avoid interference between satellite systems and ensure that communication signals are clear and reliable.

Looking ahead, the future of satellite technology is promising, with trends such as the deployment of mega-constellations, advancements in quantum communication, and the exploration of deep-space satellite networks set to revolutionize how we use satellites for communication and scientific discovery.

Conclusion

Satellite technology and communications have come a long way since the early days of Sputnik and Telstar. Today, satellites are indispensable for global communications, scientific research, and national security. As technological advancements continue to push the boundaries of what is possible, satellites will play an even more significant role in connecting the world and enabling humanity's exploration of space.

3. Robotics and Automation in Space Missions

The development of robotics and automation has been one of the most significant advancements in space exploration. These technologies allow for tasks that would be impossible or extremely dangerous for humans to perform, such as building space structures, performing maintenance on spacecraft, and exploring distant celestial bodies. Robotics and automation systems are crucial in enabling long-term missions, ensuring the safety of astronauts, and advancing scientific research.

This section explores how robotics and automation have evolved in space missions. We will delve into the historical milestones, current applications, and future possibilities, as well as the technical challenges these technologies face. Key examples, such as the Mars rovers, robotic arms on space stations, and autonomous space probes, will illustrate the immense value of automation in space.

3.1 Early Developments in Space Robotics

The history of robotics in space missions began in the 1960s, during the space race between the United States and the Soviet Union. Early efforts were focused on using remote-controlled devices for tasks such as collecting samples and performing simple mechanical tasks in space.

One of the first examples of space robotics was the Soviet **Luna 16** mission in 1970, which used a robotic arm to collect soil samples from the Moon. Around the same time, NASA launched the **Surveyor** series of landers, which also employed robotic tools to gather lunar soil and send data back to Earth.

As the complexity of space missions increased, so did the need for more advanced robotic systems. The **Viking** program in the 1970s, which sent landers to Mars, featured more sophisticated robotic instruments capable of digging into the Martian soil and performing detailed scientific analyses.

3.2 Robotic Arms in Space Stations: The Canadarm and Beyond

One of the most iconic robotic systems in space exploration is the **Canadarm**, a robotic arm first deployed on the Space Shuttle in 1981. Built by the Canadian Space Agency (CSA), the Canadarm revolutionized how astronauts performed spacewalks and deployed satellites. It was used for a variety of tasks, including moving astronauts and cargo around the spacecraft and capturing and repairing satellites.

The success of the Canadarm led to the development of the **Canadarm2**, which is installed on the International Space Station (ISS). Unlike its predecessor, the Canadarm2 can move along the exterior of the ISS, providing greater flexibility in performing repairs and maintenance. It is equipped with advanced sensors and cameras that allow it to perform tasks autonomously or be controlled remotely by astronauts or mission control.

Another critical piece of robotic technology on the ISS is **Dextre**, a two-armed robot that works alongside Canadarm2. Dextre is used for more delicate tasks, such as replacing batteries, installing new equipment, and conducting inspections. These robotic systems significantly reduce the need for astronauts to conduct extravehicular activities (EVAs), enhancing safety and efficiency on the ISS.

3.3 Robotic Exploration of Celestial Bodies

One of the most exciting applications of robotics in space exploration is the exploration of distant planets, moons, and asteroids. These missions often involve robotic rovers and landers that can traverse the surface of a celestial body, collect samples, and perform scientific analyses. Such missions have provided invaluable insights into the geology, climate, and potential habitability of other planets.

- **Mars Rovers**: NASA's **Sojourner**, which landed on Mars in 1997, was the first successful robotic rover to explore another planet. It was followed by the more advanced **Spirit** and **Opportunity** rovers, which explored the Martian surface for several years. The current **Curiosity** rover, which landed in 2012, continues to analyze Mars' surface and atmosphere, searching for signs of past water activity and organic compounds.

- **Perseverance**: In 2021, NASA's **Perseverance** rover landed on Mars with a mission to search for signs of ancient life and collect soil samples for future return to Earth. Equipped with advanced sensors, cameras, and a small helicopter named **Ingenuity**, Perseverance represents the cutting edge of robotic exploration technology.

- **Lunar Rovers**: The **Lunokhod** series, launched by the Soviet Union in the early 1970s, was the first set of robotic lunar rovers. These rovers were remotely operated and gathered valuable data about the Moon's surface. NASA followed suit with the **Apollo Lunar Roving Vehicle (LRV)**, which astronauts used during the Apollo missions to explore the Moon.

- **Asteroid Missions**: The Japanese **Hayabusa** missions are notable examples of robotic spacecraft sent to asteroids. The original **Hayabusa** mission successfully collected samples from the asteroid Itokawa in 2005, while **Hayabusa2** returned samples from the asteroid Ryugu in 2020. These missions highlight the potential of robotics for space mining and asteroid exploration.

3.4 Autonomous Systems and AI in Space Exploration

As space missions become more complex and travel to more distant destinations, autonomous systems and artificial intelligence (AI) are playing an increasingly important role. These systems allow spacecraft and robotic systems to operate without real-time input from humans, which is essential when exploring regions far from Earth where communication delays can be significant.

- **Autonomous Spacecraft**: NASA's **Deep Space 1**, launched in 1998, was a pioneering mission that tested autonomous navigation systems. Its **Autonomous Navigation System (AutoNav)** allowed the spacecraft to navigate through the solar system without human intervention, setting the stage for future autonomous missions.

- **AI for Rovers**: AI has become crucial for the operation of robotic rovers on Mars and other celestial bodies. For example, NASA's **Curiosity** rover uses AI to autonomously navigate the Martian terrain, avoiding obstacles and selecting interesting areas for scientific analysis. This reduces the need for constant oversight from mission control, allowing the rover to cover more ground in less time.

- **AI on the ISS**: On the ISS, AI-powered robotic systems assist astronauts with daily tasks. **CIMON (Crew Interactive Mobile Companion)** is an AI-powered assistant that helps astronauts with experiments, provides instructions, and offers general support. As AI systems become more advanced, their role in space missions will likely expand, including applications in spacecraft maintenance and autonomous decision-making.

3.5 Robotics in Space Manufacturing and Construction

Robotic systems are also critical for space manufacturing and construction, both of which are essential for establishing a permanent human presence in space. These technologies could eventually enable the building of space stations, habitats on the Moon or Mars, and even large-scale space infrastructure such as solar power stations or telescopic arrays.

- **In-Space Assembly**: Robotic arms and autonomous systems are being developed to build structures in space without the need for human intervention. NASA's **Restore-L** mission aims to demonstrate the use of robotic systems to refuel, repair, and even assemble spacecraft in orbit. These capabilities will be essential for maintaining satellites and building space habitats in the future.

- **Additive Manufacturing**: 3D printing is another technology being explored for space missions. In 2014, NASA successfully demonstrated 3D printing on the ISS, using a **Made In Space** printer to create tools and parts in microgravity. Future missions may use robots to print entire habitats on the Moon or Mars using local materials, drastically reducing the need to transport building materials from Earth.

3.6 Challenges and Future Directions

While robotics and automation have advanced significantly, there are still numerous challenges to overcome. Some of these challenges include:

- **Radiation Exposure**: Robots in space are exposed to high levels of radiation, which can damage sensitive electronics and reduce their operational lifespan. Developing radiation-hardened components is critical for the long-term success of robotic missions.

- **Limited Power Supply**: Many space robots rely on solar panels or batteries, which can limit their operational range and capabilities. Innovative solutions, such as nuclear-powered robots, are being explored to provide longer-lasting power for deep-space missions.

- **Autonomous Decision Making**: While AI has improved the autonomy of robotic systems, there is still much work to be done in developing truly independent robots capable of making complex decisions in unpredictable environments. The challenges of real-time decision-making in space will continue to push the boundaries of AI and machine learning.

- **Human-Robot Interaction**: As robots and astronauts work more closely together, ensuring smooth human-robot interaction will be essential. This involves improving the design of robotic systems to make them more intuitive for astronauts to control, as well as developing AI systems that can understand and respond to human needs.

Looking to the future, robotics and automation will play a central role in humanity's continued exploration of space. From autonomous spacecraft exploring the outer planets to robots constructing habitats on Mars, these technologies will enable new possibilities for space exploration and colonization.

Conclusion

Robotics and automation have transformed space missions, enabling humanity to explore distant planets, perform complex tasks in space, and advance scientific knowledge. From the early robotic arms of the Space Shuttle era to today's autonomous Mars rovers, these technologies have become indispensable tools for space exploration. As AI and automation continue to evolve, the future holds exciting possibilities for even more advanced robotic systems, which will push the boundaries of what is possible in space.

4. Earth Observation Technologies

Earth observation (EO) technologies play a critical role in gathering data about our planet's surface, atmosphere, and oceans. Through satellites and other remote sensing systems, these technologies provide essential information for applications ranging from weather forecasting and environmental monitoring to disaster management and national security. Over the years, EO technologies have evolved to become more sophisticated, offering high-resolution imagery, real-time monitoring, and advanced data analytics.

In this section, we will explore the development of Earth observation technologies, how they work, and their numerous applications. We will also discuss the challenges and future advancements in this field, focusing on the integration of artificial intelligence, machine learning, and new sensor technologies that promise to revolutionize how we observe and understand the Earth.

4.1 Evolution of Earth Observation Technologies

The history of Earth observation technologies dates back to the early 20th century, with aerial photography being one of the first methods used for gathering information about the Earth's surface. However, the development of satellite technology in the 1950s marked a turning point, allowing for comprehensive, global monitoring of the planet.

- **Landsat Program**: The launch of the **Landsat 1** satellite by NASA in 1972 was a landmark moment in EO history. Landsat 1 provided the first multi-spectral images of Earth's surface, which were used for a wide range of applications, including agriculture, forestry, and environmental monitoring. The Landsat program continues today, with **Landsat 9**, launched in 2021, offering even higher resolution images and more advanced sensors.

- **SPOT Satellite Series**: Launched in 1986, France's **SPOT** (Satellite Pour l'Observation de la Terre) satellites have provided high-resolution optical imagery of Earth. The SPOT program pioneered the use of stereo imaging, which allowed for the creation of 3D models of the Earth's surface, improving the analysis of terrain and geological features.

- **Copernicus Program**: The European Space Agency's **Copernicus** program, launched in 2014, represents one of the most advanced EO systems to date. The program consists of a fleet of **Sentinel** satellites, which provide data for environmental monitoring, climate change, and emergency response. The **Sentinel-2** satellites, for example, are capable of capturing multi-spectral images with high temporal resolution, allowing for frequent monitoring of land use, vegetation, and coastal areas.

These early systems laid the foundation for modern EO technologies, which have become indispensable for understanding and managing global challenges.

4.2 How Earth Observation Satellites Work

Earth observation satellites rely on a variety of sensors and imaging techniques to capture data. These sensors can be classified into two main types: **passive sensors** and **active sensors**.

- **Passive Sensors**: Passive sensors detect natural energy (usually sunlight) that is reflected or emitted by the Earth's surface. They measure the intensity of radiation in different parts of the electromagnetic spectrum. This type of sensing is commonly used in optical and infrared imaging systems. Satellites such as Landsat, Sentinel-2, and SPOT rely on passive sensors to capture high-resolution images of the Earth's surface.

- **Active Sensors**: Active sensors, such as radars and lidars, emit their own energy and then measure the reflection or scattering of that energy from the Earth's surface. Active sensors are particularly useful in conditions where passive sensors are limited, such as during cloudy weather or at night. **Synthetic Aperture Radar (SAR)**, used by satellites like **Sentinel-1** and **RADARSAT**, is a common type of active sensor that provides high-resolution radar imagery regardless of weather or lighting conditions.

- **Hyperspectral Imaging**: A more recent development in EO technology is the use of **hyperspectral imaging**, which captures hundreds of narrow spectral bands across the electromagnetic spectrum. This allows for more detailed analysis of surface materials and environmental conditions. Hyperspectral imaging is particularly useful in applications such as mineral exploration, precision agriculture, and environmental monitoring.

4.3 Applications of Earth Observation Technologies

The data provided by Earth observation satellites have wide-ranging applications across numerous sectors. Below are some of the key applications of EO technologies.

4.3.1 Environmental Monitoring and Climate Change

One of the most important applications of EO technologies is environmental monitoring. Satellites provide critical data for tracking changes in ecosystems, deforestation, desertification, and other environmental phenomena. For example:

- **Deforestation Monitoring**: Using high-resolution imagery from satellites like Sentinel-2 and Landsat, organizations such as the **UN Food and Agriculture Organization (FAO)** can monitor deforestation rates in real-time, helping policymakers enforce conservation efforts and reduce illegal logging.

- **Climate Change Tracking**: EO technologies play a crucial role in monitoring the impacts of climate change. For instance, satellites like **Sentinel-6** measure sea level rise, while **NASA's Aqua satellite** tracks changes in global temperatures and greenhouse gas concentrations. These data are essential for understanding how climate change is affecting the planet and for informing mitigation strategies.

- **Arctic Ice Monitoring**: Satellites such as **ICESat-2** provide detailed data on ice thickness and volume in the polar regions. This is critical for understanding the effects of climate change on sea ice and glaciers, which in turn affect global sea levels.

4.3.2 Disaster Management and Response

EO technologies are invaluable for disaster management, providing real-time data that can be used to assess the impact of natural disasters and coordinate relief efforts. Some examples include:

- **Flood Monitoring**: During flooding events, radar satellites like **Sentinel-1** can penetrate through clouds and provide high-resolution images of affected areas. This allows emergency responders to assess the extent of flooding and plan evacuation routes and relief operations.

- **Wildfire Detection**: Satellites equipped with thermal infrared sensors, such as NASA's **MODIS** (Moderate Resolution Imaging Spectroradiometer), can detect the heat signatures of wildfires in real time. This data is used to monitor the spread of fires and deploy firefighting resources more effectively.

- **Earthquake Damage Assessment**: After earthquakes, EO satellites can provide imagery to assess damage to infrastructure and communities. **Radar satellites**, such as Japan's **ALOS-2**, are particularly useful in detecting changes in the Earth's surface caused by seismic activity.

4.3.3 Agriculture and Food Security

EO technologies have become essential tools in agriculture, providing farmers and agribusinesses with valuable data for managing crops and improving productivity. Some key applications include:

- **Precision Agriculture**: Satellites like **Sentinel-2** provide multi-spectral imagery that allows farmers to monitor crop health, soil conditions, and water usage. This data can be used to optimize irrigation, fertilizer application, and pest control, improving yields and reducing environmental impact.

- **Drought Monitoring**: EO technologies are critical for tracking drought conditions, particularly in regions that rely on rain-fed agriculture. Satellites such as NASA's **GRACE (Gravity Recovery and Climate Experiment)** measure changes in water storage, helping governments and farmers plan for droughts and manage water resources more effectively.

- **Food Security**: Organizations such as the **World Food Programme (WFP)** use EO data to monitor food production and predict potential food shortages. This helps guide international aid efforts and ensure that food is delivered to regions in need.

4.3.4 National Security and Defense

Earth observation technologies are also widely used for national security and defense purposes. High-resolution satellite imagery can be used for border surveillance, maritime monitoring, and the detection of military activities.

- **Maritime Surveillance**: Satellites equipped with radar and optical sensors, such as **RADARSAT-2** and **WorldView-3**, are used to monitor shipping lanes, detect illegal fishing, and track oil spills. These capabilities are particularly important for countries with large coastlines or maritime territories.

- **Military Reconnaissance**: Defense agencies use EO satellites to gather intelligence on potential threats. For example, satellites like the United States' **KH-11** provide high-resolution images that can be used for surveillance and reconnaissance missions.

4.4 Challenges in Earth Observation Technologies

While EO technologies have advanced significantly, several challenges remain in their implementation and usage:

- **Data Overload**: The sheer volume of data generated by EO satellites is one of the biggest challenges. Managing, storing, and processing this data to extract meaningful insights requires significant computational resources and advanced algorithms.

- **Data Accuracy and Calibration**: Ensuring that satellite data is accurate and calibrated across different systems and sensors is essential for reliable analysis. Differences in sensor sensitivity, image resolution, and atmospheric conditions can introduce errors into EO data, making calibration a critical task.

- **Cost of Satellite Launch and Operation**: Although the cost of launching EO satellites has decreased with advancements in technology, it remains a significant barrier for many developing countries and smaller organizations. Moreover, maintaining and operating these satellites requires continuous investment.

4.5 Future Trends in Earth Observation Technologies

The future of Earth observation technologies looks promising, with several trends set to shape the next generation of EO systems:

- **Miniaturization and CubeSats**: The rise of **CubeSats**—small, low-cost satellites—is revolutionizing Earth observation. These miniature satellites can be deployed in large constellations, providing frequent and near-real-time data on the Earth's surface. Companies like **Planet Labs** are already using CubeSats to capture daily images of the entire Earth.

- **Artificial Intelligence and Machine Learning**: AI and machine learning are increasingly being used to analyze EO data. These technologies can process vast amounts of satellite data to identify patterns and trends, making it easier to detect changes in land use, monitor environmental conditions, and predict natural disasters.

- **Quantum Remote Sensing**: Quantum sensing technologies, which are still in the experimental stage, have the potential to significantly improve the sensitivity and accuracy of EO systems. These sensors could allow for more precise measurements of environmental parameters, such as air quality and soil moisture, leading to better decision-making in areas like agriculture and climate change mitigation.

Conclusion

Earth observation technologies have revolutionized our understanding of the planet, enabling us to monitor environmental changes, respond to disasters, and improve agricultural productivity. As these technologies continue to evolve, they will play an even greater role in addressing global challenges, from climate change to food security. However, the challenges of data management, accuracy, and cost remain, and future advancements in AI, quantum sensing, and satellite miniaturization promise to push the boundaries of what is possible in Earth observation.

5. Emerging Technologies: Space Mining and Habitats

As humanity ventures further into space, the need to exploit extraterrestrial resources and establish sustainable habitats is becoming more urgent. Emerging technologies in **space mining** and **space habitats** are pivotal to achieving this goal. Space mining promises to unlock vast quantities of valuable resources like water, metals, and rare earth elements that are essential for space exploration and even for sustaining life on Earth. Meanwhile, the development of space habitats aims to create environments that allow humans to live and work in space for extended periods, supporting missions to the Moon, Mars, and beyond.

This section explores the technological advancements and challenges associated with space mining and habitats, providing a detailed look at their potential applications and impact on the future of space exploration. Examples of current missions and projects in these areas will also be discussed, shedding light on the innovative solutions being developed to overcome the technical, economic, and ethical hurdles of space resource utilization and habitation.

5.1 Space Mining: Unlocking Extraterrestrial Resources

Space mining refers to the extraction of valuable minerals and other resources from celestial bodies, including asteroids, the Moon, and eventually Mars. The vast resources present in space could provide the raw materials needed for future space missions, making long-term human presence in space more feasible.

5.1.1 Resources Available for Mining

- **Water**: One of the most valuable resources in space is water, which can be found on the Moon and asteroids. Water is essential for human survival and can also be broken down into hydrogen and oxygen for rocket fuel. The discovery of water ice in permanently shadowed regions of the Moon's poles has sparked significant interest in lunar mining.

- **Metals**: Asteroids are rich in metals like iron, nickel, and cobalt. Some asteroids also contain precious metals like gold, platinum, and rare earth elements, which are critical for the electronics industry. The **asteroid 16 Psyche**, for example, is believed to contain metals worth trillions of dollars.

- **Helium-3**: The Moon's surface contains deposits of **Helium-3**, a rare isotope that could potentially be used in future nuclear fusion reactors to provide clean and nearly limitless energy. Helium-3 is extremely rare on Earth, making its extraction from the Moon a key goal for future space missions.

5.1.2 Mining Techniques

Several techniques are being developed to extract resources from celestial bodies, including:

- **Surface Mining**: Similar to open-pit mining on Earth, surface mining on the Moon or asteroids would involve removing surface material to access valuable resources. Robotic systems would likely perform these operations in the harsh conditions of space. For example, NASA's **Regolith Advanced Surface Systems Operations Robot (RASSOR)** is being developed to mine lunar regolith for water and other materials.

- **Drilling and Excavation**: Drilling technologies will be critical for accessing resources located beneath the surface. **Honeybee Robotics**, for instance, is working on robotic drills that could be used for mining operations on Mars or the Moon. These drills are designed to operate in extreme environments and extract core samples from deep below the surface.

- **In-Situ Resource Utilization (ISRU)**: ISRU involves using materials found in space to create the resources needed for space missions, such as water, oxygen, and building materials. NASA's **Lunar Gateway** and **Artemis missions** both plan to use ISRU technologies to extract and utilize water ice from the Moon.

5.1.3 Key Players and Missions in Space Mining

Several companies and space agencies are investing in space mining technologies:

- **Planetary Resources**: One of the pioneers in space mining, Planetary Resources aimed to extract water and metals from asteroids. Though the company has faced financial difficulties, its ambitious vision has inspired others to explore the potential of asteroid mining.

- **NASA's Artemis Program**: The **Artemis program** aims to return humans to the Moon and establish a sustainable presence by the end of the decade. NASA plans to utilize lunar resources, including water ice, to support these missions and reduce the need for resupply from Earth.

- **Luxembourg Space Resources Initiative**: Luxembourg has positioned itself as a leader in space mining by establishing policies and funding for space resource companies. The **European Space Resources Innovation Centre (ESRIC)** is developing technologies for asteroid mining and resource extraction from the Moon.

5.1.4 Challenges in Space Mining

While the potential benefits of space mining are enormous, significant challenges must be overcome:

- **Cost and Logistics**: The cost of launching mining equipment into space and transporting resources back to Earth is prohibitively high. The economic viability of space mining depends on reducing launch costs, which companies like **SpaceX** are working to achieve through reusable rockets.

- **Legal and Regulatory Issues**: The legal framework for space mining is still in its infancy. The **Outer Space Treaty** of 1967 prohibits any country from claiming ownership of celestial bodies, but it does not address private companies' rights to extract resources. Countries like the United States and Luxembourg have passed legislation that grants private companies the right to own and sell space resources, but international agreement is still needed.

- **Technical Challenges**: Mining in space is vastly different from mining on Earth. The lack of gravity, extreme temperatures, and the harsh space environment pose significant technical challenges. Developing mining systems that can operate autonomously in these conditions is essential.

5.2 Space Habitats: Building Sustainable Living Environments

As space missions extend beyond low Earth orbit and become longer in duration, there is a growing need for sustainable habitats that can support human life. Space habitats are designed to provide safe living and working environments for astronauts, ensuring they have access to air, water, food, and protection from radiation.

5.2.1 Concepts and Designs for Space Habitats

Several designs for space habitats have been proposed, each with its own approach to addressing the challenges of living in space:

- **Inflatable Habitats**: One of the most promising designs for space habitats is the use of inflatable modules, which can be compact during launch and then expanded once in space. **Bigelow Aerospace's BEAM (Bigelow Expandable Activity Module)**, which is currently attached to the International Space Station (ISS), is an example of an inflatable habitat. BEAM is made of durable materials that provide protection from micrometeoroids and radiation.

- **Cylindrical and Torus Designs**: Traditional space habitat designs include cylindrical and torus-shaped structures that rotate to generate artificial gravity through centrifugal force. The **Stanford Torus** and **O'Neill Cylinder** are two of the most famous concepts for rotating space habitats. These designs provide large living spaces and simulate Earth-like gravity, which is essential for maintaining human health during long-term missions.

- **3D-Printed Habitats**: NASA is exploring the use of **3D printing** to build habitats using local materials. The **Mars Ice House**, for example, is a concept that uses water ice found on Mars to construct protective domes for astronauts. By using in-situ resources, this approach reduces the need to transport building materials from Earth.

5.2.2 Life Support Systems

Space habitats must be equipped with life support systems that provide air, water, and food, while also managing waste. These systems are critical for ensuring the health and safety of astronauts during long missions.

- **Air and Water Recycling**: Life support systems in space habitats rely on closed-loop systems that recycle air and water. For example, the ISS uses a **Water Recovery System (WRS)** that recycles urine and sweat into drinkable water. The oxygen is generated through **electrolysis**, which splits water molecules into hydrogen and oxygen.

- **Food Production**: One of the biggest challenges for long-term space habitation is food production. NASA is exploring the use of **hydroponic** and **aeroponic** systems to grow plants in space. These systems use nutrient-rich water or air, instead of soil, to grow crops. Research is ongoing to determine which crops are best suited for growth in space.

- **Radiation Protection**: Space habitats must provide protection from cosmic rays and solar radiation, which can cause serious health problems for astronauts. One solution is to bury habitats beneath layers of lunar or Martian soil (regolith) to shield inhabitants from radiation. Another approach is to use advanced materials, such as hydrogen-rich plastics, which are effective at blocking radiation.

5.2.3 Current and Future Projects in Space Habitats

Several projects are underway to develop space habitats for future missions:

- **NASA's Lunar Gateway**: The Lunar Gateway is an orbital outpost that will serve as a staging point for missions to the Moon and beyond. It will provide living quarters for astronauts and support long-duration missions. The Gateway is part of NASA's Artemis program, which aims to establish a sustainable human presence on the Moon by the end of the decade.

- **Mars Base Camp**: SpaceX's **Starship** is designed to transport large numbers of people to Mars, with the ultimate goal of building a self-sustaining city. SpaceX envisions a base camp on Mars where habitats would be constructed using local materials, and crops would be grown using Martian soil and water extracted from the planet's ice deposits.

- **ESA's Moon Village**: The European Space Agency (ESA) has proposed the concept of a **Moon Village**, a multinational base on the lunar surface. This village would be built using 3D printing and in-situ resources, with the goal of creating a permanent human settlement on the Moon.

5.2.4 Challenges of Space Habitats

Gravity and Health: Prolonged exposure to microgravity has negative effects on human health, including muscle atrophy and bone loss. Studies conducted on astronauts aboard the International Space Station (ISS) have shown that without the constant pull of gravity, astronauts can lose up to 1% of bone density per month. This is particularly concerning for long-duration missions to destinations like Mars, where astronauts may spend several months or years in microgravity. To mitigate these effects, researchers are exploring various solutions, such as resistance exercise regimens, dietary adjustments, and the design of habitats that can generate artificial gravity through rotation. Creating a rotating habitat or incorporating exercise equipment that simulates gravitational resistance may help maintain the astronauts' physical health over extended missions.

Psychological Well-Being: Isolation and confinement in space habitats can significantly impact astronauts' mental health. Extended periods of living in a small, enclosed environment with limited social interaction can lead to feelings of loneliness, anxiety, and depression. Studies from past space missions have highlighted the importance of psychological support and the need for a well-designed habitat that encourages social interaction and teamwork.

For instance, NASA's HI-SEAS (Hawaii Space Exploration Analog and Simulation) missions have demonstrated the importance of group dynamics and the provision of recreational activities to maintain mental well-being. Designing habitats with communal spaces, recreational facilities, and opportunities for communication with loved ones on Earth can help mitigate psychological stress.

Cost and Funding: The financial costs of developing and maintaining space habitats are enormous. Securing funding for long-term space projects can be challenging, especially when competing for resources against other governmental and private sector initiatives. The cost of launching and maintaining habitats in space, along with the necessary support systems, requires substantial investment. Governments and space agencies must collaborate with private companies and international partners to share the financial burden and pool resources. Initiatives like NASA's Commercial Crew Program demonstrate how partnerships with private companies can help reduce costs while fostering innovation in habitat design and technology.

Technical Complexity: Building habitats that can withstand the harsh conditions of space is a significant technical challenge. These habitats must be equipped to handle extreme temperatures, radiation, and micrometeoroid impacts. Materials used in construction must provide sufficient insulation and protection while remaining lightweight for launch. Researchers are exploring advanced materials, such as **radiation-**

resistant composites and **self-healing materials**, that can enhance habitat durability and safety. Additionally, systems for life support, waste management, and energy production must be integrated into the habitat design, complicating the engineering process. Continuous testing and validation of these technologies in space-like environments are crucial for ensuring their effectiveness in real missions.

Supply Chain and Logistics: Establishing a sustainable supply chain for space habitats presents logistical challenges. Transporting supplies from Earth to space is costly and time-consuming. Developing habitats that can utilize in-situ resources, such as lunar regolith or Martian soil, is essential for reducing dependence on Earth. Technologies for resource extraction and processing must be developed to create a self-sufficient living environment. Additionally, the transportation of spare parts, equipment, and consumables needs to be carefully planned to ensure that astronauts have what they need throughout their mission.

Regulatory and Ethical Considerations: The establishment of space habitats raises various regulatory and ethical concerns. Questions about the ownership and utilization of extraterrestrial resources must be addressed. The **Outer Space Treaty** of 1967 stipulates that space is the province of all humankind, but it does not provide clear guidelines for resource extraction and habitat construction. International collaboration is essential to develop a legal framework that addresses these issues and ensures that space exploration benefits all nations. Ethical considerations surrounding the potential impact of human activities on extraterrestrial environments must also be taken into account, ensuring that exploration is conducted responsibly.

In summary, while the development of sustainable space habitats presents numerous challenges, advancements in technology, research, and international collaboration hold promise for overcoming these obstacles. Addressing the health, psychological, financial, technical, logistical, and regulatory aspects of space habitats will be critical to the success of long-duration missions and the future of human settlement in space.

Chapter 4: Applications of Space Technology

1. Telecommunications and Internet Services
2. Weather Forecasting and Environmental Monitoring
3. Global Navigation Systems
4. National Security and Defense Applications
5. Scientific Research and Space Exploration

Chapter 4

Applications of Space Technology

Introduction

Space technology has transformed numerous sectors on Earth, extending its influence beyond exploration to become an integral part of modern life. The advancements in satellite systems, robotics, and other space-based technologies have led to a multitude of applications that touch every aspect of society. From the way we communicate to how we monitor our planet, space technology serves as a backbone for essential services, both civilian and military.

This chapter delves into the various practical applications of space technology, highlighting how it supports telecommunications and internet services, enhances weather forecasting, and contributes to global navigation systems. Additionally, space technology plays a crucial role in national security and defense operations, while also pushing the boundaries of scientific research and discovery. Through these innovations, space technology continues to drive progress, shaping the future of our interconnected world.

1. Telecommunications and Internet Services

In recent decades, the world has witnessed rapid advancements in telecommunications and internet services, largely fueled by developments in space technology. Satellite communications have become the backbone of modern global connectivity, enabling communication across vast distances, even in the most remote and underserved regions. These technologies have not only enhanced personal and business communications but also supported critical services such as broadcasting, disaster response, and international collaboration.

This section explores the essential role space technology plays in telecommunications and internet services, detailing how satellites function, the various types of satellite systems used, and their impact on modern society. Through the use of practical examples, we will highlight how innovations in this sector continue to shape global connectivity, bridging gaps between populations and enhancing the digital economy.

1.1 The Role of Satellites in Telecommunications

Satellites serve as essential nodes in the global communications network. Positioned in space, they relay signals between distant points on Earth, enabling the transmission of data, voice, and video services across continents. There are several types of satellites used for telecommunications, categorized primarily by their orbit types: **Geostationary Earth Orbit (GEO)**, **Medium Earth Orbit (MEO)**, and **Low Earth Orbit (LEO)** satellites.

1.1.1 Geostationary Earth Orbit (GEO) Satellites

GEO satellites orbit at an altitude of approximately 35,786 kilometers above the Earth's equator. At this height, the satellite's orbital period matches the Earth's rotation, allowing it to remain stationary relative to a fixed point on the planet. These satellites are critical for services such as television broadcasting, internet backbone communications, and long-distance phone calls.

One notable example is the **Intelsat** network, which has provided reliable satellite communication services for over 50 years, facilitating international phone calls, television broadcasts, and more recently, broadband internet services. GEO satellites, due to their stationary nature, allow for continuous coverage over large areas, making them ideal for providing services to entire continents.

However, a challenge associated with GEO satellites is **signal latency**. Because of their high altitude, signals take approximately 240 milliseconds to travel from the Earth to the satellite and back, which can result in noticeable delays, especially in real-time communications such as video conferencing.

1.1.2 Medium Earth Orbit (MEO) Satellites

MEO satellites orbit at altitudes between 2,000 and 20,000 kilometers above Earth. This orbit is often used for applications requiring lower latency and higher data throughput than GEO systems. One of the most prominent examples of MEO satellites is the **O3b network** operated by **SES**, which delivers broadband internet services to remote regions. The O3b network's satellites operate at an altitude of around 8,000 kilometers, significantly reducing latency compared to GEO satellites while still covering large areas.

MEO satellites are particularly effective for services like **broadband internet** and **navigation systems**, striking a balance between coverage, cost, and performance. Their ability to provide lower-latency internet services makes them appealing to customers in areas where terrestrial infrastructure is inadequate or nonexistent.

1.1.3 Low Earth Orbit (LEO) Satellites

LEO satellites orbit much closer to the Earth's surface, at altitudes between 160 and 2,000 kilometers. The lower altitude dramatically reduces signal latency, making LEO satellites suitable for time-sensitive communications and internet services. These satellites are typically part of large constellations, where many satellites work in unison to provide continuous coverage across the globe.

One of the most ambitious LEO satellite projects is **Starlink**, developed by **SpaceX**. Starlink aims to provide high-speed, low-latency internet to underserved regions worldwide through a vast constellation of thousands of small LEO satellites. By operating in lower orbits, Starlink is capable of delivering broadband speeds with latencies as low as 20 milliseconds, comparable to fiber-optic connections.

LEO satellites also support real-time data transfer for applications such as **global positioning systems (GPS)**, earth observation, and disaster management. The main challenge with LEO constellations is the need for a large number of satellites to ensure continuous global coverage, which increases the complexity and cost of maintaining these systems.

1.2 Satellite-Based Internet Services

Space-based internet services have become a critical solution for regions where traditional infrastructure is either too expensive or technically unfeasible to deploy. This includes remote rural areas, isolated islands, and regions affected by conflict or natural disasters. Satellite internet offers an alternative to laying fiber-optic cables or building cellular towers, bridging the digital divide for billions of people.

1.2.1 Bridging the Digital Divide

One of the most significant benefits of satellite internet is its potential to bridge the digital divide. In many parts of the world, especially in developing countries, internet access is limited due to a lack of terrestrial infrastructure. **Satellite internet providers**, such as **Viasat** and **HughesNet**, have been instrumental in delivering broadband services to underserved communities.

For example, **OneWeb**, a global communications company, is deploying a LEO satellite constellation to deliver affordable internet services to rural and remote areas around the globe. OneWeb's mission is to connect schools, hospitals, and businesses that are currently offline, contributing to social and economic development in these regions.

1.2.2 Disaster Relief and Emergency Communications

Satellite internet services play a vital role in disaster relief operations, where terrestrial communication networks are often damaged or destroyed. In such scenarios, satellites can quickly restore communications, allowing emergency responders to coordinate rescue efforts. **Globalstar** and **Iridium** offer satellite phones and mobile internet solutions that are frequently used during natural disasters such as hurricanes, earthquakes, and tsunamis.

For instance, after the 2010 Haiti earthquake, satellite technology was crucial in re-establishing communication lines, enabling relief agencies to manage logistics and deliver aid more effectively. This capability demonstrates the life-saving potential of satellite-based internet during crises.

1.3 The Impact of Satellite Communications on Globalization

Satellite communications have been a major driver of globalization by enabling seamless, instant communication across borders. The ability to connect people from different parts of the world in real-time has had profound effects on international trade, diplomacy, and cultural exchange.

For businesses, satellite-based systems have facilitated **global supply chain management**, enabling real-time tracking of goods and vehicles across oceans and continents. **Multinational corporations** rely on satellite communication to maintain connectivity between offices in different countries, conduct virtual meetings, and share data securely.

In terms of media and broadcasting, satellites have revolutionized the way we consume content. **Direct-to-home (DTH)** satellite television services, like **DISH Network** and **DirecTV**, deliver hundreds of channels to households around the world, including those in remote locations. Satellite radio services such as **SiriusXM** offer uninterrupted coverage across large geographic areas, providing entertainment and news to millions of subscribers.

1.4 Challenges in Satellite Telecommunications

While satellite telecommunications have revolutionized global communication, they are not without challenges. Issues such as **signal latency**, **limited bandwidth**, and **high costs** remain significant barriers to wider adoption. For example, the cost of launching and maintaining satellites, especially in GEO and LEO orbits, is substantial, which translates into higher prices for end users.

Additionally, **space debris** poses a growing risk to satellite operations. As more satellites are launched, especially in LEO, the risk of collisions increases, potentially damaging critical communication infrastructure. Companies like **SpaceX** and **OneWeb** are actively working on collision avoidance systems and plans for deorbiting defunct satellites to mitigate this issue.

Conclusion

Space-based telecommunications and internet services have become indispensable in today's interconnected world. From providing critical communication infrastructure in remote areas to enabling seamless global connectivity, satellites play a central role in the modern digital economy. As technology continues to advance, the potential for satellite communications to improve access to information, foster economic development, and enhance global collaboration will only grow.

2. Weather Forecasting and Environmental Monitoring

Weather forecasting and environmental monitoring have evolved dramatically with the advent of space technology. Satellites orbiting the Earth now provide unprecedented levels of detail and accuracy in tracking atmospheric and environmental conditions, which are crucial for predicting weather patterns, monitoring climate change, and assessing natural disasters. Before space-based observation, meteorologists relied on ground-based systems and limited data from weather balloons, which often led to incomplete or inaccurate predictions. Today, space technology offers a more comprehensive view, providing real-time data that helps mitigate the impact of severe weather events and improve environmental conservation efforts.

This section will explore how space technology, particularly satellites, plays a key role in modern weather forecasting and environmental monitoring. It will examine the different types of satellites used, their applications in meteorology and climate studies, and how they contribute to global environmental efforts. Throughout this section, real-world examples will illustrate the importance of satellite data in our daily lives.

2.1 The Role of Satellites in Weather Forecasting

Weather satellites have become indispensable tools for meteorologists, offering continuous global coverage of atmospheric conditions. These satellites monitor various environmental factors, including cloud cover, precipitation, wind speeds, and temperature. By transmitting this data to ground stations, scientists can model weather patterns and make accurate short-term and long-term forecasts.

2.1.1 Geostationary Operational Environmental Satellites (GOES)

One of the most important satellite systems in weather forecasting is the **Geostationary Operational Environmental Satellites (GOES)**, managed by the **National Oceanic and Atmospheric Administration (NOAA)** in the United States. These satellites, positioned in geostationary orbit (around 35,786 kilometers above the Earth), provide continuous observation of the same region, making them ideal for monitoring rapidly changing weather conditions.

GOES satellites can detect early signs of storm formation, which allows for quicker responses to severe weather events. For example, the **GOES-16** satellite played a crucial role in tracking **Hurricane Harvey** in 2017, providing real-time data that helped meteorologists predict the storm's path and intensity. This advanced warning allowed emergency services to prepare and save lives in affected areas.

2.1.2 Polar-Orbiting Satellites

Unlike geostationary satellites, **polar-orbiting satellites** travel around the Earth at much lower altitudes (typically between 700 and 1,200 kilometers), covering the entire planet as the Earth rotates beneath them. These satellites, such as **NOAA's JPSS (Joint Polar Satellite System)** and **Europe's MetOp series**, provide more detailed observations of the atmosphere, land, and oceans, complementing geostationary satellite data.

Polar-orbiting satellites offer high-resolution imagery and can measure atmospheric conditions at various altitudes, which is essential for understanding global weather systems. They are particularly useful for tracking the development of weather systems in remote areas like the polar regions, where ground-based monitoring is limited.

2.1.3 Multispectral Imaging

Many weather satellites are equipped with multispectral imaging capabilities, allowing them to capture data in multiple wavelengths of light, from visible to infrared. This technology is vital for monitoring cloud formation, sea surface temperatures, and other environmental phenomena. Infrared imaging, for instance, is essential for detecting storm intensity during nighttime hours when visible light is unavailable.

One of the most famous examples of multispectral imaging in action is the **Himawari-8** satellite operated by the **Japan Meteorological Agency (JMA)**. Himawari-8 captures high-resolution images of the Asia-Pacific region, enabling real-time monitoring of typhoons and other extreme weather events.

2.2 Environmental Monitoring and Climate Observation

In addition to weather forecasting, satellites play a significant role in monitoring the environment and assessing climate change. They provide critical data on deforestation, glacier melting, ocean health, and air quality, contributing to global efforts to preserve natural resources and combat climate change.

2.2.1 Earth Observation Satellites

Earth observation satellites, such as the **Landsat** series operated by NASA and the **European Space Agency's (ESA) Sentinel satellites**, offer a wealth of information about the planet's surface. These satellites are equipped with advanced sensors that can detect changes in vegetation, land use, and water resources, helping scientists track environmental degradation and develop strategies for sustainable management.

For instance, the **Sentinel-2** satellite uses multispectral imaging to monitor deforestation in the Amazon Rainforest, providing real-time data that assists conservation efforts. By detecting illegal logging activities, satellite data helps authorities intervene and protect critical ecosystems.

2.2.2 Monitoring Climate Change

Satellites are essential tools in the study of climate change. They provide a comprehensive view of the Earth's atmosphere, oceans, and ice caps, enabling scientists to monitor long-term trends in temperature, sea level rise, and carbon dioxide concentrations. One such example is NASA's **Aqua** satellite, which is part of the **Earth Observing System (EOS)** and monitors global water cycles, including precipitation, evaporation, and ocean circulation.

Aqua has been instrumental in studying the impacts of global warming on polar ice sheets. Data from the satellite revealed that the **Antarctic Ice Sheet** is losing mass at an accelerating rate, contributing to rising sea levels. This information is critical for climate scientists, policymakers, and coastal communities planning for future sea-level rise.

2.2.3 Air Quality Monitoring

Satellites also play a key role in monitoring air quality and tracking pollution. By measuring the concentrations of gases such as nitrogen dioxide (NO2), carbon monoxide (CO), and particulate matter, satellites help scientists assess the impact of human activity on the environment and public health. For instance, ESA's **Copernicus Sentinel-5P** satellite is specifically designed to monitor air pollution levels around the globe.

During the **COVID-19 pandemic**, Sentinel-5P data showed a significant reduction in NO2 levels over major cities, such as New York and Beijing, due to the decline in industrial activity and transportation. This example highlights the potential for satellite data to contribute to environmental policy and decision-making.

2.3 Disaster Monitoring and Response

Satellite-based monitoring is crucial for managing natural disasters, such as hurricanes, floods, wildfires, and earthquakes. By providing early warnings and real-time data, satellites help governments and humanitarian organizations respond more effectively to crises.

2.3.1 Flood Monitoring and Prediction

Floods are among the most devastating natural disasters, affecting millions of people worldwide each year. Satellites can provide valuable data on precipitation, river levels, and soil moisture, enabling more accurate flood forecasting and risk assessment. **NASA's Global**

Precipitation Measurement (GPM) mission is one such example. By combining data from multiple satellites, GPM provides near real-time information on rainfall patterns, which helps meteorologists predict floods more accurately.

In 2021, satellite data from GPM was used to predict and monitor the devastating floods in Western Europe, which caused significant damage in Germany and Belgium. The early warning provided by satellites allowed for better preparedness and potentially saved many lives.

2.3.2 Wildfire Detection

Wildfires pose significant threats to both human populations and natural ecosystems. Satellites equipped with thermal imaging sensors can detect the heat signatures of wildfires, allowing for early detection and rapid response. For example, NASA's **MODIS (Moderate Resolution Imaging Spectroradiometer)** aboard the **Terra** and **Aqua** satellites has been widely used to monitor wildfires globally.

During the **2019–2020 Australian bushfire season**, known as **Black Summer**, satellite imagery played a crucial role in mapping the extent of the fires and assessing the damage to forests and wildlife habitats. Real-time data from satellites helped firefighters and emergency services allocate resources more effectively.

2.3.3 Earthquake Monitoring

Although satellites cannot predict earthquakes, they can assist in monitoring the aftermath and assessing damage. **Synthetic Aperture Radar (SAR)** satellites, such as **Sentinel-1**, can detect changes in the Earth's surface caused by seismic activity. By analyzing the displacement of land before and after an earthquake, scientists can determine the extent of the damage and prioritize rescue efforts.

In the aftermath of the **2015 Nepal earthquake**, Sentinel-1 data was used to create detailed maps of the affected areas, helping aid agencies target their response efforts to the hardest-hit regions.

2.4 Ocean Monitoring and Sea Level Rise

The world's oceans play a vital role in regulating the Earth's climate, and monitoring their health is crucial for understanding climate change. Satellites such as **Jason-3**, part of the **NASA/NOAA** partnership, monitor sea levels, ocean currents, and sea surface temperatures. These observations are essential for tracking the effects of global warming on oceanic systems.

Jason-3 has been instrumental in measuring **sea level rise**, which is a critical indicator of climate change. Rising sea levels threaten coastal cities and ecosystems, and satellite data helps scientists predict future trends and plan for mitigation strategies.

2.4.1 Coral Reef Monitoring

Coral reefs are among the most biodiverse ecosystems on the planet, but they are also highly vulnerable to changes in water temperature. Satellites equipped with thermal sensors, like NASA's **Terra** satellite, monitor sea surface temperatures and can detect heat stress on coral reefs, which is a leading cause of coral bleaching.

During the **2016 Great Barrier Reef bleaching event**, satellite data revealed elevated sea temperatures that contributed to widespread coral death. This information allowed conservationists to implement measures to protect the reef and raise awareness of the threats posed by climate change.

2.5 The Future of Weather and Environmental Monitoring

The future of weather forecasting and environmental monitoring lies in continued advancements in satellite technology. **Next-generation satellites** will feature more advanced sensors, higher-resolution imaging, and the ability to capture data in new spectral bands. These improvements will enhance the accuracy of forecasts and provide deeper insights into the Earth's changing environment.

One exciting development is the use of **CubeSats**, small and cost-effective satellites that can be deployed in large numbers to create dense networks of environmental sensors. CubeSats have already been used for localized weather monitoring and are expected to play a larger role in future climate and environmental missions.

Conclusion

Satellites have transformed weather forecasting and environmental monitoring, providing real-time data that is essential for predicting weather patterns, responding to natural disasters, and studying the impacts of climate change. From tracking hurricanes to monitoring deforestation, space-based technologies offer critical insights that help protect lives, preserve ecosystems, and guide global environmental policies. As satellite technology continues to evolve, its role in safeguarding the planet will only become more crucial.

3. Global Navigation Systems

Global Navigation Satellite Systems (GNSS) have revolutionized the way we navigate, track, and communicate on Earth. These satellite-based systems provide positioning, navigation, and timing (PNT) data to billions of users across a wide range of sectors, including transportation, defense, agriculture, and communications. The most well-known system, the **Global Positioning System (GPS)**, developed by the United States, has set the standard for satellite navigation. However, other regional and global systems such as Russia's **GLONASS**, Europe's **Galileo**, and China's **BeiDou** have emerged, contributing to a multi-system landscape that enhances global coverage and reliability.

This chapter explores the principles behind GNSS technology, how different global and regional systems operate, and their impact on everyday life and various industries. We will look into the historical development of these systems, their applications, and future trends in navigation technology. Examples from different fields will highlight the critical role GNSS plays in modern society.

3.1 Overview of Global Navigation Satellite Systems

Global Navigation Satellite Systems (GNSS) refer to constellations of satellites that provide signals for determining a user's position, velocity, and time (PVT) anywhere on or near the Earth's surface. GNSS operates through a network of satellites orbiting the Earth and ground control stations, which monitor satellite positions and the integrity of the signals.

3.1.1 Key Components of GNSS

The GNSS consists of three essential components:

- **The Space Segment:** Composed of satellites that transmit signals to users on Earth.

- **The Ground Segment:** Comprises monitoring and control stations that manage satellite orbits, synchronize their clocks, and ensure the integrity of the signals.

- **The User Segment:** Includes receivers, such as those in smartphones, vehicles, and military equipment, that interpret signals from multiple satellites to determine accurate positioning.

Each GNSS system generally has a minimum of 24 satellites to ensure global coverage. These satellites are positioned in medium Earth orbit (MEO) at approximately 20,000 kilometers above the Earth's surface, ensuring that a receiver can always "see" several satellites at once for triangulation.

3.1.2 How GNSS Works

GNSS receivers calculate their position by measuring the time it takes for signals to travel from multiple satellites to the receiver. By knowing the exact location of each satellite and the signal travel time, the receiver can compute its distance from each satellite. Using data from at least four satellites, the receiver can then determine its three-dimensional position (latitude, longitude, and altitude) as well as the precise time.

This process, called **trilateration**, forms the basis of all GNSS systems. In practice, receivers often use data from more than four satellites to improve accuracy. GNSS receivers are increasingly integrated with other technologies, such as inertial navigation systems (INS), to enhance precision, especially in environments where satellite signals may be obstructed, such as urban canyons or dense forests.

3.2 Major Global Navigation Satellite Systems

There are four major global navigation satellite systems in operation today: GPS, GLONASS, Galileo, and BeiDou. Each of these systems is independently operated by its respective government or space agency, yet they can work together to enhance global navigation services.

3.2.1 Global Positioning System (GPS)

The **Global Positioning System (GPS)**, operated by the **United States Department of Defense**, is the most widely used GNSS. Originally developed for military purposes in the 1970s, GPS was made available for civilian use in the 1980s. GPS consists of 31 operational satellites in MEO, offering global coverage and a positioning accuracy of about 5 to 10 meters for civilian users, though this can be improved with augmentation systems.

Example: GPS is widely used in consumer applications, from navigation apps like **Google Maps** to wearable fitness trackers. In addition to personal navigation, GPS plays a crucial role in agriculture, where **precision farming** techniques rely on GPS data to optimize planting, irrigation, and harvesting.

3.2.2 GLONASS

GLONASS, the Russian counterpart to GPS, was developed during the Cold War as a strategic alternative to GPS. Managed by the **Russian Aerospace Defense Forces**, GLONASS became fully operational in 1995, and today, it consists of 24 satellites. GLONASS provides global coverage, but its accuracy is slightly less than GPS, although the system performs better in high latitudes, such as in Russia.

Example: In Russia and neighboring regions, GLONASS is often integrated with GPS in smartphones and navigation systems to improve accuracy. Vehicles in Russia frequently use GLONASS as part of their navigation systems, ensuring reliable positioning even in remote or Arctic regions.

3.2.3 Galileo

Galileo is Europe's GNSS, developed by the **European Space Agency (ESA)** and the **European Union**. Operational since 2016, Galileo aims to provide independent navigation services for Europe while also complementing GPS and other systems. The full constellation of 30 satellites is expected to provide highly accurate positioning, with error margins as low as 1 meter for civilian users, making it the most accurate GNSS available.

Example: One of Galileo's unique features is its **Search and Rescue (SAR)** service, which helps locate people in distress, such as hikers or sailors. In an emergency, users can send distress signals, and Galileo can quickly locate them, reducing the response time for rescue operations.

3.2.4 BeiDou

BeiDou is China's GNSS, named after the Chinese term for the Big Dipper constellation. The BeiDou system has undergone several phases, with **BeiDou-3**, the global version, becoming fully operational in 2020. BeiDou offers not only PNT services but also short message communication and high-precision navigation services.

Example: BeiDou plays a crucial role in China's infrastructure projects, such as the **Belt and Road Initiative (BRI)**. BeiDou is used for surveying, construction, and monitoring large-scale infrastructure projects, such as bridges, roads, and railways, enhancing efficiency and safety.

3.3 Applications of GNSS in Various Sectors

GNSS is indispensable in many industries, from transportation to agriculture, defense, and scientific research. Below are some key applications of GNSS technology in different sectors:

3.3.1 Transportation and Logistics

GNSS has transformed the transportation industry by providing real-time tracking, navigation, and route optimization. **Aviation, maritime**, and **road transport** all rely heavily on satellite navigation for safe and efficient operations. Aircraft use GNSS for en-route navigation and landing approaches, while shipping companies depend on GNSS for navigating vast oceans.

Example: In the **aviation sector**, systems like GPS and Galileo allow pilots to land aircraft even in poor visibility, using precise GNSS data. This capability is essential at airports with limited infrastructure or in extreme weather conditions.

In **logistics**, companies use GNSS to track the movement of goods globally, optimizing delivery routes and reducing fuel consumption. **Fleet management systems** use GNSS to monitor vehicles, ensuring timely deliveries and improving operational efficiency.

3.3.2 Agriculture and Precision Farming

GNSS is a cornerstone of **precision agriculture**, a farming management concept that uses satellite data to optimize field-level management. Farmers use GNSS-based equipment to plan planting, monitor crop health, and control irrigation systems. GNSS allows for **automated tractor guidance**, which increases farming efficiency and reduces costs.

Example: Farmers in the United States widely use GPS for **yield monitoring**, where sensors in harvesting equipment measure and map crop yields in real-time. This information allows farmers to analyze productivity variations across fields and adjust planting techniques or resource allocation accordingly.

3.3.3 Defense and Military Applications

GNSS systems were initially developed for military purposes, and they continue to be integral to defense operations. Military forces use GNSS for **navigation, targeting, missile guidance**, and **troop movement tracking**. Military applications often require encrypted and more precise versions of GNSS signals, such as **GPS Precise Positioning Service (PPS)**.

Example: During military operations, forces rely on GNSS for **guided munitions**, where precision-guided bombs or missiles use GPS signals to strike targets accurately. This technology enhances the effectiveness of military strikes while minimizing collateral damage.

3.3.4 Timing and Synchronization in Telecommunications

GNSS provides precise timing, which is crucial for synchronizing telecommunications networks, financial transactions, and power grid operations. GNSS timing signals are used to synchronize cell towers, ensuring that mobile networks operate smoothly without interruptions.

Example: In the financial sector, stock exchanges use GNSS for **time-stamping** transactions, ensuring that trades are recorded accurately to the millisecond. This level of precision is critical for maintaining fairness in high-frequency trading environments.

3.3.5 Scientific Research and Environmental Monitoring

GNSS is widely used in **geodesy**, **seismology**, and **environmental studies** to measure the Earth's surface movements, monitor tectonic activity, and observe changes in the environment. Scientists use GNSS to study earthquakes, volcanoes, and plate tectonics by measuring ground displacements.

Example: In **geophysics**, GNSS networks detect small shifts in the Earth's crust, providing valuable data for early earthquake warning systems. In **climate research**, GNSS signals help monitor the atmosphere's water vapor content, which is crucial for weather forecasting and climate modeling.

3.4 Enhancing GNSS Accuracy: Augmentation Systems

While GNSS systems are highly accurate, there are some challenges due to signal errors caused by atmospheric interference, satellite geometry, and clock inaccuracies. To overcome these limitations, **augmentation systems** are used to improve accuracy, reliability, and availability of GNSS signals.

3.4.1 Wide Area Augmentation System (WAAS)

WAAS is a satellite-based augmentation system (SBAS) developed by the **Federal Aviation Administration (FAA)** in the United States. It provides GPS signal corrections for civil aviation by improving positioning accuracy to within 1-2 meters.

Example: WAAS is critical for aircraft using **automatic dependent surveillance-broadcast (ADS-B)** systems, which rely on highly accurate GPS data to ensure safe and efficient air traffic control.

3.4.2 European Geostationary Navigation Overlay Service (EGNOS)

EGNOS is Europe's version of an SBAS, operated by the **European Commission**. EGNOS enhances the accuracy of GPS and Galileo, particularly for aviation and maritime applications. EGNOS provides free, real-time corrections to users across Europe, offering sub-meter positioning accuracy.

3.5 Future Trends in Global Navigation Systems

The future of GNSS lies in the integration of multiple constellations, improving the accuracy and resilience of positioning services. Multi-GNSS receivers, capable of using signals from GPS, GLONASS, Galileo, and BeiDou simultaneously, are becoming standard, enhancing reliability, especially in challenging environments such as urban canyons or dense forests.

Moreover, **inter-satellite links** and the use of **low Earth orbit (LEO) satellites** are expected to further improve GNSS accuracy and reduce latency. **Quantum navigation** and **artificial intelligence** (AI)-based positioning systems are also emerging technologies that could eventually complement or even surpass traditional GNSS.

Example: In the near future, autonomous vehicles will rely on highly accurate GNSS data combined with AI to navigate cities and highways safely. These vehicles will use a combination of GNSS signals and real-time sensor data to make driving decisions, reducing accidents and improving traffic flow.

Conclusion

Global Navigation Satellite Systems (GNSS) have transformed the way we live, work, and interact with the world. From personal navigation in our smartphones to critical applications in aviation, defense, and agriculture, GNSS technology underpins many aspects of modern life. As satellite navigation systems continue to evolve and new technologies emerge, GNSS will remain at the forefront of global innovation, enabling new applications and industries that depend on precise location and timing data.

4. National Security and Defense Applications

The applications of space technology in national security and defense have been a cornerstone of military strategies and operations since the dawn of the space age. Satellites and other space-based assets provide critical capabilities in communication, reconnaissance, navigation, missile detection, and cyber warfare, giving militaries around the world a significant strategic edge. The ability to monitor vast geographical areas, detect threats in real-time, and coordinate military assets has transformed the way nations defend their interests and respond to potential conflicts.

This chapter delves into the various ways space technologies contribute to national security and defense. We will explore the role of satellites in intelligence gathering, navigation, missile warning systems, and command and control infrastructure. Additionally, we will examine how emerging technologies, such as space-based lasers, autonomous satellites, and cyber defenses, are shaping the future of military operations in space. Real-world examples will highlight the strategic importance of these technologies and the evolving challenges faced by global powers in securing the space domain.

4.1 Space-Based Surveillance and Intelligence Gathering

One of the most crucial applications of space technology in defense is surveillance and intelligence gathering. Satellites equipped with high-resolution imaging, radar, and electronic surveillance systems allow military forces to monitor activities on the ground, at sea, and in the air. These satellites provide real-time data that is vital for military planning, threat detection, and battlefield awareness.

4.1.1 Reconnaissance Satellites

Reconnaissance satellites, also known as spy satellites, have been in use since the Cold War when the United States and the Soviet Union first deployed them to monitor each other's military capabilities. Modern reconnaissance satellites, such as the **KH-11 Keyhole** operated by the United States, use optical and radar imaging systems to capture high-resolution images of military installations, troop movements, and equipment deployments.

Example: During the Gulf War, U.S. reconnaissance satellites played a critical role in locating Iraqi missile sites and guiding precision airstrikes, significantly reducing the duration of the conflict and minimizing civilian casualties. These satellites provided real-time imagery to commanders, enabling rapid decision-making and accurate targeting.

4.1.2 Signal Intelligence (SIGINT) Satellites

Signal intelligence (SIGINT) satellites intercept communications and electronic signals from adversaries, allowing defense forces to gather critical information about enemy plans, movements, and capabilities. These satellites are designed to detect and monitor radio, radar, and other electronic transmissions across the globe.

Example: The **Mercury SIGINT** satellite system, used by the U.S. National Reconnaissance Office (NRO), monitors electronic emissions from potential adversaries. This data allows the U.S. military to identify and track enemy radar systems, missile launches, and command centers, ensuring a proactive defense strategy.

4.1.3 Synthetic Aperture Radar (SAR) Satellites

Synthetic Aperture Radar (SAR) satellites can "see" through clouds, fog, and darkness by using radar waves to create detailed images of the Earth's surface. These satellites are invaluable for monitoring hostile terrain or enemy movements in all weather conditions, particularly in regions where visual imagery is limited.

Example: TerraSAR-X, a German SAR satellite, has been used in defense applications to monitor conflict zones and disaster areas where conventional satellite imagery may be obstructed by environmental factors. SAR systems provide high-precision imaging for both military and humanitarian operations.

4.2 Satellite-Based Communication Systems

Reliable and secure communication is critical for military operations, especially when deployed in remote or hostile environments. Space-based communication systems enable defense forces to maintain real-time communication with troops, ships, aircraft, and command centers across vast distances, ensuring coordination and response capabilities.

4.2.1 Military Communication Satellites

Dedicated military communication satellites, such as the **Advanced Extremely High-Frequency (AEHF)** system used by the U.S. Department of Defense, provide secure and encrypted communication channels for defense forces. These satellites support voice, data, and video communications, allowing for command and control operations in real-time.

Example: The **Wideband Global SATCOM (WGS)** system, operated by the U.S. Air Force, provides high-capacity communication links for military forces worldwide. WGS satellites are used to support U.S. and allied military operations, including secure communications for ground troops, naval vessels, and aircraft in conflict zones.

4.2.2 Tactical Satellite Communication (TACSAT)

Tactical Satellite Communication (TACSAT) systems are designed to provide real-time, high-bandwidth communication to military units operating in the field. TACSAT terminals are used by soldiers to communicate with command centers, share intelligence, and coordinate operations in challenging environments where terrestrial communication infrastructure may be unavailable or compromised.

Example: The U.S. military's **MUOS (Mobile User Objective System)** provides secure, mobile satellite communications for soldiers in remote areas. It ensures that troops have continuous access to communication networks, even in dense jungles or mountainous regions, where conventional radios may not function effectively.

4.3 Navigation and Targeting Systems

Satellites play a fundamental role in navigation and targeting for modern military operations. The integration of **Global Navigation Satellite Systems (GNSS)**, such as the U.S. **Global Positioning System (GPS)**, with military assets enables precise navigation and targeting capabilities, enhancing the accuracy and effectiveness of military strikes.

4.3.1 Precision-Guided Munitions (PGM)

Precision-guided munitions (PGM), also known as "smart bombs," use GPS data to guide themselves to their targets with remarkable accuracy. These weapons minimize collateral damage by ensuring that strikes are confined to military targets, reducing the risk to civilian populations.

Example: During the 2003 invasion of Iraq, the U.S. military used **JDAM (Joint Direct Attack Munition)** kits, which convert conventional bombs into GPS-guided smart bombs. These munitions demonstrated exceptional precision, allowing for strategic strikes on key military targets while minimizing civilian casualties.

4.3.2 Battlefield Navigation

Military vehicles, aircraft, and naval ships rely on satellite-based navigation systems to maneuver in complex battle environments. These systems provide real-time positioning and mapping data, allowing forces to navigate challenging terrains, plan operations, and coordinate troop movements effectively.

Example: During Operation Enduring Freedom in Afghanistan, U.S. and coalition forces used GPS for **ground troop navigation** through the rugged mountain regions. GPS allowed soldiers to move swiftly and avoid enemy ambushes, enhancing the effectiveness of military operations in a difficult landscape.

4.4 Missile Detection and Early Warning Systems

Space-based missile detection and early warning systems are critical components of a nation's defense infrastructure. These systems use satellites equipped with infrared sensors to detect missile launches and track their trajectories, providing early warnings to military forces and government authorities.

4.4.1 Infrared Missile Detection Satellites

Satellites such as the **Space-Based Infrared System (SBIRS)**, operated by the U.S. Air Force, use infrared sensors to detect the heat signatures of missile launches. These satellites can identify ballistic missile launches from anywhere on Earth and provide early warning to defense systems, allowing for missile interception and countermeasures.

Example: SBIRS satellites played a pivotal role during North Korea's ballistic missile tests by detecting missile launches in real time and relaying this information to U.S. and allied forces. This early detection allowed for rapid assessment of the threat and deployment of missile defense systems.

4.4.2 Anti-Missile Defense Systems

Anti-missile defense systems, such as **THAAD (Terminal High Altitude Area Defense)** and **Aegis Ballistic Missile Defense**, rely on satellite data to intercept incoming missiles. These systems use radar and infrared data from satellites to track the trajectory of incoming threats and guide interceptors to destroy the missiles before they reach their targets.

Example: THAAD has been deployed in South Korea to protect against potential missile attacks from North Korea. The system uses satellite data to track and intercept short- and medium-range ballistic missiles, providing a critical layer of defense for the region.

4.5 Space-Based Cybersecurity and Electronic Warfare

As warfare increasingly extends into the digital realm, space assets have become central to cybersecurity and electronic warfare efforts. Satellites are not only vulnerable to cyberattacks but also serve as platforms for offensive and defensive cyber operations.

4.5.1 Cybersecurity for Space Assets

Protecting satellites from cyberattacks is a growing concern for defense agencies. Satellites control critical military infrastructure, including communication networks, missile warning systems, and navigation tools. A successful cyberattack on these systems could disrupt military operations and compromise national security.

Example: In 2018, it was reported that U.S. defense satellites faced multiple cyber threats from state-sponsored hackers attempting to infiltrate military communication networks. The U.S. military has since invested heavily in improving satellite cybersecurity, including the development of **resilient satellite constellations** that can withstand cyberattacks.

4.5.2 Offensive Space Cyber Operations

Satellites are also being used as platforms for offensive cyber operations. By leveraging satellite networks, defense forces can launch cyberattacks on enemy communication systems, radar installations, and military networks, disrupting enemy operations without the need for direct physical conflict.

Example: During the **Russia-Ukraine conflict**, satellite-based cyberattacks targeted communication systems used by military forces on both sides. These cyber operations aimed to disrupt command and control capabilities, delaying military responses and complicating strategic operations.

4.6 Emerging Technologies in Space Defense

As space becomes increasingly militarized, new technologies are being developed to enhance national security and defense capabilities. These emerging technologies include autonomous satellites, space-based lasers, and advanced missile defense systems, all designed to give nations a strategic advantage in space.

4.6.1 Autonomous Defense Satellites

Autonomous satellites capable of detecting, tracking, and neutralizing threats in space are becoming a focus for defense agencies. These satellites can operate independently, making real-time decisions to protect critical space assets from threats such as enemy satellites or space debris.

Example: The U.S. military has been developing the **X-37B**, an autonomous spaceplane that can perform long-duration missions in space. Although the specific missions of the X-37B remain classified, it is believed to be used for surveillance, satellite maintenance, and potentially even offensive space operations.

4.6.2 Space-Based Laser Systems

Space-based lasers are being explored as a means of defending against missile attacks and neutralizing enemy satellites. These lasers can be deployed on satellites and used to disable incoming missiles or destroy enemy satellites, providing a non-kinetic means of space defense.

Example: In 2020, the U.S. military tested a **laser system** on board the **Boeing YAL-1**, an airborne laser-equipped aircraft designed to shoot down ballistic missiles during their boost phase. While the project has since been canceled, similar technologies are being explored for space-based missile defense.

Conclusion

Space technology plays a pivotal role in national security and defense, providing critical capabilities that are essential for modern military operations. From intelligence gathering and communication to missile detection and cybersecurity, satellites and space-based systems have transformed the defense landscape. As new technologies continue to emerge and the space domain becomes more contested, nations will need to adapt their strategies and invest in cutting-edge space technologies to maintain their defense capabilities and protect their interests in space.

5. Scientific Research and Space Exploration

The intersection of scientific research and space exploration has been a driving force behind humanity's quest for knowledge about the universe. Since the launch of Sputnik 1 in 1957, space exploration has opened up new frontiers in science, enabling researchers to study everything from planetary systems to the origins of life. Space missions have not only advanced our understanding of the cosmos but have also led to technological innovations that benefit life on Earth. This chapter explores the significant contributions of space exploration to scientific research, highlighting key missions, discoveries, and the technologies developed through these endeavors.

Through the lens of various space missions, we will delve into the fields of planetary science, astrobiology, Earth science, and fundamental physics, emphasizing how space exploration has transformed our understanding of the universe and our place within it. Examples from historical and contemporary missions will illustrate the profound impact of space research on scientific knowledge, technology, and international collaboration. Finally, we will consider the future of space exploration and its potential to address some of humanity's most pressing challenges.

5.1 The Role of Space Exploration in Scientific Research

Space exploration serves as a unique platform for scientific inquiry, providing an environment where researchers can conduct experiments and gather data that would be impossible to achieve on Earth. The microgravity conditions of space, the ability to observe celestial bodies up close, and the access to cosmic phenomena have led to groundbreaking discoveries across multiple scientific disciplines.

5.1.1 Microgravity Research

The microgravity environment aboard the International Space Station (ISS) allows scientists to study physical, biological, and chemical processes in ways that are not possible under the influence of Earth's gravity. Experiments conducted in microgravity provide insights into fundamental scientific questions and have applications in various fields, including medicine, materials science, and fluid dynamics.

Example: The **Protein Crystallization Experiment** aboard the ISS has revealed how proteins behave in microgravity. Understanding protein structures at a high resolution aids in drug design and the development of treatments for diseases such as cancer and diabetes.

5.1.2 Astronomy and Astrophysics

Space telescopes and observatories, such as the **Hubble Space Telescope** and the **James Webb Space Telescope (JWST)**, have revolutionized our understanding of the universe. By observing celestial phenomena beyond Earth's atmosphere, these instruments provide data on the formation of stars, galaxies, and exoplanets.

Example: The Hubble Space Telescope has captured stunning images of distant galaxies and nebulae, leading to discoveries such as the acceleration of the universe's expansion, which supports the existence of dark energy. The JWST, launched in December 2021, aims to delve deeper into the early universe, potentially providing insights into the formation of the first stars and galaxies.

5.2 Planetary Science and Exploration

The exploration of other planets and celestial bodies has been a central focus of space missions. Robotic spacecraft, landers, and rovers have allowed scientists to study the geology, atmospheres, and potential habitability of planets and moons within our solar system.

5.2.1 Mars Exploration

Mars has been a primary target for scientific research due to its similarities to Earth and its potential for past or present life. Various missions, including NASA's **Mars Rovers** (Spirit, Opportunity, Curiosity, and Perseverance), have contributed significantly to our understanding of the Martian environment.

Example: NASA's Perseverance rover, which landed on Mars in February 2021, is equipped with advanced scientific instruments to analyze soil samples and search for signs of ancient microbial life. Its mission includes the collection of samples for future return to Earth, which will provide deeper insights into the planet's history and geology.

5.2.2 Lunar Exploration

The Moon has also been a focal point of exploration, with missions aimed at understanding its geology, history, and potential resources. The **Apollo program** marked a significant achievement in lunar exploration, bringing back valuable samples that have informed our understanding of the Moon's formation and evolution.

Example: The Apollo lunar samples revealed that the Moon is about 4.5 billion years old, providing crucial information about the early solar system. The upcoming **Artemis program**, set to return humans to the Moon, aims to establish a sustainable presence and prepare for future human exploration of Mars.

5.3 Astrobiology: The Search for Life Beyond Earth

Astrobiology is a rapidly evolving field that seeks to understand the potential for life beyond our planet. Space missions have been instrumental in investigating extreme environments on Earth, other celestial bodies, and the chemical precursors necessary for life.

5.3.1 Moons of the Outer Planets

Several moons of the outer planets, such as Europa (moon of Jupiter) and Enceladus (moon of Saturn), are believed to harbor subsurface oceans, raising the possibility of extraterrestrial life.

Example: The **Europa Clipper mission**, planned for launch in the 2020s, aims to explore Europa's icy surface and investigate its ocean's potential habitability. By analyzing surface composition and searching for signs of water plumes, scientists hope to gather evidence of conditions suitable for life.

5.3.2 Martian Atmosphere and Life

Mars missions have focused on the planet's atmospheric composition and surface conditions, which could provide clues about its potential to support life. The detection of methane spikes in the Martian atmosphere raises intriguing questions about biological activity.

Example: The **Curiosity rover** detected seasonal methane emissions, leading to speculation about possible microbial life in the subsurface. Future missions will aim to investigate these emissions further and assess their origins.

5.4 Earth Science and Environmental Monitoring

Space technology has proven invaluable for studying Earth's climate, weather patterns, and environmental changes. Satellites equipped with remote sensing technology monitor natural disasters, track climate change, and provide data for sustainable resource management.

5.4.1 Climate Monitoring Satellites

Satellites such as NASA's **Earth Observing System (EOS)** provide critical data on Earth's climate systems, allowing scientists to analyze changes in temperature, sea level, and ice cover. These observations are essential for understanding the impacts of climate change and informing policy decisions.

Example: The **MODIS (Moderate Resolution Imaging Spectroradiometer)** on board the Terra satellite collects data on land surface changes, forest cover, and ocean temperature. This information is crucial for climate modeling and assessing the health of ecosystems.

5.4.2 Natural Disaster Response

Satellites play a vital role in disaster monitoring and response efforts. Remote sensing technology allows for rapid assessments of areas affected by natural disasters such as hurricanes, earthquakes, and floods.

Example: After Hurricane Katrina in 2005, satellite imagery was used to assess damage, track the storm's path, and coordinate emergency response efforts. This technology has since improved disaster response planning and recovery efforts.

5.5 Technological Innovations from Space Research

The technological advancements derived from space exploration have far-reaching applications beyond scientific research. Innovations developed for space missions often find their way into everyday life, enhancing various industries and improving quality of life on Earth.

5.5.1 Advancements in Materials Science

The extreme conditions of space require the development of advanced materials that can withstand harsh environments. Research in materials science for space missions has led to the creation of lightweight, durable materials used in aerospace and other industries.

Example: The development of **carbon-fiber composites** for spacecraft has revolutionized aircraft and automotive manufacturing, resulting in lighter and more fuel-efficient vehicles.

5.5.2 Medical Technologies

Space research has also contributed to advancements in medical technology. Research on the effects of microgravity on the human body has led to innovations in health monitoring and treatment.

Example: The development of portable ultrasound devices for astronauts aboard the ISS has translated to improved medical diagnostics and emergency care capabilities in remote locations on Earth.

5.6 International Collaboration in Space Research

Scientific research and space exploration often require international collaboration, bringing together countries, institutions, and organizations to achieve common goals. Joint missions and partnerships enhance the exchange of knowledge and resources, fostering goodwill among nations.

5.6.1 The International Space Station (ISS)

The ISS is a testament to international cooperation in space research, involving contributions from space agencies such as NASA, ESA, Roscosmos, JAXA, and CSA. The ISS serves as a laboratory for scientific research and technology demonstration, enabling countries to work together on shared objectives.

Example: Research on the ISS has yielded valuable insights into various fields, including human physiology, materials science, and Earth observation. The collaboration among different countries exemplifies the importance of teamwork in advancing space exploration.

5.6.2 Global Scientific Partnerships

Space exploration has led to numerous partnerships between nations and organizations, facilitating the exchange of data, technology, and expertise. Collaborative missions, such as the **Mars Science Laboratory** (Curiosity rover), demonstrate the potential for global cooperation in addressing scientific challenges.

Conclusion

Scientific research and space exploration are deeply intertwined, driving our understanding of the universe and addressing critical challenges on Earth. The contributions of space missions to various scientific disciplines have led to significant discoveries, technological advancements, and international collaboration. As we look to the future, the continued exploration of space promises to yield even greater insights, enabling us to tackle some of the most pressing issues facing humanity and deepening our understanding of our place in the cosmos.

Chapter 5: Key Players in the Space Industry

1. Overview of Major Space Agencies (NASA, ESA, etc.)
2. Leading Private Space Companies (SpaceX, Blue Origin, etc.)
3. Collaborations and Partnerships in Space Missions
4. Startups and Emerging Companies in the Space Sector
5. Competitive Landscape and Market Share

Chapter 5

Key Players in the Space Industry

Introduction

The space industry has grown into a global sector involving various stakeholders, ranging from government agencies to private enterprises. Historically, space exploration was dominated by a handful of national space agencies, such as NASA (National Aeronautics and Space Administration) in the United States and ESA (European Space Agency) in Europe. These agencies played a pivotal role in shaping early advancements in space exploration and establishing international collaborations.

However, in recent years, the landscape of the space industry has transformed with the rise of private companies like SpaceX and Blue Origin, which have introduced groundbreaking innovations in launch services and space missions. This shift has fostered new partnerships between public and private entities, creating a dynamic environment where startups and emerging companies also find opportunities to contribute to space exploration and technology development.

Understanding the key players—both traditional and new entrants—is essential to grasp the industry's current competitive landscape. This chapter explores the major space agencies, leading private companies, and the growing presence of startups, highlighting the collaborations and market forces that shape this ever-evolving sector.

1.Overview of Major Space Agencies (NASA, ESA, etc.)

The development of space exploration has been significantly driven by the establishment of major space agencies across the globe. Since the mid-20th century, these government organizations have taken the lead in exploring outer space, developing space technologies, and conducting scientific research. NASA (the National Aeronautics and Space Administration) and ESA (the European Space Agency) stand out as two of the most influential players, but other key agencies like Roscosmos (Russia), CNSA (China), and ISRO (India) have also made remarkable contributions.

This chapter will provide a comprehensive overview of these major space agencies, examining their historical background, mission objectives, achievements, and current activities. We will explore how these agencies differ in their goals, capabilities, and collaborative efforts, using examples where appropriate. By the end of this section, the reader will have a clearer understanding of the significant role these agencies play in advancing space exploration, technology, and international cooperation.

1.1 National Aeronautics and Space Administration (NASA)

1.1.1 History and Establishment

NASA was established in 1958 in response to the Soviet Union's launch of the first artificial satellite, Sputnik, in 1957. The creation of NASA marked a critical point in the United States' commitment to space exploration. NASA's predecessor, the National Advisory Committee for Aeronautics (NACA), had already laid the groundwork in aeronautics research, but NASA was tasked with a broader mandate: the civilian exploration of space and aeronautics.

Example: One of NASA's most significant achievements is the Apollo 11 mission, which successfully landed the first humans on the Moon in 1969. This mission demonstrated NASA's technological prowess and solidified its position as a global leader in space exploration.

1.1.2 Mission and Vision

NASA's mission is "to pioneer the future in space exploration, scientific discovery, and aeronautics research." The agency focuses on four key areas: space exploration, scientific discovery, advancing aeronautics, and developing new space technologies.

NASA's vision aims to "reach for new heights and reveal the unknown for the benefit of humankind." This vision drives their efforts in missions such as Mars exploration, studying exoplanets, and space observatories like the Hubble Space Telescope.

1.1.3 Key Achievements

NASA has achieved numerous milestones, including manned missions to the Moon, robotic exploration of Mars, and the development of satellite systems that have revolutionized telecommunications and earth observation.

- **Apollo Program:** The Apollo program is widely regarded as one of NASA's crowning achievements, culminating in the Apollo 11 Moon landing.

- **Hubble Space Telescope:** Launched in 1990, the Hubble Space Telescope has provided unprecedented images of distant galaxies, advancing our understanding of the universe.

- **International Space Station (ISS):** NASA played a key role in the development and maintenance of the ISS, a collaborative project involving several space agencies.

1.1.4 Current Projects

NASA is currently focused on ambitious projects like the Artemis program, which aims to return humans to the Moon by 2024, and Mars exploration missions like the Perseverance rover, which is tasked with searching for signs of past life on Mars.

1.2 European Space Agency (ESA)

1.2.1 History and Establishment

The European Space Agency was founded in 1975, merging two precursor organizations: ESRO (European Space Research Organisation) and ELDO (European Launcher Development Organisation). ESA was created to unify Europe's space efforts and provide a platform for scientific cooperation.

Example: One of ESA's most notable contributions is the development of the Ariane family of launch vehicles, which have become highly successful in commercial satellite launches.

1.2.2 Mission and Vision

ESA's mission is to ensure that investment in space continues to deliver benefits to the citizens of Europe and the world. It works closely with its 22 member states to develop space capabilities that support scientific, economic, and security needs.

ESA's vision is to "explore space for peaceful purposes, ensuring that space benefits everyone on Earth." The agency also focuses heavily on Earth observation, space science, and human spaceflight.

1.2.3 Key Achievements

ESA has made several significant contributions to space exploration, especially in collaboration with other agencies.

- **Rosetta Mission:** ESA's Rosetta mission successfully landed a probe on the comet 67P/Churyumov–Gerasimenko in 2014, marking a historic first in space exploration.

- **ExoMars:** In partnership with Roscosmos, ESA launched the ExoMars mission, which aims to search for signs of life on Mars.

- **Galileo Navigation System:** ESA developed the Galileo satellite navigation system, Europe's answer to the American GPS.

1.2.4 Current Projects

ESA's current projects include its participation in the Artemis program and its involvement in the development of new technologies for space exploration, such as the upcoming JUICE mission to explore Jupiter's moons.

1.3 Roscosmos (Russian Space Agency)

1.3.1 History and Establishment

Roscosmos, officially known as the State Corporation for Space Activities, is Russia's governmental body responsible for space exploration. It was formed in 1992 following the dissolution of the Soviet Union, inheriting the legacy of the Soviet space program.

Example: The Soviet Union's launch of Sputnik in 1957, and later Yuri Gagarin's historic flight as the first human in space in 1961, remain two of the most defining moments in space history.

1.3.2 Mission and Vision

Roscosmos is tasked with the development of space exploration programs, the advancement of space technology, and maintaining Russia's position as a leader in space activities.

1.3.3 Key Achievements

Roscosmos has been responsible for numerous significant space missions.

- **Sputnik and Vostok:** The first artificial satellite and the first human spaceflight, respectively, marked the Soviet Union's dominance in the early space race.

- **ISS Contributions:** Roscosmos is a major partner in the ISS, providing transportation and scientific capabilities.

1.3.4 Current Projects

Roscosmos continues to play a critical role in global space activities, with missions aimed at deep-space exploration, such as the Luna-25 mission to explore the Moon's south pole, and collaborations with China on lunar exploration.

1.4 China National Space Administration (CNSA)

1.4.1 History and Establishment

The China National Space Administration (CNSA) was established in 1993, overseeing China's burgeoning space exploration efforts. Since then, China has rapidly become one of the leading players in space.

Example: In 2019, CNSA successfully landed the Chang'e 4 spacecraft on the far side of the Moon, the first mission of its kind.

1.4.2 Mission and Vision

CNSA's mission is to advance China's space capabilities for peaceful purposes, with a focus on scientific research, technology development, and international cooperation.

1.4.3 Key Achievements

CNSA has made remarkable progress in recent years, establishing itself as a global leader in space.

- **Chang'e Lunar Missions:** The Chang'e series of lunar missions represent China's most significant achievements in space exploration, with plans to establish a lunar research base by 2030.

- **Tiangong Space Station:** CNSA launched the Tiangong space station, marking China's capability to build and operate a long-term human outpost in space.

1.4.4 Current Projects

CNSA's future plans include missions to Mars, further lunar exploration, and international partnerships in space missions, including collaborations with Russia and ESA.

1.5 Indian Space Research Organisation (ISRO)

1.5.1 History and Establishment

The Indian Space Research Organisation (ISRO) was founded in 1969 with the aim of advancing space technology and using its applications for India's development.

Example: ISRO gained global recognition with the Mars Orbiter Mission (Mangalyaan) in 2014, which made India the first country to reach Mars on its first attempt.

1.5.2 Mission and Vision

ISRO's mission is to harness space technology for national development while pursuing space science and planetary exploration.

1.5.3 Key Achievements

ISRO's achievements are notable for their cost-effectiveness and technological innovation.

- **Mars Orbiter Mission:** A milestone in space exploration, the Mars Orbiter Mission demonstrated ISRO's capabilities in deep-space exploration.

- **PSLV and GSLV Launch Vehicles:** ISRO has developed reliable and cost-effective launch vehicles, particularly the Polar Satellite Launch Vehicle (PSLV).

1.5.4 Current Projects

ISRO continues to focus on satellite development, interplanetary exploration, and human spaceflight, with the Gaganyaan mission aiming to send Indian astronauts to space.

Conclusion

In summary, the major space agencies—NASA, ESA, Roscosmos, CNSA, and ISRO—have collectively advanced humanity's understanding of space, achieved groundbreaking scientific discoveries, and fostered international cooperation. These agencies continue to lead the way in space exploration and will play a pivotal role in the future of space technology, exploration, and innovation.

2.Leading Private Space Companies (SpaceX, Blue Origin, etc.)

In recent decades, the space industry has evolved from a domain dominated by government agencies into a competitive marketplace where private companies play an increasingly prominent role. These private players are pioneering technological innovations, lowering the cost of space access, and reshaping the vision for future space exploration and utilization. Leading the charge are companies like SpaceX, Blue Origin, and Virgin Galactic, which have brought in a new era of reusable rockets, commercial space tourism, and ambitious plans for interplanetary colonization.

This chapter delves into the most influential private space companies, exploring their history, goals, key achievements, technological innovations, and their influence on the broader space economy. Through real-world examples and case studies, we will see how these firms are shaping the future of space exploration and development.

2.1 SpaceX

2.1.1 History and Founding

Founded in 2002 by Elon Musk, Space Exploration Technologies Corp., or SpaceX, began with an ambitious goal: to reduce the cost of space travel and ultimately enable the colonization of Mars. Musk's desire to make humanity a multi-planetary species drove the company's early focus on developing reusable rockets and lowering the cost of launching payloads into orbit.

Example: SpaceX's first successful orbital launch came in 2008 with Falcon 1, making it the first privately funded liquid-fueled rocket to reach orbit. This breakthrough set the stage for the company's rapid growth and success in the space industry.

2.1.2 Mission and Vision

SpaceX's mission is clear: "to revolutionize space technology, with the ultimate goal of enabling people to live on other planets." At the core of this vision is the development of reusable rocket systems that can reduce the cost of space travel and open new possibilities for deep-space exploration.

Visionary Goal: Colonization of Mars by the mid-21st century is SpaceX's long-term objective, with ongoing developments in their Starship program aimed at making interplanetary travel a reality.

2.1.3 Key Achievements

SpaceX has accomplished several groundbreaking feats in space exploration:

- **Falcon 9 and Reusability:** The development of Falcon 9, which successfully became the first orbital rocket capable of reusability, was a major milestone. In December 2015, SpaceX landed the first stage of a

Falcon 9 rocket after an orbital launch, a feat previously thought to be impossible.

- **Crew Dragon and NASA Partnership:** SpaceX's Crew Dragon spacecraft became the first privately built spacecraft to carry NASA astronauts to the International Space Station (ISS) in May 2020. This achievement marked a pivotal moment in NASA's reliance on private companies for human spaceflight.

- **Starlink Satellite Constellation:** SpaceX's ambitious Starlink project aims to provide global high-speed internet via a constellation of thousands of low-Earth orbit satellites. With thousands of satellites already deployed, Starlink is offering broadband services across the globe, including remote and underserved regions.

Example: In 2020, SpaceX completed over 25 successful Falcon 9 launches, many of which carried Starlink satellites. This accomplishment demonstrates the company's ability to perform frequent and reliable launches at a scale unprecedented in the space industry.

2.1.4 Impact on Space Industry

SpaceX's introduction of reusable rockets has dramatically reduced the cost of sending payloads into space. The company's innovations have pressured other space agencies and companies to focus on cost-efficiency and reusability, setting a new industry standard. SpaceX's Falcon 9 and Falcon Heavy rockets are now leading choices for launching commercial satellites, cargo, and crewed missions.

Economic Impact: SpaceX has driven down the cost of launching to space from approximately $18,000 per kilogram (Space Shuttle era) to about $2,700 per kilogram using Falcon 9. This has not only benefited private industries but also government space programs like NASA.

2.1.5 Current Projects and Future Plans

- **Starship Development:** SpaceX is actively working on Starship, a fully reusable spacecraft designed for deep-space missions, including Mars colonization. Starship is intended to carry up to 100 passengers and cargo, and it aims to revolutionize both interplanetary travel and Earth-to-Earth transport.

- **NASA Artemis Program:** SpaceX has been selected as a key partner in NASA's Artemis program, which aims to return humans to the Moon by 2024. SpaceX's Starship will be used as the lunar lander for NASA's crewed missions.

- **Mars Colonization:** Musk's ultimate vision for SpaceX is to enable the colonization of Mars. The company plans to develop large-scale spacecraft capable of transporting humans to Mars within the next few decades, with the goal of establishing a permanent human settlement on the Red Planet.

2.2 Blue Origin

2.2.1 History and Founding

Founded by Amazon CEO Jeff Bezos in 2000, Blue Origin's motto, "Gradatim Ferociter" (Latin for "Step by Step, Ferociously"), reflects its methodical approach to space exploration. Unlike SpaceX, which made headlines with frequent public displays of its technology, Blue Origin maintained a lower profile during its early years, focusing on long-term research and development.

Example: Blue Origin gained public attention in 2015 when its New Shepard suborbital vehicle successfully completed a vertical landing after a spaceflight, marking the first time a reusable rocket returned safely to Earth after reaching space.

2.2.2 Mission and Vision

Blue Origin's mission is to build a future where millions of people live and work in space, driven by the belief that space exploration is essential for the long-term survival of humanity. The company aims to create a path for future generations to tap into the limitless resources of space.

Bezos envisions the creation of **space colonies** in Earth's orbit, where industries can flourish, and humanity can expand without straining Earth's resources.

2.2.3 Key Achievements

- **New Shepard:** The successful development and multiple launches of the New Shepard rocket, designed for suborbital space tourism, is a significant achievement for Blue Origin. This fully reusable rocket and crew capsule are intended to take paying passengers on short trips to the edge of space, providing a new frontier in commercial spaceflight.

- **BE-4 Rocket Engine:** Blue Origin is developing the BE-4 engine, which will be used in its upcoming New Glenn orbital launch vehicle as well as ULA's (United Launch Alliance) Vulcan Centaur rocket. This next-generation engine is designed to be reusable, powerful, and efficient.

Example: The BE-4 engine was selected by ULA as the replacement for the Russian-made RD-180, signaling confidence in Blue Origin's capabilities in engine development.

2.2.4 Impact on Space Industry

Blue Origin has played a key role in advancing the concept of space tourism and the commercialization of space. While not as aggressive in launch cadence as SpaceX, Blue Origin is set to challenge the space industry with its **New Glenn** rocket, which promises to be a heavy-lift vehicle for both commercial and government payloads.

Tourism Impact: Blue Origin's New Shepard flights, which are expected to carry paying customers to space in the near future, represent a breakthrough in the space tourism industry, potentially making suborbital space travel accessible to the public.

2.2.5 Current Projects and Future Plans

- **New Glenn Rocket:** Blue Origin is developing the New Glenn rocket, a heavy-lift orbital launch vehicle capable of sending large payloads into space. New Glenn is expected to compete with SpaceX's Falcon Heavy in terms of payload capacity and cost.

- **Orbital Reef:** In partnership with Sierra Space, Blue Origin is developing the Orbital Reef, a proposed commercial space station that will serve as a "mixed-use business park" in low Earth orbit. This project aims to support various industries, including research, tourism, and manufacturing in space.

- **Lunar Exploration:** Blue Origin is a key player in NASA's Artemis program, with plans to develop a lunar lander named Blue Moon. This lander is designed to deliver payloads and astronauts to the Moon's surface.

2.3 Virgin Galactic

2.3.1 History and Founding

Virgin Galactic, founded by billionaire Richard Branson in 2004, was created with the goal of making space tourism accessible to the general public. Unlike SpaceX and Blue Origin, which are primarily focused on orbital and interplanetary missions, Virgin Galactic's focus has been suborbital spaceflight for private individuals.

Example: In 2018, Virgin Galactic's SpaceShipTwo completed a successful test flight, reaching the edge of space with a crew on board. This was a major step toward the company's goal of providing commercial suborbital spaceflights.

2.3.2 Mission and Vision

Virgin Galactic's vision is to be the world's first commercial spaceline, offering suborbital flights to passengers seeking a few minutes of weightlessness and a view of Earth from space. Branson's ambition is to democratize space travel and make it a viable option for non-professional astronauts.

2.3.3 Key Achievements

- **SpaceShipTwo:** Virgin Galactic's SpaceShipTwo is a reusable suborbital spaceplane designed to carry tourists to the edge of space. Its design is based on the successful SpaceShipOne, which won the Ansari X Prize in 2004 for the first non-governmental crewed spaceflight.

- **Commercial Space Tourism:** Virgin Galactic became the first company to sell tickets for commercial space tourism, with over 600 people reportedly signing up to experience suborbital spaceflight.

Example: On July 11, 2021, Richard Branson flew aboard the SpaceShipTwo during its Unity 22 mission, reaching an altitude of approximately 86 kilometers, marking the company's first fully crewed spaceflight.

2.3.4 Impact on Space Industry

Virgin Galactic is a pioneer in the nascent space tourism industry, and its efforts have inspired other companies, such as Blue Origin and SpaceX, to explore space travel for private individuals. The company's progress toward regular suborbital flights has opened up new markets for luxury tourism, scientific research, and microgravity experiments.

Tourism and Entertainment Impact: Virgin Galactic's promise of space tourism has not only captured public imagination but also demonstrated the commercial viability of space as a destination for recreational travel.

2.3.5 Current Projects and Future Plans

- **Commercial Flights:** Virgin Galactic aims to begin regular commercial spaceflights, with paying customers expected to fly on SpaceShipTwo in the coming years. The company is targeting individuals, researchers, and organizations that want to experience space or conduct microgravity experiments.

- **Next-Generation Spaceplanes:** Virgin Galactic is also developing new, more advanced spaceplanes that will offer longer and higher-altitude flights, increasing both the experience for passengers and the potential for research applications.

2.4 Other Emerging Companies

- **Rocket Lab:** A key player in the small satellite launch market, Rocket Lab, based in New Zealand and the U.S., has made significant strides with its Electron rocket. Its mission is to provide frequent, cost-effective access to orbit for small payloads.

Example: Rocket Lab has launched numerous commercial payloads and is working on developing a reusable small rocket system, further emphasizing the trend toward cost reduction in space access.

- **Relativity Space:** Specializing in 3D-printed rockets, Relativity Space is an innovative startup that aims to disrupt the space launch industry. Their use of automation and 3D printing allows for rapid production and flexibility in rocket design.

- **OneWeb:** OneWeb is another company focusing on satellite constellations, similar to SpaceX's Starlink. The company aims to deploy a large network of small satellites to provide global internet coverage.

Conclusion

The rise of private companies in the space industry has ushered in a new era of space exploration and commercialization. These companies have not only brought about technological advancements but also challenged the traditional norms of space access, making space more accessible than ever before. Whether through reusable rockets, satellite constellations, or space tourism, private companies like SpaceX, Blue Origin, and Virgin Galactic are reshaping the space industry and setting the stage for future developments in space travel and exploration.

3. Collaborations and Partnerships in Space Missions

The complexity and high costs associated with space exploration have historically driven governments, private companies, and international organizations toward collaboration. In the early days of space missions, partnerships were largely between governments, exemplified by international treaties and cooperative space station programs. However, in today's space landscape, private companies and commercial entities are playing an increasingly significant role in partnerships, driving innovation, reducing costs, and expanding opportunities for exploration.

Collaborations in the space industry are vital for achieving ambitious objectives like deep-space exploration, lunar landings, Mars colonization, and the development of space technologies such as reusable rockets and satellite constellations. These collaborations range from public-private partnerships (PPPs) to international collaborations between space agencies, as well as joint ventures between private companies and scientific organizations.

This chapter will provide a detailed examination of the various forms of collaborations and partnerships in space missions, highlighting specific case studies such as the International Space Station (ISS), the Artemis Program, and the partnerships between private entities like SpaceX and NASA. The discussion will also explore the role of partnerships in advancing space tourism, satellite technology, and interplanetary exploration.

3.1 Public-Private Partnerships (PPPs) in Space Exploration

3.1.1 Defining Public-Private Partnerships

Public-private partnerships (PPPs) refer to collaborative agreements between government agencies and private companies. In the space industry, PPPs have emerged as a key strategy to share the burden of cost, risk, and development in space missions. Governments benefit from the private sector's technological innovations and efficiency, while private companies gain access to government contracts and the prestige of participating in high-profile missions.

Example: One of the most notable examples of PPPs is NASA's Commercial Crew Program, which partnered with companies like SpaceX and Boeing to develop spacecraft capable of transporting astronauts to and from the International Space Station (ISS). This partnership allowed NASA to reduce costs while fostering competition and innovation in the private sector.

3.1.2 NASA's Commercial Crew and Cargo Programs

The Commercial Crew Program, initiated by NASA in 2010, sought to develop private spacecraft to carry astronauts to the ISS. Prior to this program, NASA relied on Russian Soyuz spacecraft after the retirement of the Space Shuttle in 2011. NASA selected SpaceX and Boeing to develop the Dragon and Starliner spacecraft, respectively, creating a collaborative environment where private companies were directly involved in manned spaceflight missions.

In parallel, NASA's Commercial Orbital Transportation Services (COTS) program, under which SpaceX and Northrop Grumman (formerly Orbital ATK) were selected to develop cargo vehicles, further highlighted the effectiveness of these partnerships in reducing reliance on government-built systems.

Case Study: SpaceX's Crew Dragon successfully completed its first manned mission to the ISS in 2020, marking the first time a private company launched humans into orbit. This achievement underlines the benefits of public-private collaboration, as NASA was able to reduce its costs and focus on more complex exploration missions, while SpaceX gained valuable experience and credibility.

3.1.3 The Role of PPPs in Technological Innovation

PPPs have played a significant role in driving technological advancements in the space industry. Private companies, motivated by competition and commercial interests, have accelerated the development of reusable rocket technology, satellite networks, and spacecraft.

Example: SpaceX's development of reusable rockets under NASA contracts has been a game-changer for the space industry. With NASA supporting SpaceX through contracts for ISS resupply and crew transportation, SpaceX was able to focus on developing Falcon 9 and Falcon Heavy reusable rockets, which have drastically reduced launch costs.

3.2 International Collaborations in Space Missions

3.2.1 The International Space Station (ISS)

The International Space Station (ISS) is the most prominent example of global collaboration in space. A joint project between NASA (USA), Roscosmos (Russia), ESA (Europe), JAXA (Japan), and CSA (Canada), the ISS has been continuously inhabited since 2000 and serves as a hub for scientific research and international cooperation.

Example: Countries that do not possess independent human spaceflight programs, such as Japan and Canada, have contributed to the ISS through scientific modules (like Japan's Kibo laboratory) and technology (such as Canada's robotic arm, the Canadarm2), in exchange for access to the station for their astronauts and experiments.

The ISS is a powerful example of how international cooperation can achieve what no single country could accomplish alone. It has provided a platform for research that benefits humanity in areas ranging from medicine to environmental science, while also fostering peace and diplomacy through collaboration.

3.2.2 The Artemis Program and the Lunar Gateway

NASA's Artemis Program, which aims to return humans to the Moon by 2024, has fostered international collaboration on an unprecedented scale. The Lunar Gateway, a space station set to orbit the Moon, will be built in partnership with multiple space agencies, including ESA, JAXA, and CSA.

Example: The Artemis Accords, a set of international agreements initiated by NASA, outline the principles of cooperation for nations participating in lunar exploration. Signatories, including the UK, Australia, and Italy, have committed to working together on the development of lunar infrastructure and scientific exploration.

The collaboration between NASA and international partners in the development of the Lunar Gateway underscores the importance of cooperative efforts in achieving long-term goals like lunar colonization and deep-space exploration. Each partner brings its own expertise and technology, such as ESA's contribution of the European Service Module, which powers the Orion spacecraft.

3.2.3 Russia-China Collaborations in Space Exploration

While NASA has traditionally led international space cooperation, recent years have seen increased collaboration between Russia and China in space exploration. In 2021, the two countries signed a memorandum of understanding to build a joint lunar base, signaling a shift toward a multipolar space industry.

Example: The Russian and Chinese space agencies, Roscosmos and CNSA, have announced plans to cooperate on lunar exploration, including the development of robotic missions and infrastructure for a future lunar base. This partnership is expected to provide both nations with the resources and knowledge necessary to challenge the dominance of NASA and its partners in lunar exploration.

3.2.4 Global Navigation Satellite Systems (GNSS)

International collaboration is also critical in the development and operation of global navigation satellite systems (GNSS). The United States' GPS, Russia's GLONASS, Europe's Galileo, and China's BeiDou are all examples of GNSS programs that serve a global population and often involve cooperation between multiple countries.

Example: Europe's Galileo system, which became operational in 2016, was developed with contributions from several EU member states and represents Europe's commitment to maintaining an independent GNSS system that complements and competes with the U.S. GPS system.

3.3 Private Sector Partnerships and Joint Ventures

3.3.1 SpaceX and NASA

The collaboration between SpaceX and NASA represents one of the most successful partnerships in space exploration. Through programs such as the Commercial Crew and Commercial Resupply Services, NASA has enabled SpaceX to become a dominant force in space travel.

Example: SpaceX's partnership with NASA began with cargo missions to the ISS and expanded to include crewed missions with the successful launch of the Crew Dragon in 2020. These collaborations have not only benefited NASA by lowering costs and increasing efficiency but have also positioned SpaceX as a global leader in spaceflight.

3.3.2 Blue Origin and NASA

Blue Origin, founded by Jeff Bezos, has partnered with NASA on various projects, including the development of lunar landers under NASA's Artemis program. The company's **Blue Moon** lander is designed to carry scientific payloads and potentially humans to the lunar surface.

Example: In 2020, NASA selected Blue Origin as one of the companies to develop a human landing system for the

Artemis program. This partnership underscores the growing role of private companies in critical space missions.

3.3.3 Collaboration Between SpaceX and Google

SpaceX and Google have entered into a partnership to integrate Starlink's satellite internet with Google Cloud infrastructure. This collaboration exemplifies how the space industry intersects with other sectors, such as telecommunications and cloud computing, to deliver innovative services.

Example: The collaboration allows Google to use SpaceX's Starlink satellite network to provide high-speed internet to remote areas and improve data storage and processing capabilities for its cloud services. This partnership not only enhances global internet access but also demonstrates the commercial potential of space technologies.

3.4 Scientific Collaborations and Academic Partnerships

3.4.1 CERN and Space Research

Scientific organizations like CERN, the European Organization for Nuclear Research, often collaborate with space agencies on research related to particle physics and astrophysics. The insights gained from space-based experiments help advance understanding in areas such as dark matter and the origins of the universe.

Example: CERN has partnered with ESA to use data from the Planck satellite, which maps cosmic microwave background radiation, to explore fundamental questions about the early universe and the nature of dark matter.

3.4.2 University Partnerships and Space Research

Many universities worldwide have partnered with space agencies and private companies to conduct cutting-edge research in fields like astrophysics, planetary science, and materials engineering. These partnerships often involve the development of satellite technology, space experiments, and even the training of future astronauts.

Example: MIT and NASA's collaboration on the Transiting Exoplanet Survey Satellite (TESS) mission has resulted in the discovery of thousands of exoplanets. This collaboration demonstrates the critical role that academic institutions play in advancing space science.

3.5 Collaborations in Space Tourism and Commercial Spaceflight

3.5.1 SpaceX, Blue Origin, and Commercial Spaceflight

Partnerships in space tourism are becoming more prominent, particularly as companies like SpaceX and Blue Origin collaborate with investors, tourism agencies, and private individuals to expand access to space.

Example: In 2021, SpaceX launched the **Inspiration4** mission, the first all-civilian spaceflight, in collaboration with billionaire Jared Isaacman, highlighting how partnerships in the private sector are enabling space tourism to become a reality.

3.5.2 Virgin Galactic and Academic Institutions

Virgin Galactic has partnered with universities and research institutions to offer microgravity research opportunities aboard its spaceplanes. These partnerships are expanding the scope of scientific research that can be conducted in space, allowing more organizations to participate in space-based experiments.

Example: The University of Central Florida partnered with Virgin Galactic to conduct experiments on fluid dynamics in microgravity, leveraging the company's spaceplane for cost-effective research.

Conclusion

Collaborations and partnerships have become a cornerstone of modern space exploration. From public-private partnerships that have revolutionized space travel to international collaborations like the ISS and Artemis programs, cooperation has proven essential for achieving complex, large-scale space missions. As the space industry continues to grow, the role of partnerships will expand, bringing together governments, private companies, scientific organizations, and academic institutions in a shared pursuit of advancing human knowledge and capabilities in space.

4. Startups and Emerging Companies in the Space Sector

In recent years, the space sector has experienced a remarkable transformation, characterized by the rise of startups and emerging companies that are reshaping the landscape of space exploration and commercialization. Once dominated by government agencies and a few large corporations, the industry is now witnessing an influx of innovative companies driven by advances in technology, changing market dynamics, and new funding models.

These startups are not only developing novel technologies but also introducing disruptive business models that challenge the traditional paradigms of space exploration and commercial satellite services. They are playing a pivotal role in various areas, including satellite manufacturing, launch services, space tourism, and even lunar mining. This chapter will explore the growth of startups in the space sector, examine key players, and highlight examples of how these companies are contributing to the future of space exploration and commercialization.

4.1 The Emergence of the Space Startup Ecosystem

4.1.1 Growth Factors for Space Startups

The emergence of startups in the space sector can be attributed to several factors:

- **Reduced Launch Costs:** Advances in reusable rocket technology and competition among launch service providers have significantly lowered the cost of sending payloads to space. This affordability has opened the door for startups to enter the market.

- **Access to Funding:** The rise of venture capital firms and private equity investment in the space sector has provided startups with the necessary capital to develop their technologies and scale their operations.

- **Government Support:** Governments around the world are increasingly supporting space startups through grants, contracts, and initiatives aimed at fostering innovation in the space industry.

Example: NASA's Small Business Innovation Research (SBIR) program provides funding to startups and small businesses developing innovative technologies for space exploration, allowing them to advance their research and development efforts.

4.1.2 The Role of Incubators and Accelerators

Incubators and accelerators focused on space technology have emerged as essential resources for startups. These programs offer mentorship, funding, and networking opportunities to help fledgling companies navigate the complexities of the space industry.

Example: The **Space Accelerator** program, launched by the Techstars network, supports early-stage companies in the space sector, providing them with resources, industry connections, and access to investors. Participants receive mentorship from industry experts, which can significantly enhance their chances of success.

4.2 Key Startups in the Space Sector

4.2.1 Rocket Lab

Founded in 2006, Rocket Lab is a prominent startup focused on providing launch services for small satellites. With its Electron rocket, Rocket Lab aims to offer frequent and cost-effective access to space.

Example: Rocket Lab successfully launched its first satellite in 2018 and has since conducted multiple missions, establishing itself as a key player in the small satellite launch market. The company is also developing a reusable version of its Electron rocket to further reduce costs and increase launch frequency.

4.2.2 Relativity Space

Relativity Space is a groundbreaking startup that leverages 3D printing technology to manufacture rockets. The company's innovative approach enables rapid prototyping and production, significantly reducing the time and cost associated with traditional rocket manufacturing.

Example: Relativity Space's Terran 1 rocket, designed for small satellite launches, is made up of 95% 3D-printed components. This manufacturing technique allows for greater flexibility and customization in rocket design, positioning the company as a leader in innovation within the space industry.

4.2.3 Planet Labs

Planet Labs is a startup that operates a fleet of small satellites, known as Doves, for Earth observation. The company's mission is to democratize access to satellite imagery and provide actionable insights for various industries, including agriculture, forestry, and urban planning.

Example: Planet Labs successfully launched its first satellites in 2014 and has since built a constellation of over 200 satellites. Their imagery is used by governments and businesses worldwide for applications ranging from environmental monitoring to disaster response.

4.3 Innovations in Satellite Technology

4.3.1 OneWeb

OneWeb is a satellite communications startup focused on deploying a global satellite internet constellation. The company aims to provide high-speed internet access to underserved areas around the world.

Example: OneWeb has launched hundreds of satellites as part of its constellation, with plans for a total of around 648 satellites. The company's mission is to bridge the digital divide by providing internet access in remote and rural areas.

4.3.2 Swarm Technologies

Swarm Technologies is a startup specializing in low-cost satellite communications. The company's focus is on enabling IoT devices to communicate via a constellation of small satellites.

Example: Swarm's network is designed to provide global coverage at a fraction of the cost of traditional satellite communications systems, making it an attractive option for businesses looking to connect remote assets.

4.4 Space Tourism Startups

4.4.1 Virgin Galactic

Virgin Galactic is a pioneer in the space tourism industry, aiming to make space travel accessible to civilians. The company's SpaceShipTwo spacecraft is designed for suborbital flights, allowing passengers to experience a few minutes of weightlessness.

Example: In July 2021, Virgin Galactic successfully conducted its first fully crewed test flight, marking a significant milestone for commercial space tourism. The company has sold tickets for future flights, with plans to expand its operations and increase the frequency of flights.

4.4.2 Blue Origin

Blue Origin, founded by Jeff Bezos, is also focused on the space tourism market. The company's New Shepard rocket is designed for suborbital flights and has successfully completed multiple test missions.

Example: In July 2021, Blue Origin conducted its first crewed flight of New Shepard, carrying Jeff Bezos and three other passengers. This mission showcased the company's capabilities in space tourism and its commitment to making space accessible to private individuals.

4.5 Emerging Technologies and Their Impact

4.5.1 Lunar Mining Startups

With the renewed interest in lunar exploration, several startups are exploring the potential for mining resources on the Moon. These companies are developing technologies for extracting water, minerals, and other materials that could support human habitation and exploration.

Example: Astrobotic is a startup focused on lunar landers and payload delivery services. The company aims to enable lunar mining operations by providing transportation for scientific instruments and commercial payloads to the Moon's surface.

4.5.2 In-Space Manufacturing

Startups are also exploring in-space manufacturing technologies that could revolutionize the way materials are produced and utilized in space. This innovation has the potential to reduce the need to transport materials from

Earth, making space missions more sustainable and cost-effective.

Example: Made In Space is a company specializing in 3D printing technology for use in space. Their Archinaut technology allows for the construction of large structures in orbit, such as satellites and space habitats, using materials sourced in space.

4.6 Challenges Faced by Space Startups

4.6.1 Funding and Investment

While there has been a surge in investment in space startups, securing funding remains a challenge for many companies. The capital-intensive nature of the industry requires startups to demonstrate their viability and potential for profitability to attract investors.

Example: Many startups rely on government contracts or grants to support their development efforts, but competition for funding can be intense, particularly as more companies enter the space sector.

4.6.2 Regulatory Hurdles

Navigating the regulatory landscape can be challenging for space startups. Compliance with national and international laws, including those related to satellite launches and space debris management, requires significant resources and expertise.

Example: Startups must work closely with regulatory bodies such as the Federal Aviation Administration (FAA) in the United States to obtain the necessary permits for launches and ensure compliance with safety regulations.

Conclusion

Startups and emerging companies in the space sector are driving innovation and transforming the landscape of space exploration and commercialization. With advancements in technology, reduced costs, and increased access to funding, these companies are positioning themselves as key players in various areas, from satellite manufacturing and launch services to space tourism and lunar mining. As they continue to push the boundaries of what is possible in space, startups will play an increasingly vital role in shaping the future of the space industry.

5. Competitive Landscape and Market Share

The space industry has undergone a dramatic transformation in recent years, transitioning from a government-dominated sector to a vibrant marketplace characterized by the active participation of private companies, startups, and international collaborations. This chapter delves into the competitive landscape of the space industry, examining the key players, their market positions, and the dynamics that drive competition.

As the demand for space services continues to grow, companies are increasingly vying for market share across various segments, including satellite manufacturing, launch services, and space exploration. Understanding the competitive landscape is crucial for stakeholders looking to navigate this complex and evolving industry. This chapter will analyze market trends, key players, and the factors that influence competition and market share within the space sector.

5.1 Overview of the Space Market

5.1.1 Market Segmentation

The space industry can be broadly segmented into several key areas:

- **Launch Services:** Companies that provide launch capabilities for satellites, payloads, and space missions.

- **Satellite Manufacturing:** Firms engaged in designing and producing satellites for various applications, including communications, Earth observation, and scientific research.

- **Space Exploration:** Organizations focused on missions beyond Earth, including lunar and Martian exploration.

- **Space Tourism:** Companies offering commercial space travel experiences to private individuals.

- **Ground Services:** Providers of data analysis, ground control operations, and other support services related to space operations.

5.1.2 Market Size and Growth

The global space economy is estimated to be worth over $400 billion, with projections suggesting significant growth in the coming years. The increasing demand for satellite services, advances in launch technology, and the emergence of new markets, such as space tourism, are driving this growth.

Example: According to a report by the Space Foundation, the global space economy grew by 7% in 2021, reflecting a strong recovery following the pandemic and highlighting the resilience of the industry.

5.2 Key Players in the Space Industry

5.2.1 Major Government Agencies

Government space agencies continue to play a pivotal role in the space sector. Organizations like NASA, the European Space Agency (ESA), and the Russian Federal Space Agency (Roscosmos) remain key players in space exploration and research.

- **NASA:** As a leading space agency, NASA is involved in various missions, including crewed exploration, robotic missions, and international collaborations.

- **ESA:** The European Space Agency conducts numerous satellite missions and participates in collaborative projects like the International Space Station (ISS).

5.2.2 Leading Private Companies

Private companies have emerged as significant competitors in the space industry, often focusing on cost-effective solutions and innovative technologies.

- **SpaceX:** Founded by Elon Musk, SpaceX is a dominant player in the launch services market, known for its reusable Falcon rockets and ambitious plans for Mars colonization.

- **Blue Origin:** Founded by Jeff Bezos, Blue Origin focuses on suborbital and orbital flight, emphasizing space tourism and lunar exploration.

- **Boeing and Lockheed Martin:** These traditional aerospace companies are heavily involved in both government contracts and commercial space initiatives, including partnerships for satellite launches and exploration missions.

5.3 Market Share Analysis

5.3.1 Launch Services Market

The launch services market is one of the most competitive segments in the space industry, characterized by numerous players vying for contracts.

- **SpaceX:** Currently holds a significant share of the commercial launch market, attributed to its cost-effective services and frequent launches. In 2021, SpaceX conducted over 30 successful launches, establishing itself as a leader in the industry.

- **Arianespace:** A traditional player in the market, Arianespace focuses on heavy-lift launches and maintains a strong presence in Europe and beyond.

- **Rocket Lab:** Specializing in small satellite launches, Rocket Lab has captured a growing share of the small satellite market with its Electron rocket.

5.3.2 Satellite Manufacturing Market

The satellite manufacturing segment is dominated by several key players, including traditional aerospace companies and specialized startups.

- **Boeing and Airbus:** These aerospace giants have established a strong foothold in satellite manufacturing, producing a wide range of satellites for various applications, including communications and Earth observation.

- **Planet Labs:** As a significant player in the small satellite market, Planet Labs operates a large fleet of Earth observation satellites, catering to a diverse range of customers.

- **OneWeb:** This startup focuses on manufacturing satellites for global internet coverage, aiming to deploy a constellation of low-Earth orbit satellites.

5.4 Competitive Strategies

5.4.1 Innovation and Technology

In the competitive landscape of the space industry, innovation is crucial for companies seeking to differentiate themselves. Advanced technologies, such as reusable rockets and satellite miniaturization, are reshaping the industry.

Example: SpaceX's development of the Falcon 9 rocket, which features a reusable first stage, has significantly reduced launch costs and set new standards for the industry.

5.4.2 Cost Leadership

Cost leadership is a key strategy employed by many emerging companies to capture market share. By optimizing operations and reducing costs, startups can offer competitive pricing.

Example: Rocket Lab's focus on small satellite launches has allowed it to provide services at lower costs than traditional providers, enabling it to gain traction in the competitive launch market.

5.4.3 Strategic Partnerships

Collaborations and partnerships are essential for companies looking to expand their capabilities and market reach. By leveraging the strengths of other organizations, companies can enhance their offerings and improve competitiveness.

Example: NASA's partnerships with private companies through initiatives like the Commercial Crew Program have facilitated the development of new technologies and increased access to space.

5.5 Challenges in the Competitive Landscape

5.5.1 Regulatory Hurdles

Navigating the regulatory environment can pose challenges for companies operating in the space sector. Compliance with national and international laws, as well as coordination with government agencies, can be time-consuming and complex.

Example: Startups may face challenges in obtaining launch licenses from regulatory bodies like the Federal Aviation Administration (FAA), which can impact their ability to compete effectively.

5.5.2 Market Saturation

As more companies enter the space industry, competition is intensifying across various segments. Market saturation can lead to price wars and reduced profit margins.

Example: The increasing number of companies offering satellite launch services has created a competitive environment where price competition is fierce, potentially impacting the sustainability of smaller providers.

Conclusion

The competitive landscape of the space industry is evolving rapidly, driven by the emergence of private companies and the increasing participation of startups. As the market continues to grow, understanding the dynamics of competition, key players, and market share will be essential for stakeholders navigating this complex environment. The interplay of innovation, cost leadership, strategic partnerships, and regulatory challenges will shape the future of the space sector, influencing which companies thrive and which face obstacles.

Chapter 6: Global Markets and Economic Impact

1. Growth Trends in the Space Industry
2. Regional Markets for Space Exploration
3. Economic Contributions of the Space Sector
4. Challenges and Opportunities in Space Investment
5. Future Market Predictions

Chapter 6

Global Markets and Economic Impact

Introduction

The space industry has evolved into a multifaceted global market that plays a pivotal role in shaping economies and driving technological advancements. Over the past few decades, the growth trends in the space sector have garnered significant attention from governments, private companies, and investors alike. This chapter delves into the various dimensions of global markets associated with space exploration, highlighting the growth trends that define the industry and the regional markets that contribute to its expansion.

As nations recognize the strategic importance of space, they are investing heavily in developing their capabilities and infrastructure. This investment not only fosters scientific discovery and technological innovation but also has substantial economic implications. The economic contributions of the space sector are far-reaching, impacting a wide array of industries, from telecommunications to national security.

However, the landscape of space investment is not without its challenges. From regulatory hurdles to the complexities of public-private partnerships, stakeholders must navigate a myriad of obstacles to capitalize on the opportunities presented by the expanding space economy.

This chapter will also explore these challenges while identifying key opportunities for growth and innovation.

Finally, looking ahead, we will examine future market predictions and trends that are expected to shape the space sector in the coming years. As we stand on the brink of a new era in space exploration, understanding the dynamics of global markets and their economic impact is crucial for stakeholders aiming to navigate this exciting and evolving landscape.

1. Growth Trends in the Space Industry

The space industry has experienced remarkable growth over the past few decades, driven by advancements in technology, increased investment, and a growing recognition of the strategic importance of space exploration. From government-funded missions to the rise of private companies, the landscape of space exploration has changed dramatically, leading to new opportunities and challenges. This section will explore the growth trends in the space industry, examining key factors that contribute to this expansion, highlighting examples of successful ventures, and discussing the implications for the future.

1.1 Technological Advancements

Technological innovation has been a significant driver of growth in the space industry. The development of reusable rocket technology, for instance, has revolutionized the economics of space travel. SpaceX's Falcon 9 rocket, which can land vertically and be reused for multiple missions, has drastically reduced launch costs. This advancement not only makes space more accessible for private companies but also opens new avenues for research and commercial ventures in orbit.

Another critical area of technological advancement is satellite technology. Smaller, more efficient satellites, often referred to as CubeSats or smallsats, have made it possible for organizations to conduct scientific research and commercial activities at a fraction of the cost of traditional satellites. Companies like Planet Labs and Spire Global have successfully launched constellations of small satellites to provide Earth observation data, demonstrating the potential of these innovations in addressing various societal challenges, such as climate monitoring and disaster response.

1.2 Increased Investment

Investment in the space sector has surged in recent years, with both public and private sectors recognizing its potential. According to a report by the Space Foundation, global space economy revenues reached approximately $469 billion in 2020, with projections indicating continued growth. Governments worldwide are allocating more funds for space exploration, science missions, and technology development. For instance, NASA's budget has consistently increased, reflecting a commitment to ambitious missions like Artemis, which aims to return humans to the Moon and eventually send astronauts to Mars.

Private investment has also played a pivotal role in the industry's growth. Venture capital firms and private equity are increasingly directing funds toward space startups. Companies like Blue Origin and Rocket Lab have attracted significant funding, enabling them to develop innovative technologies and expand their operations. The success of SpaceX's Starlink project, which aims to provide global internet coverage through a network of satellites, has also highlighted the lucrative opportunities available in the commercial space market.

1.3 Emergence of New Market Segments

The growth of the space industry has given rise to new market segments that cater to diverse needs. Space tourism is one of the most exciting developments, with companies like Virgin Galactic and Blue Origin actively pursuing commercial spaceflight experiences for tourists. This emerging sector promises to democratize access to space, allowing civilians to experience weightlessness and view Earth from above.

Additionally, the demand for satellite services continues to expand. As more industries rely on satellite data for various applications—ranging from agriculture and environmental monitoring to telecommunications—the market for satellite services has grown significantly. Companies are increasingly exploring partnerships with governments and organizations to provide critical data and insights for decision-making processes.

1.4 Global Collaboration and Partnerships

Global collaboration has become increasingly essential in driving growth in the space industry. International partnerships allow countries to share resources, knowledge, and expertise. The International Space Station (ISS) serves as a prime example of such collaboration, with contributions from space agencies worldwide, including NASA, Roscosmos, ESA, JAXA, and CSA. This collaborative effort has enabled groundbreaking scientific research and technological advancements, demonstrating the benefits of shared goals in space exploration.

Moreover, public-private partnerships are on the rise, facilitating collaboration between government agencies and private companies. NASA's Commercial Crew Program is a notable example, wherein NASA partnered with private companies like SpaceX and Boeing to develop spacecraft capable of transporting astronauts to the ISS. These partnerships have accelerated innovation and increased the pace of space exploration, making it more efficient and cost-effective.

1.5 Challenges and Risks

While the growth trends in the space industry are promising, several challenges and risks must be addressed. Regulatory hurdles, for instance, can impede the pace of innovation. Governments need to establish clear guidelines for satellite launches, space debris mitigation, and space traffic management to ensure safe and sustainable operations in space.

Another challenge is the competition for talent and skilled workforce. As the space industry expands, there is a growing need for engineers, scientists, and technicians who can support the development of advanced technologies. Educational institutions and industry players must work together to cultivate a skilled workforce capable of meeting the demands of a rapidly evolving industry.

Conclusion

The growth trends in the space industry underscore the dynamic and transformative nature of this sector. Technological advancements, increased investment, the emergence of new market segments, and global collaboration are all contributing to the industry's expansion. However, addressing challenges and risks is crucial to sustaining this growth and ensuring a sustainable future for space exploration. As we move forward, the continued evolution of the space industry will rely on innovation, cooperation, and a commitment to addressing the pressing challenges facing humanity.

2. Regional Markets for Space Exploration

The space industry has evolved into a truly global endeavor, with various regions of the world playing distinct roles in space exploration and commercialization. Each region brings its unique strengths, challenges, and market dynamics, contributing to the overall growth of the space economy. This section explores the regional markets for space exploration, highlighting key players, specific initiatives, and the overall impact of these markets on the global space landscape.

By examining the distinct characteristics of regional space markets—such as North America, Europe, Asia-Pacific, the Middle East, and Africa—we gain a comprehensive understanding of the diverse contributions to space exploration and the implications for future developments. As we delve into these regions, it becomes evident that collaboration and competition coexist, shaping the evolution of the space sector.

2.1 North America

North America, particularly the United States, is a leader in space exploration and the commercial space industry. With NASA at the forefront, the U.S. has achieved significant milestones, from the Apollo moon landings to the ongoing Artemis program, which aims to return humans to the Moon by the mid-2020s.

The commercial space sector in North America has also witnessed explosive growth. Companies like SpaceX, Blue Origin, and Boeing are at the forefront, developing innovative technologies and launching missions at an unprecedented pace. For example, SpaceX's Falcon 9 has become the workhorse of the space industry, regularly delivering payloads to the International Space Station (ISS) and deploying satellite constellations for global internet coverage through its Starlink project.

In addition to commercial launches, the U.S. market is bolstered by the presence of venture capital and private equity investments. As of 2020, U.S. private investments in space-related ventures reached over \$5 billion, highlighting the growing interest in space commercialization and innovation.

2.2 Europe

Europe's space market is characterized by collaboration among member states through the European Space Agency (ESA). Established in 1975, ESA plays a pivotal role in coordinating space activities across Europe, enabling joint missions, research, and development projects.

Key initiatives, such as the Galileo satellite navigation system and the Copernicus Earth observation program, underscore Europe's commitment to leveraging space technology for societal benefits. Galileo, Europe's alternative to the U.S. GPS, aims to provide accurate positioning services, while Copernicus monitors the Earth's environment and contributes to climate change research.

The European commercial space sector is also thriving, with companies like Airbus, Thales Alenia Space, and Arianespace leading the way. Arianespace's Ariane rockets have established a strong reputation for reliability, catering to commercial satellite launches. The rise of small satellite manufacturers in Europe further illustrates the region's adaptability to changing market demands.

2.3 Asia-Pacific

The Asia-Pacific region has emerged as a significant player in the global space market, driven by countries like China, India, and Japan. China's ambitious space program, spearheaded by the China National Space Administration (CNSA), has made remarkable strides in recent years. The successful landing of the Tianwen-1 rover on Mars in 2021 and the construction of the Tiangong space station demonstrate China's growing capabilities in space exploration.

India's space program, led by the Indian Space Research Organisation (ISRO), has also garnered global attention. With cost-effective satellite launches and successful missions like the Mars Orbiter Mission (Mangalyaan), India has positioned itself as a key player in the commercial launch market.

Japan, known for its advanced technology and robotics, has made significant contributions to space exploration through initiatives like the Hayabusa asteroid missions. The collaboration among these countries in the Asia-Pacific region reflects a trend toward increased cooperation in space research and development.

2.4 Middle East

The Middle East has recognized the strategic importance of space exploration and has invested in developing its capabilities. The United Arab Emirates (UAE) has emerged as a leader in the region, launching the Hope Probe to Mars in 2020, marking the first Arab mission to the Red Planet. This ambitious project underscores the UAE's commitment to advancing its space program and inspiring future generations.

Saudi Arabia and Israel are also making strides in space activities, focusing on satellite development and research. The establishment of the Saudi Space Commission in 2018 signifies the kingdom's intent to invest in space exploration and technology, while Israel's space agency continues to advance its capabilities in satellite technology and research.

The growing interest in space exploration in the Middle East presents opportunities for international collaborations and partnerships, contributing to the global space economy.

2.5 Africa

Africa's involvement in the space industry is gaining momentum, driven by the recognition of space technology's potential to address local challenges. Various African nations are establishing their space agencies and launching satellite programs to support development goals.

For instance, South Africa has made significant contributions to space science and technology through the South African National Space Agency (SANSA), focusing on Earth observation and satellite communications. Kenya's successful launch of its first satellite, NaVStar-1, in 2018 marked a milestone for the country, showcasing the growing interest in leveraging space technology for national development.

Regional cooperation is also evident through initiatives like the African Union's Agenda 2063, which emphasizes the need for collaboration in space science and technology to promote sustainable development across the continent.

Conclusion

Regional markets for space exploration play a crucial role in shaping the global space economy. Each region brings unique strengths, initiatives, and contributions, fostering a dynamic and interconnected landscape. North America's dominance in commercial space, Europe's collaborative efforts, the Asia-Pacific's ambitious programs, the Middle East's growing capabilities, and Africa's emerging initiatives all highlight the diverse contributions to space exploration.

As countries continue to invest in their space programs, the potential for collaboration and innovation will shape the future of the space industry. Understanding the dynamics of regional markets is essential for stakeholders seeking to navigate this rapidly evolving sector and leverage the opportunities it presents.

3. Economic Contributions of the Space Sector

The space sector has become a vital component of the global economy, contributing significantly to technological advancements, job creation, and economic growth. With a growing number of private companies entering the market and increased governmental investments in space exploration, the economic contributions of the space industry are more pronounced than ever. This section explores the various ways in which the space sector impacts the economy, including direct contributions through job creation, indirect contributions through technological innovations, and the broader implications for national and global economic development.

The economic contributions of the space sector can be analyzed through several lenses, including revenue generation, employment opportunities, technological advancements, and benefits to other industries. By understanding these contributions, we can better appreciate the space sector's role in shaping a more prosperous and innovative future.

3.1 Revenue Generation

The space sector generates significant revenue through various activities, including satellite services, launch services, and government contracts. According to the Space Foundation, the global space economy was valued at approximately $447 billion in 2020, reflecting growth across multiple segments.

3.1.1 Satellite Services

Satellite services are one of the most substantial revenue generators within the space sector. These services include telecommunications, broadcasting, and internet access, contributing billions to the global economy. The global satellite services market alone is projected to reach $100 billion by 2025, driven by the increasing demand for connectivity and data transmission.

For instance, companies like SpaceX, with its Starlink project, aim to provide high-speed internet access to underserved regions around the world, tapping into a market that promises substantial returns. The growth of satellite internet services is particularly crucial as remote work and online education continue to expand globally.

3.1.2 Launch Services

The commercial launch services market is another significant revenue stream. Companies such as SpaceX, Blue Origin, and Arianespace have transformed the landscape by providing cost-effective launch options for satellites and cargo missions. In 2020, SpaceX completed over 20 launches, generating substantial revenue from both government and commercial clients.

As more countries and companies invest in satellite technology, the demand for launch services will continue to grow. The increasing frequency of launches presents lucrative opportunities for both established players and new entrants in the market.

3.2 Job Creation

The space sector is a significant source of employment, creating high-quality jobs across various fields, including engineering, research, manufacturing, and support services. According to NASA, the U.S. space industry alone employed over 1 million people in 2020, with projections for continued job growth.

3.2.1 High-Skill Employment

Jobs in the space sector often require specialized skills and training, contributing to a highly skilled workforce. Engineers, scientists, and technicians are essential for the design, development, and operation of space missions. The growth of the commercial space industry has further fueled demand for skilled labor, with many companies competing for talent.

3.2.2 Indirect Job Creation

In addition to direct employment, the space sector creates indirect job opportunities in related industries. For example, the construction of launch facilities, manufacturing of spacecraft components, and the development of ground support systems all contribute to job creation beyond the space industry itself. The ripple effect of space-related employment extends to education, health care, and technology sectors, enhancing overall economic development.

3.3 Technological Advancements

The space sector is a catalyst for technological innovation, leading to advancements that benefit various industries and society as a whole. The research and development associated with space exploration often result in new technologies that can be applied to commercial markets.

3.3.1 Spin-Off Technologies

Many technologies initially developed for space missions have found applications in everyday life. For instance, NASA's work in materials science has led to the development of advanced materials used in aerospace, automotive, and consumer goods. Technologies such as satellite-based GPS navigation, weather forecasting, and remote sensing have become integral to various sectors, enhancing efficiency and safety.

3.3.2 Research and Development Investments

Governments and private companies are increasingly recognizing the importance of investing in research and development within the space sector. For example, the European Space Agency (ESA) has invested in various innovative projects, such as Earth observation satellites that monitor climate change and natural disasters. These investments not only drive technological advancements but also create economic opportunities in research and development sectors.

3.4 Broader Economic Implications

The economic contributions of the space sector extend beyond revenue generation and job creation. The sector plays a crucial role in fostering innovation, enhancing national security, and promoting international collaboration.

3.4.1 National Security

Many nations view their space capabilities as vital to national security. The development of satellite technology for defense purposes enhances situational awareness and intelligence gathering. For instance, the U.S. Department of Defense relies on satellite systems for communication, navigation, and reconnaissance. The economic impact of these capabilities contributes to a robust defense industry, generating jobs and revenue.

3.4.2 International Collaboration

Space exploration fosters collaboration among nations, leading to diplomatic relations and shared technological advancements. Collaborative projects, such as the International Space Station (ISS), involve multiple countries working together toward common goals. These partnerships often extend beyond space, fostering cooperation in areas such as science, technology, and education.

3.5 Challenges and Future Outlook

Despite its substantial contributions, the space sector faces challenges that could impact its economic growth. Funding constraints, regulatory hurdles, and competition among countries can pose risks to ongoing development.

3.5.1 Funding Constraints

While government investments in space exploration remain significant, budget constraints can affect the pace of progress. Countries must balance their space ambitions with other pressing domestic needs, which can impact the long-term sustainability of space programs.

3.5.2 Regulatory Hurdles

The rapid expansion of the commercial space sector raises questions about regulatory frameworks. As new players enter the market, establishing clear regulations and guidelines will be essential to ensure safety and sustainability.

3.5.3 Future Outlook

Looking ahead, the space sector is poised for continued growth. The increasing demand for satellite services, advancements in launch technologies, and the rise of new players in the market will contribute to the sector's economic contributions. Governments and private companies must work collaboratively to overcome challenges and leverage opportunities for innovation and exploration.

Conclusion

The economic contributions of the space sector are profound and multifaceted. From revenue generation and job creation to technological advancements and broader economic implications, the space industry plays a critical role in shaping the global economy. As countries invest in their space capabilities and private companies continue to innovate, the economic impact of the space sector will only grow, underscoring its significance in the modern world.

4. Challenges and Opportunities in Space Investment

The space sector has witnessed significant growth over the past few decades, driven by advancements in technology, increased private sector involvement, and growing interest from governments worldwide. However, this growth is not without challenges. Navigating the complexities of space investment requires a deep understanding of the unique hurdles that companies and governments face. This section will explore the key challenges and opportunities present in the realm of space investment, emphasizing the need for strategic planning and collaboration to overcome obstacles and capitalize on emerging trends.

Investing in space presents both high risks and potential high rewards. The challenges include regulatory hurdles, funding constraints, technological uncertainties, and market volatility. On the other hand, opportunities arise from the increasing demand for satellite services, the rise of commercial space ventures, and international partnerships. By analyzing these challenges and opportunities, stakeholders can make informed decisions that foster the sustainable growth of the space sector.

4.1 Key Challenges in Space Investment

4.1.1 Regulatory Hurdles

One of the most significant challenges facing space investment is the complex regulatory environment. Various national and international regulations govern space activities, which can create barriers to entry for new companies and impede the progress of existing ones.

Example: In the United States, the Federal Aviation Administration (FAA) oversees commercial space launch operations. Companies must navigate a lengthy and often complicated licensing process to obtain the necessary permits for launching rockets. This regulatory maze can delay projects and increase costs, deterring potential investors.

4.1.2 Funding Constraints

Space ventures often require substantial capital investments, which can be difficult to secure. While venture capital has begun to flow into the space sector, many startups struggle to find funding due to the high risk and long timelines associated with space projects.

Example: Many promising space startups have faced challenges in securing initial funding rounds. A notable case is Planet Labs, a company focused on Earth observation satellites. Despite its innovative technology, the company initially struggled to secure funding until it established a track record of successful satellite launches and operational satellites.

4.1.3 Technological Uncertainties

Investing in space technology involves inherent risks due to the rapidly evolving nature of the industry. Innovations in propulsion, materials, and satellite technology can quickly render existing technologies obsolete.

Example: The rapid advancements in small satellite technology have disrupted the traditional satellite manufacturing industry. Companies that once dominated the market, such as Boeing and Lockheed Martin, now face competition from smaller companies that can produce satellites more efficiently and at lower costs.

4.1.4 Market Volatility

The space industry is susceptible to market fluctuations driven by economic conditions, geopolitical events, and shifts in consumer demand. Investors must navigate this volatility while making strategic investment decisions.

Example: The COVID-19 pandemic highlighted vulnerabilities in the space sector, with delays in satellite launches and disruptions in supply chains. As a result, some companies faced revenue declines, leading to reevaluations of their business models and investment strategies.

4.2 Opportunities in Space Investment

4.2.1 Growing Demand for Satellite Services

The demand for satellite services is projected to grow significantly in the coming years, driven by increased reliance on telecommunications, internet connectivity, and data analytics.

Example: The rise of the Internet of Things (IoT) has created new opportunities for satellite connectivity. Companies like SpaceX, with its Starlink project, aim to provide high-speed internet access globally, especially in underserved areas. This growing demand presents a lucrative opportunity for investors willing to back innovative satellite service providers.

4.2.2 Rise of Commercial Space Ventures

The commercial space sector has seen a surge in investment and innovation, with numerous startups entering the market to offer services ranging from satellite manufacturing to launch capabilities.

Example: Rocket Lab, a private aerospace manufacturer, has gained traction in the small satellite launch market. By providing affordable and reliable launch services, the company has attracted significant investment and expanded its customer base. The rise of such commercial ventures indicates a shift in how space activities are approached, opening doors for investors.

4.2.3 International Partnerships and Collaboration

Collaborative efforts between governments, private companies, and international organizations present unique opportunities for investment. These partnerships can leverage resources, share risks, and drive innovation.

Example: The Artemis program, led by NASA, aims to return humans to the Moon by the mid-2020s and establish a sustainable presence there. This initiative involves collaboration with international partners, including the European Space Agency (ESA) and the Japan Aerospace Exploration Agency (JAXA). Investments in technologies developed for the Artemis program can yield benefits beyond lunar exploration, such as advancements in Earth-based applications.

4.2.4 Advancements in Technology and Innovation

Continuous advancements in technology present opportunities for investment in new solutions and applications. Innovations in propulsion, robotics, and materials science are transforming the landscape of space exploration.

Example: The development of reusable rocket technology, pioneered by SpaceX, has revolutionized the economics of space launches. By significantly reducing the cost of access to space, this innovation has attracted interest from various sectors, including government and commercial clients looking to deploy satellites more affordably.

4.3 Strategic Approaches for Investors

To effectively navigate the challenges and seize the opportunities in space investment, investors must adopt strategic approaches:

4.3.1 Conducting Thorough Due Diligence

Investors should conduct comprehensive due diligence on potential investment opportunities, assessing the technical feasibility, market demand, and competitive landscape.

4.3.2 Building Strategic Partnerships

Forming partnerships with established players in the space industry can provide access to resources, expertise, and market insights, reducing the risks associated with investment.

4.3.3 Fostering Innovation and Research

Investors can support innovation by funding research initiatives and startups that focus on disruptive technologies. Engaging with universities and research institutions can also foster collaboration and drive technological advancements.

4.3.4 Staying Informed on Regulatory Developments

Staying updated on regulatory changes and emerging trends in the space sector will help investors make informed decisions and adapt to evolving market conditions.

Conclusion

The space sector offers a dynamic landscape for investment, characterized by both significant challenges and abundant opportunities. Understanding the complexities of the industry, from regulatory hurdles to technological uncertainties, is crucial for investors seeking to navigate this evolving market. By leveraging the growing demand for satellite services, the rise of commercial ventures, and international collaborations, investors can position themselves to capitalize on the economic potential of the space sector. With strategic planning and a proactive approach, stakeholders can help shape the future of space exploration and contribute to the continued growth of this exciting industry.

5. Future Market Predictions

As the space industry continues to evolve, predicting future market trends becomes essential for stakeholders looking to capitalize on opportunities and navigate challenges. The space sector is experiencing unprecedented growth, driven by technological advancements, increased commercial participation, and a rising demand for satellite services. This section will delve into future market predictions for the space industry, focusing on growth trajectories, emerging technologies, potential market disruptions, and the overall economic impact. By examining these factors, stakeholders can better prepare for the future landscape of space exploration and investment.

Forecasting future market trends in space requires a multifaceted approach that considers technological innovations, geopolitical influences, economic conditions, and consumer demands. As countries and private entities invest heavily in space initiatives, understanding these dynamics will enable investors and policymakers to make informed decisions. The predictions presented in this section will highlight key areas of growth, the potential for market disruptions, and the ongoing shift toward commercial and international collaboration in space endeavors.

5.1 Growth Trajectories in the Space Industry

5.1.1 Satellite Services Market Expansion

The satellite services market is expected to experience significant growth in the coming years. With the increasing demand for communication, earth observation, and data analytics, satellite operators are expanding their fleets to meet global needs.

Example: According to a report by Euroconsult, the global satellite services market is projected to reach $300 billion by 2025, driven by the demand for broadband services and the rise of IoT applications. As industries like agriculture, healthcare, and transportation increasingly rely on satellite data, the market for satellite services will expand, creating opportunities for investors.

5.1.2 Space Launch Industry Growth

The space launch industry is also on a growth trajectory, with an increasing number of satellite launches anticipated in the coming years. This growth is fueled by the rise of small satellites and the decreasing costs of launch services.

Example: Companies like SpaceX and Rocket Lab have pioneered cost-effective launch solutions, enabling a new generation of small satellites to enter the market. It is estimated that over 10,000 small satellites will be launched by 2028, presenting significant investment opportunities for launch service providers and satellite manufacturers.

5.1.3 Deep Space Exploration Investments

Investments in deep space exploration are expected to increase as governments and private companies set ambitious goals for interplanetary missions. This focus on exploration will lead to new technologies and opportunities in various sectors.

Example: NASA's Artemis program aims to return humans to the Moon by 2024, with plans for eventual missions to Mars. The global interest in deep space exploration will encourage investment in technologies such as propulsion systems, life support, and habitat construction, creating opportunities for companies involved in these areas.

5.2 Emerging Technologies Shaping the Future

5.2.1 Artificial Intelligence and Machine Learning

Artificial intelligence (AI) and machine learning (ML) are set to revolutionize various aspects of the space industry, from satellite data analysis to mission planning. These technologies will enhance operational efficiency and improve decision-making processes.

Example: AI-powered algorithms can analyze vast amounts of satellite imagery to monitor environmental changes, track deforestation, and assess natural disasters. Companies like Planet Labs leverage AI to provide actionable insights from their satellite data, creating value for a wide range of industries.

5.2.2 Space Robotics and Automation

Advancements in robotics and automation will play a crucial role in the future of space exploration and operations. Autonomous systems will enable more efficient and safer missions, reducing the need for human intervention.

Example: NASA's Mars 2020 mission utilized the Perseverance rover, equipped with advanced robotics and autonomous navigation capabilities. As robotic technology continues to evolve, it will become integral to lunar and Martian exploration, paving the way for human missions and sustainable presence on other celestial bodies.

5.2.3 Launch System Innovations

Innovations in launch systems, including reusable rockets and advanced propulsion technologies, will significantly impact the economics of space travel and satellite deployment.

Example: SpaceX's Falcon 9 rocket, designed for reusability, has transformed the launch market by drastically reducing costs. This innovation has made space more accessible, allowing smaller companies and countries to participate in space activities, leading to a more competitive landscape.

5.3 Potential Market Disruptions

5.3.1 Geopolitical Factors

Geopolitical tensions and international relations will continue to influence the space industry. As nations compete for dominance in space, regulatory changes and trade policies may impact investments and collaborations.

Example: The ongoing competition between the United States and China in space exploration has led to increased funding for NASA and the establishment of the Space Force. Such geopolitical dynamics can create uncertainties for international partnerships and investments.

5.3.2 Environmental Concerns and Sustainability

Growing concerns about space debris and the environmental impact of space activities may lead to stricter regulations and market disruptions. Stakeholders must prioritize sustainability to ensure the long-term viability of the space sector.

Example: The increasing number of satellites in orbit has raised alarms about space debris. Companies and organizations are exploring solutions to mitigate this issue, such as active debris removal technologies. Investors focusing on sustainable practices may find opportunities in companies addressing these challenges.

5.4 Economic Impact and Job Creation

5.4.1 Job Creation in the Space Sector

The growth of the space industry will lead to significant job creation across various sectors, from engineering and manufacturing to data analysis and project management. As new companies enter the market, the demand for skilled professionals will rise.

Example: A report by the Space Foundation indicated that the global space economy employed over 1.1 million people in 2020, and this number is expected to grow as the industry expands. Investment in workforce development and education will be crucial to meeting this demand.

5.4.2 Contributions to Economic Growth

The space industry contributes to economic growth by driving innovation, creating jobs, and supporting a wide range of sectors. Investments in space-related technologies often yield benefits that extend beyond the industry itself.

Example: The development of satellite technologies has enabled advancements in telecommunications, agriculture, and disaster management, demonstrating the far-reaching economic impact of space investments. As the industry grows, its contributions to the global economy will become increasingly significant.

Conclusion

The future of the space industry is poised for remarkable growth, driven by emerging technologies, increasing demand for satellite services, and ambitious exploration goals. However, stakeholders must remain vigilant in addressing challenges such as regulatory hurdles, geopolitical factors, and environmental concerns. By staying informed and adapting to market dynamics, investors, governments, and private companies can seize the opportunities presented by this rapidly evolving sector. As the space industry continues to expand, its potential for economic impact and job creation will shape the future of exploration and innovation.

Chapter 7: Regulatory and Ethical Framework

1. Space Law and International Treaties
2. Ethical Considerations in Space Exploration
3. Environmental Impact of Space Activities
4. The Role of National and International Regulations
5. Future Directions for Space Governance

Chapter 7

Regulatory and Ethical Framework

Introduction

As humanity ventures further into the cosmos, the need for a comprehensive regulatory and ethical framework governing space exploration becomes increasingly critical. The rapid advancement of technology and the increasing number of stakeholders in the space sector necessitate clear guidelines and standards to ensure safe, sustainable, and equitable access to outer space. This chapter will explore the complex interplay between space law, ethical considerations, environmental impacts, and the role of national and international regulations in shaping the future of space governance.

The exploration and utilization of outer space present unique challenges that require careful consideration of legal and ethical issues. Space law, rooted in international treaties and agreements, establishes the foundational principles that govern activities in space, including the rights and responsibilities of nations and private entities. Additionally, ethical considerations surrounding the exploration of celestial bodies and the potential colonization of other planets raise important questions about our responsibilities to preserve these environments for future generations.

Moreover, the environmental impact of space activities, particularly the proliferation of space debris, poses significant risks to both current and future missions. Addressing these challenges requires robust regulations and proactive measures to mitigate environmental harm while promoting responsible exploration.

As we look toward the future, it is essential to consider how emerging technologies and evolving geopolitical landscapes will influence space governance. This chapter will examine existing frameworks, identify gaps, and propose future directions for enhancing the regulatory and ethical landscape of space exploration. By doing so, we can ensure that our endeavors in space are conducted responsibly, equitably, and with respect for the unique environments we seek to explore.

1. Space Law and International Treaties

Space exploration, once a domain of national pride and technological advancement, has evolved into a complex arena that necessitates the establishment of legal and regulatory frameworks. As various nations and private enterprises aim to explore and exploit outer space, understanding space law and the international treaties that govern these activities becomes crucial. This section delves into the foundations of space law, the key treaties that shape its framework, and their implications for current and future space activities.

1.1 The Genesis of Space Law

The concept of space law emerged during the early years of space exploration, primarily in response to the rapid advancements in technology and the launch of artificial satellites. The launching of Sputnik by the Soviet Union in 1957 marked a pivotal moment, igniting international discussions on how to regulate outer space activities. Consequently, the need for legal norms governing the use of outer space became apparent, leading to the development of various treaties and agreements.

1.2 Key International Treaties

1.2.1 The Outer Space Treaty (1967)

The cornerstone of international space law, the Outer Space Treaty, was adopted by the United Nations in 1967. This treaty establishes several key principles, including:

- **Peaceful Use of Outer Space**: Article IV states that the exploration and use of outer space shall be carried out for the benefit of all countries, emphasizing that outer space is not subject to national appropriation by claim of sovereignty.

- **Non-Militarization of Space**: The treaty prohibits the placement of nuclear weapons in space and asserts that celestial bodies shall be used exclusively for peaceful purposes.

- **Responsibility for National Activities**: Article VI mandates that countries are responsible for national space activities, including those conducted by private entities, ensuring accountability and oversight.

1.2.2 The Rescue Agreement (1968)

The Agreement on the Rescue of Astronauts and the Return of Objects Launched into Outer Space, commonly known as the Rescue Agreement, emphasizes the duty of countries to assist astronauts in distress and ensure the safe return of space objects that may land on foreign territory. This agreement underlines the principle of cooperation among nations in space activities.

1.2.3 The Liability Convention (1972)

The Convention on International Liability for Damage Caused by Space Objects outlines the liability of states for damages caused by their space objects. It establishes a framework for compensation and the legal responsibilities of launching states, promoting accountability in space operations.

1.2.4 The Registration Convention (1976)

The Registration Convention mandates that launching states provide information about their space objects to the United Nations. This transparency enhances tracking and monitoring of space activities, thereby contributing to accountability and reducing potential conflicts.

1.2.5 The Moon Agreement (1984)

Although not widely adopted, the Moon Agreement aims to govern the exploration and use of celestial bodies, particularly the Moon. It emphasizes the Moon's resources as the "common heritage of mankind" and calls for international cooperation in their exploration and utilization.

1.3 The Role of National Legislation

While international treaties provide a foundational framework for space law, individual countries have enacted national legislation to address specific aspects of space activities. These laws often complement international agreements and establish regulations governing licensing, liability, and compliance for national space endeavors. For instance, the United States' Commercial Space Launch Competitiveness Act of 2015 facilitates commercial space activities by providing a regulatory structure for private companies to operate in compliance with international obligations.

1.4 Challenges in Space Law

Despite the establishment of treaties and national laws, challenges persist in the field of space law:

- **Emerging Technologies**: The rapid advancement of technologies, such as satellite mega-constellations and space tourism, presents challenges in ensuring compliance with existing treaties.

- **Private Space Enterprises**: The rise of private companies in space exploration raises questions about accountability, liability, and adherence to international norms.

- **Space Debris**: The increasing amount of space debris poses risks to operational satellites and future missions, necessitating regulatory measures to mitigate this hazard.

1.5 Conclusion

Space law, anchored by international treaties, provides a crucial framework for governing the exploration and utilization of outer space. As humanity embarks on ambitious missions beyond Earth, understanding and adhering to these legal principles is essential for ensuring sustainable and peaceful exploration. Continued collaboration among nations and adaptation of legal frameworks will be vital in addressing emerging challenges and promoting responsible practices in the rapidly evolving space sector.

2. Ethical Considerations in Space Exploration

As humanity reaches beyond our planet, venturing into the cosmos, the exploration of space raises profound ethical questions. These considerations are not merely theoretical; they have practical implications for how we conduct missions, interact with celestial bodies, and understand our responsibilities to future generations. Ethical considerations in space exploration encompass a range of issues, including the protection of extraterrestrial environments, the rights of potential extraterrestrial life forms, and the equitable use of space resources. This section explores these ethical dimensions, providing examples to illustrate the complexities involved.

2.1 The Ethics of Environmental Stewardship

The principle of environmental stewardship extends to space exploration, where the potential for contamination and degradation of celestial bodies raises ethical concerns. The exploration of planets, moons, and asteroids may inadvertently lead to the introduction of Earth-based microorganisms, jeopardizing the integrity of extraterrestrial ecosystems. For instance, the contamination of Mars with Earth life forms could compromise future scientific research aimed at understanding whether life ever existed on the planet.

2.1.1 The Planetary Protection Policy

In recognition of these concerns, space agencies like NASA and ESA (European Space Agency) have developed planetary protection policies aimed at minimizing biological contamination. These policies enforce strict sterilization protocols for spacecraft destined for celestial bodies to ensure that our explorations do not irreparably damage pristine environments. The Outer Space Treaty of 1967 implicitly supports this by promoting the responsible use of outer space, highlighting the need to avoid harmful interference with extraterrestrial environments.

2.1.2 Case Study: Mars Exploration

Mars exploration serves as a pertinent example of environmental stewardship in space. NASA's Perseverance rover is equipped with advanced sterilization technologies and follows stringent protocols to ensure that it does not contaminate Martian soil and atmosphere. The rover's mission not only aims to search for signs of ancient life but also to preserve the Martian environment for future study. Ethical dilemmas arise when considering the balance between exploration and preservation, prompting debates about the limits of human intervention on other planets.

2.2 The Rights of Extraterrestrial Life

As we search for signs of life beyond Earth, ethical considerations expand to include the potential rights of any extraterrestrial life forms we might discover. The question arises: should we regard extraterrestrial organisms as sentient beings deserving of protection? If intelligent life is found, how should we approach communication and interaction? These questions challenge our anthropocentric perspectives and require a reevaluation of our ethical frameworks.

2.2.1 The Ethical Treatment of Extraterrestrial Intelligence

The discovery of intelligent extraterrestrial life would necessitate an ethical approach to interaction. Historical examples, such as the colonization of indigenous peoples on Earth, serve as cautionary tales of exploitation and harm. The Galactic Civilizations model proposed by science fiction author C.S. Lewis emphasizes a moral imperative to treat intelligent extraterrestrial beings with respect and dignity, fostering an ethical discourse around potential future encounters.

2.3 Space Resource Utilization and Equity

The increasing interest in the extraction of resources from celestial bodies, such as asteroids and the Moon, raises ethical questions about ownership and exploitation. The Outer Space Treaty asserts that space shall be the province of all mankind, promoting equitable access to its resources. However, as private companies and nations pursue resource extraction, the potential for conflict and inequality grows.

2.3.1 The Ethical Implications of Resource Mining

The prospect of mining asteroids for precious metals and rare minerals has attracted significant interest, with companies like Planetary Resources and Deep Space Industries leading the charge. Ethical dilemmas arise when considering who benefits from these resources and how profits are distributed. Should nations with advanced technology monopolize access to space resources, or should there be regulations ensuring that benefits are shared equitably among all humanity?

2.4 The Impact of Space Exploration on Society

The ethical considerations surrounding space exploration also extend to its impact on society. As funds are allocated to space missions, it is crucial to assess the opportunity costs associated with these expenditures. How do investments in space exploration affect critical social issues such as poverty, healthcare, and education on Earth? Striking a balance between ambitious space programs and addressing pressing terrestrial challenges poses ethical questions about priorities and responsibilities.

2.4.1 Case Study: NASA's Budget Allocation

NASA's budget allocation serves as a prime example of the ethical dilemmas involved. The agency's significant investments in space exploration and technology must be weighed against the urgent needs of marginalized communities on Earth. Advocates argue that while space exploration fosters innovation and scientific advancement, there is an ethical imperative to ensure that the benefits of such advancements are accessible to all.

2.5 Conclusion

The ethical considerations in space exploration are multifaceted and demand thoughtful deliberation as we navigate this uncharted frontier. Issues of environmental stewardship, the rights of potential extraterrestrial life, resource utilization, and societal impact present complex challenges that require collaboration and engagement across disciplines. As humanity embarks on its journey into the cosmos, we must commit to upholding ethical principles that ensure responsible exploration, equitable access, and the preservation of both our planet and the celestial realms we seek to explore.

3. Environmental Impact of Space Activities

The exploration of space has ushered in significant advancements in science, technology, and our understanding of the universe. However, it also poses unique environmental challenges that warrant careful examination. The environmental impact of space activities encompasses the effects of satellite launches, space debris, planetary exploration, and potential contamination of celestial bodies. This section delves into these environmental considerations, providing examples and discussing their implications for current and future space missions.

3.1 The Carbon Footprint of Rocket Launches

Rocket launches contribute to greenhouse gas emissions, primarily through the combustion of rocket fuels. The environmental footprint of a single launch can be substantial, with some estimates suggesting that one launch can produce as much carbon dioxide as a car would emit over its entire lifetime. As the frequency of launches increases, especially with the rise of commercial spaceflight, the cumulative impact on the atmosphere raises concerns about climate change.

3.1.1 Case Study: Falcon Heavy Launches

SpaceX's Falcon Heavy, one of the most powerful rockets, has conducted multiple launches since its debut in 2018. Each launch utilizes a significant amount of rocket fuel, contributing to atmospheric emissions. While SpaceX has made strides in developing reusable rockets to mitigate costs and emissions, the environmental implications of frequent launches remain a topic of ongoing research and debate.

3.2 Space Debris and Orbital Pollution

One of the most pressing environmental issues related to space activities is the growing problem of space debris. Millions of fragments from defunct satellites, spent rocket stages, and other debris orbit Earth, posing risks to operational spacecraft and astronauts. This pollution can also impact future space exploration efforts and satellite communications.

3.2.1 The Kessler Syndrome

The Kessler Syndrome is a theoretical scenario where the density of objects in low Earth orbit becomes so high that collisions between objects create a cascade of debris, leading to an unmanageable environment. This phenomenon raises significant concerns for space agencies and private companies alike, emphasizing the need for effective debris mitigation strategies. Organizations like NASA and ESA have implemented guidelines for the responsible disposal of satellites and debris tracking to minimize the risks associated with space debris.

3.2.2 Mitigation Efforts

To combat the issue of space debris, various mitigation strategies have been proposed. These include end-of-life protocols for satellites, such as deorbiting procedures and the use of "space tugs" to remove defunct satellites from orbit. The development of innovative technologies, such as lasers and nets for capturing debris, is also being explored to reduce the impact of orbital pollution.

3.3 Planetary Protection and Extraterrestrial Environments

As humanity extends its reach into the solar system, the ethical responsibility to protect celestial environments becomes paramount. The contamination of other planets, particularly Mars and Europa, raises concerns about preserving their scientific integrity and potential for harboring life.

3.3.1 The Case of Mars

Mars exploration missions, such as NASA's Perseverance rover, follow strict planetary protection protocols to prevent the introduction of Earth microorganisms to the Martian environment. This effort aims to ensure that future research on the planet remains uncontaminated, preserving its potential to reveal insights about the existence of past or present life. The measures include sterilization of spacecraft and monitoring for biological contamination before landing.

3.4 The Environmental Impact of In-Situ Resource Utilization (ISRU)

In-situ resource utilization (ISRU) refers to the practice of utilizing resources found on celestial bodies, such as water, minerals, and gases, to support space missions. While ISRU can reduce the need to transport materials from Earth, it also raises environmental questions about the extraction processes and their potential impact on extraterrestrial environments.

3.4.1 Case Study: Water Extraction on the Moon

The Artemis program aims to establish a sustainable human presence on the Moon by utilizing lunar resources, including water ice located at the poles. Extracting water from the Moon will support life support systems and fuel for future missions to Mars. However, careful planning and assessment are required to minimize disruption to the lunar environment and ensure the long-term sustainability of the extraction processes.

3.5 Conclusion

The environmental impact of space activities poses complex challenges that must be addressed as humanity expands its presence in the cosmos. From the carbon footprint of rocket launches to the growing problem of space debris and the ethical responsibility of planetary protection, these considerations necessitate a collaborative approach among space agencies, private companies, and policymakers. As we move forward in our quest for exploration, it is essential to prioritize sustainable practices that minimize harm to both our planet and the celestial bodies we seek to understand.

4. The Role of National and International Regulations

As humanity ventures deeper into space, the importance of regulations governing space activities cannot be overstated. Both national and international regulatory frameworks play a crucial role in ensuring that space exploration and utilization are conducted safely, responsibly, and sustainably. This chapter delves into the complex landscape of space regulations, highlighting key examples, the significance of various treaties, and the evolving role of regulatory bodies in managing the growing activities in outer space.

4.1 The Evolution of Space Regulations

The regulatory landscape surrounding space exploration has evolved significantly since the launch of Sputnik 1 in 1957. The initial response to the advent of space exploration was largely reactive, focusing on ensuring peaceful uses of outer space and establishing a framework for international cooperation. As technology advanced and more nations and private entities engaged in space activities, the need for comprehensive regulations became increasingly apparent.

4.1.1 The Outer Space Treaty of 1967

One of the cornerstone documents in space law is the Outer Space Treaty (OST), established in 1967. This treaty serves as a foundational framework for international space law, outlining principles such as the prohibition of the militarization of space, the commitment to peaceful exploration, and the non-appropriation of celestial bodies by any one nation. The OST has been ratified by over 100 countries and remains a critical reference point for national and international regulations in space activities.

4.2 National Regulatory Frameworks

Each nation engaging in space activities develops its regulatory framework to manage its interests, safety, and responsibilities in outer space. National regulations can vary significantly in scope and stringency, often influenced by a country's space ambitions, technological capabilities, and international commitments.

4.2.1 The United States: NASA and FAA

In the United States, the regulatory framework for space activities is primarily divided between two agencies: NASA (National Aeronautics and Space Administration) and the FAA (Federal Aviation Administration). NASA oversees governmental space missions and ensures compliance with international treaties, while the FAA regulates commercial spaceflight activities, including licensing launches and ensuring safety for the public and the environment.

4.2.1.1 Example: Commercial Space Launch Competitiveness Act

The Commercial Space Launch Competitiveness Act, enacted in 2015, serves as a key regulatory instrument promoting the U.S. commercial space industry. This act encourages private investment and innovation in space activities while establishing safety guidelines and liability measures for commercial launch operators.

4.2.2 The European Space Agency (ESA)

The European Space Agency (ESA) serves as an intergovernmental organization dedicated to space exploration and technology development. ESA member states collaborate to establish common regulatory frameworks that facilitate cooperative missions and promote compliance with international treaties. ESA has developed various guidelines addressing space debris, launch safety, and environmental protection.

4.3 International Regulatory Frameworks

While national regulations are essential, the interconnected nature of space activities necessitates international cooperation and regulatory frameworks. Various treaties and agreements have been established to foster collaboration and address the challenges posed by increased space activities.

4.3.1 The Registration Convention

The Convention on Registration of Objects Launched into Outer Space, known as the Registration Convention, was adopted in 1976 and requires states to provide information about space objects they launch. This treaty enhances transparency and accountability in space operations, allowing nations to track and identify objects in orbit.

4.3.2 The Liability Convention

The Convention on International Liability for Damage Caused by Space Objects, established in 1972, outlines the liability of launching states for damage caused by their space objects. This treaty provides a framework for compensation claims in cases of damage to property or injury resulting from space activities, fostering accountability among space-faring nations.

4.4 The Role of International Organizations

International organizations play a vital role in the development and enforcement of space regulations. The United Nations Office for Outer Space Affairs (UNOOSA) is a key body facilitating international cooperation in space exploration and ensuring compliance with treaties.

4.4.1 The United Nations Committee on the Peaceful Uses of Outer Space (COPUOS)

COPUOS, established in 1959, serves as a forum for member states to discuss and develop policies on space activities. The committee has produced various guidelines and recommendations addressing issues such as space debris mitigation, long-term sustainability, and capacity-building for developing countries in space exploration.

4.5 Challenges in Regulatory Frameworks

Despite the established regulatory frameworks, several challenges persist in effectively managing space activities. The rapid pace of technological advancements, the emergence of new actors in the space sector, and the increasing frequency of launches pose significant challenges for existing regulations.

4.5.1 The Rise of Commercial Space Companies

The growing involvement of private companies in space exploration, such as SpaceX, Blue Origin, and Virgin Galactic, has introduced complexities into regulatory frameworks. National authorities must adapt existing regulations to accommodate the unique challenges posed by commercial space activities while ensuring safety and compliance with international treaties.

4.6 Future Directions for Space Regulation

As humanity continues to push the boundaries of space exploration, the regulatory landscape must evolve to address emerging challenges. Future regulations should prioritize sustainability, cooperation, and transparency in space activities. Additionally, increased dialogue among nations and stakeholders is essential to foster a collaborative approach to space governance.

Conclusion

The role of national and international regulations in space activities is paramount in ensuring the safe, responsible, and sustainable exploration of outer space. As technology continues to advance and new actors enter the field, the regulatory frameworks must adapt to the evolving landscape. A collaborative approach among nations, international organizations, and commercial entities will be crucial in addressing the challenges and opportunities that lie ahead in space exploration.

5. Future Directions for Space Governance

As humanity continues its journey into the cosmos, the need for robust space governance has never been more critical. Future directions for space governance encompass a wide array of issues, including the sustainable use of outer space, the role of emerging technologies, international cooperation, and the ethical implications of space exploration. This chapter examines potential pathways for evolving governance structures, highlighting the necessity for adaptable frameworks that can address the complexities of modern space activities. Through examples and case studies, we will explore how future space governance can ensure that exploration remains peaceful, equitable, and beneficial for all humanity.

5.1 The Need for Sustainable Space Governance

The increasing number of satellites, space debris, and planned missions to other celestial bodies underscores the necessity for sustainable governance in space activities. As more nations and private entities venture into space, the potential for conflicts and environmental degradation rises. Sustainable governance must focus on the responsible use of resources and the long-term health of the space environment.

5.1.1 Addressing Space Debris

One of the foremost challenges in space governance is the growing issue of space debris. According to the European Space Agency (ESA), thousands of pieces of debris, including defunct satellites and spent rocket stages, currently orbit the Earth. Effective governance will require international cooperation to establish guidelines for debris mitigation and removal. For example, the ESA's "Space Debris Mitigation Guidelines" aim to promote best practices for minimizing the creation of space debris, emphasizing the need for compliance by all space-faring nations.

5.2 The Role of Emerging Technologies

Emerging technologies, such as artificial intelligence (AI), robotics, and advanced materials, are reshaping the landscape of space exploration. These advancements can enhance safety, efficiency, and sustainability in space operations. However, they also pose ethical and regulatory challenges that must be addressed.

5.2.1 AI in Space Operations

The integration of AI into space missions can optimize data analysis, improve spacecraft navigation, and enhance decision-making processes. For instance, NASA's Mars Rover, Perseverance, employs AI to navigate the Martian surface autonomously. While AI offers significant benefits, it raises questions about accountability and transparency in decision-making. Future governance frameworks must establish clear guidelines on the use of

AI in space missions, ensuring that ethical considerations are prioritized.

5.3 International Cooperation and Collaboration

As space activities become more complex and diverse, international cooperation will be essential for effective governance. The spirit of collaboration can lead to shared knowledge, resources, and technologies, ultimately enhancing the safety and sustainability of space exploration.

5.3.1 Public-Private Partnerships

The increasing involvement of private companies in space exploration presents opportunities for innovative public-private partnerships. For example, NASA's Commercial Crew Program partners with private companies like SpaceX and Boeing to develop crewed spacecraft for missions to the International Space Station (ISS). Such collaborations can accelerate technological advancements and reduce costs, but they also necessitate clear regulations and accountability measures to ensure public safety and compliance with international agreements.

5.3.2 International Treaties and Agreements

To foster international cooperation, new treaties and agreements may be necessary to address emerging challenges in space governance. For example, a potential "Space Resources Treaty" could regulate the extraction and use of resources from celestial bodies, ensuring that such activities are conducted in a manner that benefits all humanity. Collaborative efforts among nations can help establish a framework for responsible resource management and equitable access to outer space.

5.4 Ethical Considerations in Space Exploration

The ethical implications of space exploration must be at the forefront of future governance discussions. As humanity expands its presence in space, questions about the rights of future generations, the protection of extraterrestrial environments, and the potential exploitation of resources arise.

5.4.1 The Ethical Use of Space Resources

The extraction of resources from celestial bodies, such as asteroids and the Moon, raises ethical questions about ownership and benefit-sharing. Future governance frameworks should ensure that resource extraction is conducted responsibly and transparently, with a focus on equitable distribution of benefits. For instance, initiatives like the Lunar Gateway project, which aims to establish a sustainable human presence on the Moon, can serve as models for ethical resource use and international collaboration.

5.5 Education and Capacity Building

Education and capacity building are crucial for fostering a culture of responsible space governance. As more nations engage in space activities, there is a need for education and training programs that emphasize the importance of sustainable practices, compliance with international agreements, and ethical considerations.

5.5.1 Developing National Capacity

Countries with emerging space programs should prioritize developing national capacity for space governance. This includes training experts in space law, policy, and technology, as well as creating institutions that facilitate compliance with international regulations. Collaborations with established space-faring nations can provide valuable support and knowledge-sharing opportunities.

Conclusion

The future of space governance is shaped by the complexities and challenges of modern space exploration. As humanity continues to push the boundaries of what is possible in outer space, adaptive and robust governance frameworks are essential. Emphasizing sustainability, international cooperation, ethical considerations, and education will pave the way for a responsible and inclusive approach to space exploration. Through collaborative efforts, we can ensure that the final frontier remains a domain that benefits all of humanity.

Chapter 8: Challenges and Opportunities

1. Technical Challenges in Space Exploration
2. Economic Barriers and Funding Issues
3. Public Perception and Support for Space Missions
4. The Role of Education and Workforce Development
5. Opportunities for Innovation and Collaboration

Chapter 8

Challenges and Opportunities

Introduction

The exploration of outer space is one of humanity's most ambitious endeavors, driven by curiosity and the quest for knowledge. However, this journey is not without its challenges. Chapter 8 delves into the multifaceted obstacles and opportunities that characterize contemporary space exploration. As we push the boundaries of technology and venture into the unknown, we encounter a range of technical challenges that must be addressed to ensure the success of missions beyond our planet. Simultaneously, economic barriers and funding issues pose significant hurdles that can impede progress.

Public perception and support for space missions play a crucial role in determining the sustainability of these endeavors. As the public becomes increasingly aware of the importance of space exploration, understanding their concerns and aspirations is essential for garnering support. Furthermore, the role of education and workforce development is critical in preparing the next generation of innovators and leaders who will shape the future of space exploration.

In addition to challenges, this chapter will explore the myriad opportunities for innovation and collaboration that arise in the realm of space exploration. As nations, organizations, and private entities come together to share knowledge and resources, new possibilities emerge for advancing our capabilities in space. This chapter aims to provide a comprehensive overview of the challenges and opportunities that define the current landscape of space exploration, emphasizing the importance of adaptability, collaboration, and foresight in navigating this exciting frontier.

1. Technical Challenges in Space Exploration

Space exploration has always been an endeavor fraught with technical challenges. From the very first launch of a rocket to sending humans to the Moon and exploring distant planets, the complexities involved in these missions have demanded unprecedented innovation and collaboration. As we advance further into the cosmos, understanding and overcoming these technical challenges become more critical than ever. This section delves into the key technical obstacles faced in space exploration, offering examples and insights that illustrate the importance of addressing these issues to ensure the future success of humanity's ventures into space.

1.1. Launch Vehicle Limitations

One of the most significant technical challenges in space exploration is the development and deployment of launch vehicles capable of overcoming Earth's gravity. Launch vehicles must generate enough thrust to carry payloads, which can weigh several tons, into space. The engineering involved in designing rockets that can withstand the extreme conditions of launch, including high pressures and temperatures, is complex.

For example, the Saturn V rocket, which was used in the Apollo missions, remains one of the most powerful rockets ever built. It was capable of lifting about 140 metric tons to low Earth orbit. However, building such powerful launch systems is not only a technical feat but also an expensive undertaking. The development of reusable launch systems, such as SpaceX's Falcon 9, has demonstrated potential cost savings but comes with its own set of engineering challenges.

1.2. Life Support Systems

Human space exploration introduces additional technical challenges, particularly in designing effective life support systems. These systems must provide astronauts with essential resources such as oxygen, water, and food, while also managing waste and maintaining a stable environment in the spacecraft.

For instance, the International Space Station (ISS) employs a closed-loop life support system that recycles air and water, making it one of the most advanced life support systems in operation. However, creating a reliable life support system for long-duration missions, such as trips to Mars, poses challenges due to the need for sustainable resource management over extended periods without resupply from Earth.

1.3. Propulsion Technology

Advancements in propulsion technology are vital for expanding the reach of space exploration. Traditional chemical propulsion systems, while effective for launching payloads from Earth, have limitations when it comes to interplanetary travel. The development of new propulsion methods, such as ion propulsion and nuclear thermal propulsion, is essential for reducing travel times and enabling missions to more distant destinations.

For example, NASA's Dawn spacecraft utilized ion propulsion to travel to the asteroid belt, allowing it to efficiently reach and study celestial bodies like Vesta and Ceres. This technology represents a significant advancement but requires further research and development to become viable for crewed missions to Mars or beyond.

1.4. Navigation and Communication

Navigating and communicating in space are formidable technical challenges. Spacecraft must be equipped with sophisticated navigation systems to ensure accurate trajectory calculations and maneuvers. The vast distances in space introduce delays in communication, complicating real-time decision-making.

For instance, the Mars rovers rely on a combination of autonomous navigation and Earth-based commands to traverse the Martian landscape. The time delay in communication between Earth and Mars, which can range from 4 to 24 minutes depending on their relative positions, means that real-time control is impossible. This necessitates the development of autonomous systems capable of making critical decisions on their own.

1.5. Space Environment Hazards

The space environment presents various hazards that pose technical challenges for spacecraft and their occupants. Space debris, radiation exposure, and micrometeoroids are significant threats that must be mitigated to ensure the safety and longevity of missions.

For example, the increasing amount of space debris in low Earth orbit poses a collision risk for operational satellites and the ISS. Strategies for debris tracking and mitigation, as well as the design of spacecraft capable of withstanding impacts, are critical areas of research.

1.6. Engineering and Material Science

The materials used in spacecraft must withstand extreme temperatures, radiation, and mechanical stresses. Advances in materials science are essential for developing lighter, stronger, and more resilient materials that can endure the harsh conditions of space.

Innovations such as carbon fiber composites and heat-resistant ceramics are being explored for use in spacecraft design. The development of these materials involves rigorous testing and validation to ensure their performance under space conditions.

1.7. Human Factors Engineering

Human factors engineering focuses on optimizing the interaction between astronauts and their environment. Designing spacecraft that are comfortable and user-friendly is essential for the success of long-duration missions.

For instance, the layout of controls and displays in spacecraft must facilitate ease of use, even under stressful conditions. Research into human factors is crucial for ensuring that astronauts can effectively manage complex tasks and respond to emergencies.

1.8. Budget Constraints

Technical challenges are often exacerbated by budget constraints. Funding for space missions is subject to political and economic fluctuations, which can lead to project delays or cancellations. Balancing the desire for ambitious exploration goals with fiscal realities is a continuous challenge for space agencies and private enterprises alike.

For example, NASA's Constellation program aimed to return humans to the Moon but faced significant budgetary issues that ultimately led to its cancellation. Sustainable funding models and international collaboration may help alleviate some of these financial pressures.

Conclusion

The technical challenges faced in space exploration are vast and varied, encompassing everything from launch vehicle design to human factors engineering. Overcoming these challenges requires continuous innovation, collaboration, and investment in research and development. As we strive to explore the cosmos, addressing these technical hurdles will be paramount to ensuring the success and safety of future missions. The examples highlighted in this section underscore the importance of a comprehensive approach to problem-solving in the face of these challenges.

2. Economic Barriers and Funding Issues

The pursuit of space exploration is inherently linked to significant economic barriers and funding issues that can impact the success and sustainability of missions. As countries and private entities embark on ambitious space programs, they often encounter financial limitations, fluctuating budgets, and complex funding structures. This section explores the economic barriers faced in space exploration, including the challenges of securing funding, the influence of political and economic climates, and the potential solutions that could pave the way for more sustainable financing in the space sector. By examining case studies and historical examples, we can gain insight into how economic factors shape the landscape of space exploration.

2.1. High Costs of Space Missions

One of the most significant barriers to space exploration is the high cost associated with designing, building, and launching spacecraft. Space missions require substantial investments in research and development, engineering, and operational costs, which can quickly escalate into billions of dollars. For instance, NASA's Space Shuttle program, which operated from 1981 to 2011, had a total program cost exceeding $196 billion, making it one of the most expensive space programs in history.

The costs of launching payloads into space are also a significant consideration. Traditional launch vehicles can charge anywhere from $10,000 to $30,000 per kilogram of payload. This financial barrier limits the number of missions that can be conducted and restricts access to space for smaller organizations and countries.

2.2. Fluctuating Budgets

Space programs are often subject to the vagaries of political priorities and economic conditions, leading to fluctuating budgets that can jeopardize mission timelines and goals. In many cases, funding for space exploration is allocated on a yearly basis, making it vulnerable to political changes and shifting government priorities.

For example, the Constellation program, aimed at returning humans to the Moon, was initiated by NASA but faced severe budget constraints that ultimately led to its cancellation in 2010. Such fluctuations can result in delays and re-evaluations of mission objectives, hampering long-term planning and execution.

2.3. Dependency on Government Funding

Many space agencies, particularly those in developing countries, rely heavily on government funding to support their programs. This dependency can create significant barriers to growth, especially in times of economic downturn when governments may prioritize other areas over space exploration.

For example, India's Indian Space Research Organisation (ISRO) has made significant strides in space exploration, yet its budget remains contingent on government allocations. While India has successfully launched missions like Mangalyaan (Mars Orbiter Mission), any reduction in funding could hinder its future aspirations, including crewed spaceflight and lunar exploration.

2.4. The Role of Private Investment

The emergence of private companies in the space sector has introduced new funding avenues but also brought about economic challenges. While private investment can lead to innovation and cost reduction, it also creates a competitive environment where funding is often directed toward projects with high commercial potential rather than exploratory missions.

SpaceX, for example, has revolutionized the launch industry with its reusable rocket technology, attracting billions in private investment. However, this shift in focus may lead to underfunding of important scientific missions that do not have immediate commercial viability. Balancing private and public investment is crucial for ensuring a diverse range of missions can be pursued.

2.5. International Collaboration and Funding

International collaboration in space exploration can alleviate some economic barriers by pooling resources and sharing costs. Programs like the International Space Station (ISS), which involves multiple countries, demonstrate the benefits of collaborative funding models.

However, securing contributions from various nations can be challenging due to differing priorities, economic conditions, and political climates. For instance, the European Space Agency (ESA) faces funding challenges as member states grapple with their own economic issues, which can affect their contributions to joint missions.

2.6. Cost-Effective Technology Development

Investing in cost-effective technology development is essential for addressing funding issues in space exploration. Innovations in materials, manufacturing processes, and propulsion systems can reduce mission costs while maintaining safety and effectiveness.

For example, the development of 3D printing technology has the potential to revolutionize how spacecraft are built, allowing for on-demand manufacturing of components in space. This could significantly reduce transportation costs and create more sustainable missions.

2.7. The Importance of Public Support

Public support for space exploration is a vital economic factor that can influence funding decisions. Positive public sentiment can lead to increased governmental budget allocations and private investments in space programs.

Engaging the public through education and outreach initiatives can help garner support for space exploration efforts. For instance, NASA's Mars rover missions have captivated global audiences, leading to increased interest and funding for future projects.

2.8. Future Funding Models

As the landscape of space exploration evolves, new funding models must be explored to address economic barriers effectively. Public-private partnerships, international collaborations, and innovative funding mechanisms, such as crowdfunding and grants, could provide alternative sources of funding.

An example of this is the XPRIZE Foundation, which incentivizes innovation through competitions that offer cash prizes for achieving specific technological goals in space exploration. This model not only promotes technological advancement but also attracts diverse funding sources.

Conclusion

Economic barriers and funding issues pose significant challenges to space exploration, affecting the feasibility and scope of missions. Understanding the complexities of funding in this field is crucial for developing strategies that can address these issues effectively. By leveraging innovative funding models, fostering public support, and promoting international collaboration, the space sector can continue to thrive and expand its horizons, paving the way for a new era of exploration and discovery.

3. Public Perception and Support for Space Missions

Public perception and support play a crucial role in shaping the trajectory of space missions and the broader field of space exploration. As humanity ventures deeper into space, understanding the attitudes, beliefs, and emotional connections that the public holds towards space activities becomes increasingly vital. This section delves into how public perception affects funding, policy-making, and the overall success of space missions. It also explores historical examples and case studies to illustrate the impact of public support and sentiment on space exploration endeavors.

3.1. The Role of Public Perception in Space Exploration

Public perception encompasses the beliefs, attitudes, and emotional responses of individuals and communities regarding space exploration. These perceptions can significantly influence government policies, funding allocations, and the priorities of space agencies. Positive public sentiment can lead to increased support for ambitious missions, while negative perceptions may result in skepticism and reduced funding.

For example, the Apollo program, which landed humans on the Moon in 1969, was initially met with skepticism from some segments of the public who questioned the expenditure of taxpayer dollars on space exploration. However, as the program progressed and the achievements of the missions were broadcast globally, public perception shifted dramatically. The sense of national pride and technological achievement fostered strong public support, ultimately leading to increased funding for NASA.

3.2. Historical Case Studies of Public Support

Throughout history, several key missions have demonstrated the profound impact of public perception on space exploration. The following case studies illustrate how public sentiment can shape the success of missions.

3.2.1. Apollo 11: A Triumph of Public Engagement

The Apollo 11 mission, which successfully landed humans on the Moon, serves as a prime example of how public engagement can bolster support for space initiatives. NASA's extensive public outreach, educational programs, and televised broadcasts of the lunar landing captivated millions worldwide. This engagement not only inspired a generation but also fostered a sense of ownership and pride among the public.

The "Earthrise" photo taken during the Apollo 8 mission, showcasing Earth from lunar orbit, sparked a global environmental movement. It shifted public perception regarding the fragility of our planet and emphasized the importance of space exploration in understanding our place in the universe.

3.2.2. Mars Rover Missions: Building Community Enthusiasm

NASA's Mars rover missions, including Spirit, Opportunity, and Curiosity, have generated substantial public interest and support. The use of social media platforms, interactive websites, and live streaming of mission events has allowed the public to engage directly with scientists and engineers. For instance, the "Curiosity Rover" landing in 2012 was watched by millions online, creating a sense of shared achievement and excitement.

The success of these missions has reinforced public perception of NASA as a leader in space exploration, resulting in increased support for subsequent missions and research initiatives. The emotional connection cultivated through these engagements has proven crucial in securing funding and political backing for future endeavors.

3.3. Factors Influencing Public Perception

Various factors influence public perception of space missions, including media representation, educational outreach, and the framing of space exploration narratives. Understanding these factors is essential for fostering positive public sentiment.

3.3.1. Media Representation

Media portrayal of space exploration plays a significant role in shaping public perception. Sensationalized reporting or negative framing can lead to skepticism and distrust. For example, coverage of high-profile failures, such as the Space Shuttle Challenger disaster in 1986, initially resulted in a decline in public support for NASA.

Conversely, positive media coverage showcasing scientific breakthroughs and successful missions can enhance public enthusiasm. Documentaries, films, and news segments that highlight the benefits of space exploration for society, such as advancements in technology and medicine, can further bolster public support.

3.3.2. Educational Outreach

Educational outreach initiatives are vital in fostering public interest and understanding of space exploration. Programs targeting schools and communities can engage students and families, creating a more informed public.

NASA's "STEM (Science, Technology, Engineering, and Mathematics) Engagement" programs aim to inspire the next generation of scientists and engineers, fostering a culture of curiosity and support for space initiatives. By emphasizing the educational aspects of space missions, organizations can cultivate long-term public enthusiasm.

3.4. The Impact of Social Media

The rise of social media has transformed how space agencies engage with the public. Platforms like Twitter, Facebook, and Instagram provide direct communication channels that enable agencies to share real-time updates, images, and stories from missions.

This shift has allowed for immediate public engagement and feedback. NASA's social media campaigns, such as the #JourneyToMars initiative, have successfully created buzz and excitement around upcoming missions, fostering a sense of community among space enthusiasts. The viral nature of social media also amplifies positive messaging, attracting a broader audience to space exploration.

3.5. The Role of Public Support in Funding and Policy

Public support directly influences funding decisions and policy-making in space exploration. When the public perceives space missions as beneficial and inspiring, lawmakers are more likely to allocate resources to support these initiatives.

For example, the successful landing of the Mars Perseverance rover in 2021 was met with widespread enthusiasm and media coverage, leading to increased public interest in space exploration. In turn, this public enthusiasm can translate into stronger political support and funding for NASA and other space agencies.

3.6. Challenges to Public Perception

Despite the positive aspects of public perception, challenges remain. Misinformation and lack of understanding about the complexities of space exploration can lead to skepticism and apathy. The portrayal of space exploration as purely a "race to Mars" or a competition among nations can undermine public interest in the collaborative aspects of space missions.

Moreover, economic factors, such as budget cuts and competing priorities, can also affect public perception. When citizens perceive space missions as diverting funds from pressing social issues, they may become less supportive of space exploration initiatives.

3.7. Enhancing Public Engagement Strategies

To foster a more informed and engaged public, space agencies must prioritize outreach and education. Innovative strategies, such as interactive exhibits, virtual reality experiences, and public lectures, can help demystify space exploration and create lasting interest.

Engaging with diverse communities, including underrepresented groups in STEM, is essential for broadening public support. Initiatives aimed at increasing access to space-related education and experiences can cultivate a more inclusive and enthusiastic public.

Conclusion

Public perception and support are vital components of the success and sustainability of space missions. By understanding the factors that influence public sentiment, space agencies can develop effective engagement strategies that foster enthusiasm, support, and funding for future endeavors. As humanity continues its journey into space, cultivating positive public perception will be crucial for inspiring the next generation of explorers and innovators.

4. The Role of Education and Workforce Development

As humanity continues to push the boundaries of space exploration, the role of education and workforce development becomes increasingly vital. A robust education system and a skilled workforce are essential to support the growing demands of the space industry, ensuring that we have the necessary talent to innovate, design, and execute complex space missions. This section explores the critical intersection between education, workforce development, and the evolving landscape of space exploration. It highlights current educational initiatives, workforce training programs, and the importance of fostering a culture of STEM (Science, Technology, Engineering, and Mathematics) to prepare future generations for careers in the space sector.

4.1. The Importance of STEM Education

STEM education forms the foundation for the skills and knowledge required in the space industry. The rapidly advancing nature of space technology necessitates a workforce that is not only technically proficient but also capable of critical thinking and problem-solving.

4.1.1. Developing Critical Skills

STEM programs cultivate essential skills, including mathematics, engineering principles, programming, and scientific inquiry. For instance, robotics competitions, such as FIRST Robotics and VEX Robotics, engage students in hands-on projects that promote teamwork, creativity, and technical proficiency. These competitions allow students to apply theoretical knowledge in practical scenarios, fostering a deeper understanding of engineering and technology.

4.1.2. Encouraging Interest in Space Careers

Early exposure to STEM subjects is crucial for inspiring students to pursue careers in the space industry. Programs that emphasize the relevance of space exploration—such as NASA's educational initiatives—help students see the connection between their studies and real-world applications. By highlighting careers in aerospace engineering, astrophysics, and space policy, educators can spark interest and enthusiasm for the field.

4.2. Educational Initiatives in Space Exploration

Numerous educational initiatives are designed to engage students and foster interest in space exploration. These programs aim to provide hands-on learning experiences and mentorship opportunities, thereby nurturing the next generation of space professionals.

4.2.1. NASA's Education Programs

NASA has implemented various education programs aimed at enhancing STEM education and workforce development. The agency's "NASA Educator Resource Center" offers teachers access to materials and training to incorporate space science into their curricula. Additionally, NASA's "Student Launch" program invites high school and college students to design and build their own rockets, providing a practical introduction to engineering principles and teamwork.

4.2.2. University Partnerships

Collaboration between universities and space agencies is essential for advancing research and development in the field. Programs like NASA's "Space Grant Consortium" support university-level research and provide scholarships to students pursuing careers in aerospace and related fields. These partnerships enhance the educational landscape by fostering innovation and providing students with access to cutting-edge research and facilities.

4.3. Workforce Development Programs

As the space industry evolves, workforce development programs play a crucial role in preparing professionals for the challenges of modern space exploration. These programs ensure that individuals possess the necessary skills to thrive in a competitive and rapidly changing environment.

4.3.1. Internships and Apprenticeships

Internships and apprenticeships provide valuable hands-on experience that is essential for students entering the workforce. Organizations such as SpaceX and Blue Origin offer internship programs that allow students to work alongside industry professionals, gaining practical insights into space engineering and operations.

For example, SpaceX's internship program has become highly competitive, attracting top talent from universities across the country. Participants engage in projects that contribute directly to ongoing missions, providing them with a unique opportunity to apply their knowledge in real-world scenarios.

4.3.2. Continuing Education and Training

The fast-paced nature of the space industry necessitates ongoing education and training for professionals. Organizations such as the American Institute of Aeronautics and Astronautics (AIAA) offer workshops, webinars, and certification programs that help professionals stay current with emerging technologies and best practices.

These continuing education programs not only enhance the skills of the workforce but also foster a culture of lifelong learning that is essential for innovation in space exploration.

4.4. Fostering Diversity and Inclusion in Space Education

A diverse and inclusive workforce is essential for driving innovation in the space industry. Efforts to promote diversity in STEM education help to ensure that individuals from all backgrounds have equal access to opportunities in space exploration.

4.4.1. Outreach Programs for Underrepresented Groups

Initiatives aimed at underrepresented groups—such as women, minorities, and individuals from low-income backgrounds—are crucial for fostering diversity in the workforce. Programs like NASA's "Women in STEM" initiative encourage young girls to explore careers in space science and engineering.

Additionally, organizations such as Black Girls Code work to empower young girls of color by providing coding and technology training. These outreach efforts help to create a more equitable representation of diverse voices within the space sector.

4.4.2. Mentorship and Support Networks

Mentorship programs play a significant role in supporting underrepresented individuals in their pursuit of careers in the space industry. By connecting students with experienced professionals, these programs provide guidance, encouragement, and valuable networking opportunities.

Organizations such as the Society of Women Engineers (SWE) offer mentorship programs that connect aspiring engineers with female role models in the industry. This support helps to foster confidence and resilience in the next generation of space professionals.

4.5. The Future of Space Education and Workforce Development

The future of space exploration hinges on the continuous development of a skilled workforce and innovative educational programs. As the industry expands, educational institutions, government agencies, and private companies must collaborate to create pathways for aspiring space professionals.

4.5.1. Integration of Emerging Technologies

Incorporating emerging technologies, such as artificial intelligence (AI), data analytics, and virtual reality (VR), into educational programs will enhance the learning experience and prepare students for the complexities of the space industry. For example, VR simulations of space missions can provide students with immersive experiences that deepen their understanding of spacecraft operations and mission planning.

4.5.2. Lifelong Learning in a Changing Industry

The space industry will continue to evolve, requiring professionals to adapt to new challenges and opportunities. Emphasizing a culture of lifelong learning and continuous skill development will be critical in ensuring that the workforce remains agile and innovative.

Conclusion

Education and workforce development are fundamental components of a thriving space exploration ecosystem. By prioritizing STEM education, fostering diversity, and investing in training programs, society can equip the next generation of space professionals with the skills and knowledge needed to tackle the challenges of the future. As humanity looks to the stars, the commitment to education and workforce development will ensure that we are well-prepared to explore and inhabit the cosmos.

5. Opportunities for Innovation and Collaboration

The field of space exploration is characterized by rapid advancements and an increasing demand for innovation. As humanity endeavors to explore beyond our planet, the need for collaboration among various stakeholders—governments, private companies, educational institutions, and international organizations—has never been more critical. This section delves into the opportunities for innovation and collaboration in the space sector, emphasizing how diverse partnerships can drive technological advancements, improve mission success rates, and ultimately expand our capabilities in space exploration. We will explore successful case studies, emerging trends, and the potential impact of collaborative efforts on the future of space exploration.

5.1. The Role of Public-Private Partnerships

Public-private partnerships (PPPs) have become a vital mechanism for fostering innovation in the space industry. These collaborations leverage the strengths of both the public sector and private companies to achieve shared goals, often resulting in groundbreaking advancements and cost efficiencies.

5.1.1. NASA and Commercial Spaceflight

One of the most prominent examples of successful public-private collaboration is NASA's Commercial Crew Program. This initiative aims to develop safe, reliable, and cost-effective crew transportation to the International Space Station (ISS) through partnerships with private aerospace companies such as SpaceX and Boeing. By contracting these companies to develop spacecraft, NASA has significantly reduced costs and accelerated the timeline for launching astronauts into space.

For instance, SpaceX's Crew Dragon spacecraft successfully transported astronauts to the ISS in May 2020, marking the first crewed launch from U.S. soil since 2011. This collaboration not only enhanced NASA's capabilities but also stimulated growth in the commercial space sector.

5.1.2. Collaboration on Lunar Exploration

NASA's Artemis program, aimed at returning humans to the Moon by the mid-2020s, exemplifies the potential for innovation through collaboration. NASA is partnering with various private companies and international space agencies to develop the necessary technologies and infrastructure for lunar exploration. By engaging partners like SpaceX, Blue Origin, and the European Space Agency (ESA), NASA is fostering innovation that will facilitate sustainable exploration on the Moon and beyond.

5.2. International Collaboration in Space Exploration

The complexity and cost of space exploration often necessitate international collaboration. By pooling resources, knowledge, and expertise, countries can achieve common objectives and expand the frontiers of space exploration.

5.2.1. The International Space Station (ISS)

The ISS serves as a prime example of successful international collaboration. Launched in 1998, the ISS is a partnership involving five space agencies: NASA (United States), Roscosmos (Russia), ESA (European Space Agency), JAXA (Japan), and CSA (Canada). This collaboration has enabled scientific research, technology development, and international cooperation in space.

Research conducted on the ISS has led to significant advancements in various fields, including medicine, materials science, and environmental monitoring. By fostering an environment of collaboration among nations, the ISS demonstrates the potential for shared knowledge and innovation in space exploration.

5.2.2. Global Initiatives for Planetary Defense

International collaboration is also critical for addressing global challenges, such as planetary defense against potential asteroid threats. Initiatives like the "Asteroid Impact & Near-Earth Object (NEO) Program" bring together scientists and researchers from multiple countries to share data, conduct studies, and develop strategies for detecting and mitigating potential asteroid impacts.

By pooling resources and expertise, countries can enhance their ability to respond to potential threats, demonstrating the importance of collaboration in ensuring the safety and security of our planet.

5.3. Innovation through Technology Transfer

Collaboration between the space industry and other sectors, such as technology, healthcare, and environmental science, can lead to innovative solutions that benefit society as a whole. Technology transfer initiatives facilitate the sharing of knowledge and technologies developed for space applications to other industries.

5.3.1. Advancements in Telecommunications

Technological innovations derived from space exploration have significantly impacted the telecommunications industry. Satellite technology, developed for space missions, has revolutionized global communication, enabling high-speed internet access,

GPS navigation, and real-time data transmission. Companies like Intelsat and SES, which provide satellite communication services, benefit from the advancements made through space research.

5.3.2. Medical Innovations from Space Research

Space research has also contributed to advancements in healthcare. For instance, research on the ISS has led to breakthroughs in drug development, telemedicine, and medical imaging technologies. The zero-gravity environment of the ISS allows scientists to study biological processes in ways that are not possible on Earth, leading to innovations that enhance medical treatments.

5.4. Fostering Innovation through Open Data and Collaboration Platforms

The increasing availability of open data and collaborative platforms has transformed the landscape of space exploration, providing new opportunities for innovation and research.

5.4.1. Open Data Initiatives

Open data initiatives, such as NASA's "Open Data" program, allow researchers, developers, and the public to access vast amounts of data collected during space missions. This democratization of information fosters innovation by enabling individuals and organizations to develop new applications, technologies, and scientific insights.

For example, the availability of satellite imagery data has led to innovations in agriculture, disaster response, and urban planning. Researchers and entrepreneurs can analyze this data to create solutions that address real-world challenges.

5.4.2. Collaborative Research Platforms

Collaborative research platforms, such as the "International Space Exploration Coordination Group (ISECG)," facilitate partnerships among countries and organizations to share resources, knowledge, and expertise. These platforms promote joint research initiatives, technology development, and data sharing, ultimately driving innovation in space exploration.

5.5. The Role of Education and Outreach in Fostering Collaboration

Education and outreach initiatives play a critical role in fostering collaboration and innovation within the space sector. By engaging the public, students, and emerging professionals, these initiatives create a culture of collaboration and inspire future generations to contribute to space exploration.

5.5.1. Public Engagement and Citizen Science

Citizen science programs encourage public participation in scientific research, fostering a sense of ownership and engagement in space exploration. Initiatives like the "Galaxy Zoo" project allow volunteers to classify galaxies and contribute to scientific discoveries, demonstrating the potential for collaboration between scientists and the public.

5.5.2. STEM Education and Workforce Development

Investing in STEM education and workforce development initiatives ensures that the next generation of innovators and collaborators is well-prepared to tackle the challenges of space exploration. By providing students with opportunities to engage in hands-on projects, internships, and mentorship programs, educational institutions can cultivate a skilled workforce that drives innovation.

Conclusion

The opportunities for innovation and collaboration in the space sector are vast and multifaceted. Through public-private partnerships, international collaboration, technology transfer, and open data initiatives, the space industry can harness the collective knowledge and expertise of diverse stakeholders. By fostering a culture of collaboration and investing in education and outreach, we can inspire future generations to contribute to the exciting frontier of space exploration.

Chapter 9: Future Trends in the Space Industry

1. Innovations on the Horizon
2. The Role of Space in Sustainable Development
3. Predictions for the Future of Space Exploration
4. The Impact of Artificial Intelligence in Space
5. Space Colonization: Possibilities and Challenges

Chapter 9

Future Trends in the Space Industry

Introduction

The space industry stands at a pivotal juncture, with advancements in technology and increasing global interest in exploration shaping its future. As we gaze into the horizon, we find an array of innovations poised to transform the landscape of space exploration and utilization. This chapter explores key future trends that will influence the space sector, including cutting-edge innovations, the role of space in promoting sustainable development, and the impact of artificial intelligence on mission efficiency and data analysis.

Moreover, we will delve into predictions for the future of space exploration, considering how human endeavors may extend beyond Earth and into the realms of space colonization. These developments present both exciting opportunities and significant challenges that will require careful consideration and strategic planning.

By examining these trends, we aim to provide insights into the dynamic evolution of the space industry, highlighting how emerging technologies, international collaborations, and innovative approaches will shape humanity's journey beyond our home planet. As we embark on this exploration of future trends, it is essential to recognize that the decisions made today will have lasting implications for generations to come in the realm of space exploration and development.

1. Innovations on the Horizon

As the space industry rapidly evolves, numerous innovations are on the horizon, poised to redefine our understanding of space exploration and utilization. These advancements encompass a broad spectrum of technologies and methodologies, enhancing our capabilities in launching, operating, and maintaining space missions. This section explores various innovations that are expected to shape the future of the space industry, providing examples of current projects and developments that exemplify these trends.

1.1. Advanced Propulsion Systems

One of the most significant areas of innovation in space technology is the development of advanced propulsion systems. Traditional chemical rockets, while effective, have limitations in terms of efficiency and speed. Researchers and companies are exploring alternatives such as:

- **Electric Propulsion:** Technologies like ion thrusters and Hall-effect thrusters offer higher efficiency and are capable of long-duration missions. For instance, NASA's Dawn spacecraft used ion propulsion to travel to the asteroid belt, allowing it to enter orbit around both Vesta and Ceres.

- **Nuclear Thermal Propulsion:** This technology uses nuclear reactions to heat a propellant, offering a significant increase in thrust compared to conventional systems. The NASA Nuclear Thermal Propulsion (NTP) project aims to develop this technology for future crewed missions to Mars, reducing travel time and enhancing safety.

- **Solar Sails:** Utilizing the pressure of sunlight, solar sails can propel spacecraft without fuel. The Planetary Society's LightSail project successfully demonstrated this technology, showcasing the potential for low-cost, long-duration space missions.

1.2. Reusable Launch Systems

The push for reusability in launch systems is another transformative innovation. Traditional expendable rockets incur high costs for each launch, while reusable systems offer significant savings and efficiency. Notable examples include:

- **SpaceX's Falcon 9:** With its first stage designed for reusability, the Falcon 9 has successfully returned to land after launching payloads into orbit. This innovation has revolutionized the economics of spaceflight, allowing for more frequent launches at lower costs.

- **Blue Origin's New Shepard:** This suborbital vehicle is designed for space tourism and scientific research, featuring a fully reusable rocket and capsule system.

Its successful flights have demonstrated the viability of reusability for commercial applications.

- **Arianespace's Ariane 6:** This upcoming launch vehicle incorporates a partially reusable first stage, which aims to reduce launch costs while maintaining high performance.

1.3. Small Satellites and CubeSats

The rise of small satellites, particularly CubeSats, has democratized access to space and spurred innovation in satellite technology. These compact, cost-effective satellites are being used for various applications:

- **Earth Observation:** Companies like Planet Labs operate fleets of small satellites to provide high-resolution imagery for environmental monitoring, urban planning, and agriculture. Their ability to capture daily images of the Earth offers unprecedented insights into global changes.

- **Communication:** Small satellites are increasingly being deployed in constellations to provide global internet coverage. For instance, SpaceX's Starlink aims to create a network of thousands of small satellites, improving internet access in remote areas.

- **Scientific Research:** CubeSats are being utilized for scientific missions, such as NASA's MarCO mission, which sent two CubeSats to Mars to provide communications during the InSight lander's descent. These missions demonstrate the potential for small satellites to contribute to significant scientific endeavors.

1.4. Artificial Intelligence and Machine Learning

The integration of artificial intelligence (AI) and machine learning (ML) into space operations is poised to enhance efficiency and decision-making capabilities:

- **Autonomous Spacecraft:** AI can enable spacecraft to make real-time decisions during missions, reducing reliance on ground control. For example, the European Space Agency's (ESA) BepiColombo mission to Mercury utilizes AI algorithms to optimize its trajectory and operations.

- **Data Analysis:** With the increasing volume of data generated by satellites and missions, AI and ML algorithms can process and analyze data more effectively than traditional methods. This capability is crucial for applications such as Earth monitoring and astrophysics.

- **Predictive Maintenance:** AI can be employed to predict equipment failures in spacecraft, improving reliability and reducing costs. This technology is being tested in various missions to enhance operational safety.

1.5. Space Habitats and Life Support Systems

As the prospect of long-duration space missions and human colonization of other celestial bodies becomes more tangible, innovations in habitats and life support systems are critical:

- **Closed-Loop Life Support Systems:** These systems aim to recycle air, water, and waste, minimizing the need for resupply missions. NASA's Veggie experiment aboard the International Space Station (ISS) explores growing food in space, demonstrating the potential for sustainable life support.

- **Modular Habitats:** Companies like Bigelow Aerospace are developing expandable habitats that can be deployed in space, providing living and working spaces for astronauts. These habitats can be tailored to specific mission needs, enhancing flexibility.

- **In-Situ Resource Utilization (ISRU):** Technologies that enable the use of local resources for sustaining human life are being explored. For example, NASA's Artemis program plans to utilize lunar ice for producing water and oxygen, supporting long-term lunar missions.

1.6. International Collaborations and Partnerships

The future of space exploration will increasingly rely on international collaborations, pooling resources and expertise:

- **International Space Station (ISS):** The ISS serves as a model for international cooperation in space, involving multiple space agencies and private partners. Its success demonstrates the benefits of shared knowledge and resources.

- **Global Partnerships:** Initiatives like the Lunar Gateway, which involves collaboration between NASA, ESA, JAXA, and other space agencies, highlight the importance of partnerships in advancing space exploration.

- **Public-Private Partnerships:** Collaborations between governments and private companies are fostering innovation. For instance, NASA's Commercial Crew Program has partnered with SpaceX and Boeing to develop crew transportation systems, accelerating access to the ISS.

Conclusion

The innovations on the horizon in the space industry are not only exciting but also essential for overcoming the challenges of future exploration. As advanced propulsion systems, reusable launch vehicles, small satellites, artificial intelligence, space habitats, and international collaborations emerge, they will collectively reshape our approach to space missions. The potential for new discoveries, enhanced capabilities, and sustainable practices will pave the way for humanity's continued exploration of the cosmos.

2. The Role of Space in Sustainable Development

The intersection of space exploration and sustainable development represents a crucial frontier for both scientific advancement and the enhancement of life on Earth. As the global community faces significant challenges—such as climate change, resource depletion, and food security—the role of space technologies in promoting sustainable development has become increasingly prominent. This section explores how space capabilities can contribute to sustainable development goals (SDGs), focusing on applications in Earth observation, satellite communications, and technological innovations. By leveraging the unique vantage point of space, we can address pressing challenges and foster a more sustainable future.

2.1. Earth Observation and Monitoring

Earth observation (EO) satellites play a pivotal role in sustainable development by providing critical data for environmental monitoring, resource management, and disaster response.

- **Climate Change Monitoring:** EO satellites, such as NASA's Landsat program, have been instrumental in tracking changes in land use, deforestation, and greenhouse gas emissions. For instance, the Sentinel-2 satellites of the European Space Agency (ESA) provide high-resolution imagery that helps monitor vegetation health and assess the impact of climate change on ecosystems.

- **Disaster Management:** Satellites facilitate rapid assessments during natural disasters, such as hurricanes, floods, and wildfires. The use of remote sensing data enables emergency responders to identify affected areas and coordinate relief efforts more effectively. For example, the United Nations Office for Outer Space Affairs (UNOOSA) utilizes satellite data to support disaster risk reduction initiatives globally.

- **Water Resources Management:** Satellites equipped with radar and optical sensors monitor water bodies, providing vital information on water quality and availability. The GRACE (Gravity Recovery and Climate Experiment) mission, for example, tracks changes in groundwater and surface water, aiding in sustainable water resource management.

2.2. Satellite Communications and Connectivity

Satellite communication technologies enhance global connectivity, bridging the digital divide and supporting various sectors crucial for sustainable development.

- **Telecommunication Services:** Satellites provide essential communication services to remote and underserved regions, enabling access to education, healthcare, and information. For instance, the OneWeb project aims to deploy a constellation of low Earth orbit (LEO) satellites to provide high-speed internet access to rural communities, enhancing educational opportunities and economic development.

- **Disaster Communication:** During emergencies, terrestrial communication networks may fail. Satellites offer reliable communication channels for first responders and humanitarian organizations. The Inmarsat network, for instance, provides satellite communication services to aid agencies during disaster recovery efforts.

- **Telemedicine and Distance Learning:** Satellite technology facilitates telemedicine and online education in remote areas. Programs leveraging satellite communications enable healthcare providers to deliver services to isolated communities and allow students to access quality education, regardless of their geographical location.

2.3. Technological Innovations for Sustainability

Innovations driven by space technologies contribute significantly to sustainable practices in various sectors.

- **Agriculture and Food Security:** Satellite imagery helps monitor crop health, predict yields, and optimize agricultural practices. The Global Agricultural Monitoring initiative utilizes satellite data to assess food production, enabling timely interventions to prevent food shortages and improve food security.

- **Renewable Energy Development:** Satellite data assists in identifying optimal locations for renewable energy projects, such as solar farms and wind turbines. For example, NASA's Surface Meteorology and Solar Energy (SSE) project provides solar radiation data to support the development of solar energy initiatives worldwide.

- **Urban Planning and Development:** Remote sensing technology informs urban planners about land use changes, population density, and infrastructure development. By analyzing satellite imagery, cities can develop more sustainable urban policies, improve transportation systems, and enhance the quality of life for residents.

2.4. International Cooperation and Capacity Building

The role of space in sustainable development extends beyond national efforts; it necessitates international collaboration and capacity building.

- **Global Partnerships:** Initiatives like the Group on Earth Observations (GEO) promote international collaboration in EO data sharing and capacity building. By fostering partnerships between countries, organizations can enhance their capabilities to utilize satellite data for sustainable development.

- **Capacity Building in Developing Countries:** Programs aimed at building capacity in developing nations empower them to leverage space technologies for sustainable development. The United Nations Office for Outer Space Affairs (UNOOSA) offers training and resources to support the integration of space applications into national development strategies.

- **Collaborative Research and Innovation:** Joint research projects involving multiple countries can lead to innovative solutions for sustainability challenges. For example, the European Space Agency's Copernicus program collaborates with various nations to provide data for environmental monitoring and climate action.

2.5. Addressing Challenges and Ensuring Sustainability

While space technologies offer immense potential for sustainable development, certain challenges must be addressed to maximize their benefits.

- **Space Debris:** The increasing number of satellites raises concerns about space debris, which poses risks to operational satellites and future missions. Sustainable practices in satellite design, launch, and end-of-life disposal are essential to mitigate this issue.

- **Equitable Access:** Ensuring equitable access to space technologies and data is crucial for fostering sustainable development worldwide. Efforts must be made to support developing countries in accessing satellite data and technologies to address their unique challenges.

- **Policy and Regulation:** Effective governance frameworks are needed to guide the use of space technologies in support of sustainable development. Policymakers must consider the environmental, social, and economic implications of space activities to ensure alignment with sustainability goals.

Conclusion

The role of space in sustainable development is multifaceted, encompassing Earth observation, satellite communications, technological innovations, international collaboration, and addressing challenges. By harnessing space capabilities, we can enhance our understanding of environmental changes, improve connectivity, and develop innovative solutions to pressing global challenges. As we continue to explore the cosmos, the potential for space technologies to contribute to a sustainable future for all becomes increasingly apparent, highlighting the importance of integrated efforts in this vital area.

3. Predictions for the Future of Space Exploration

As we advance further into the 21st century, the landscape of space exploration is poised for transformative change. Technological advancements, increased international collaboration, and growing interest from the private sector are converging to create a vibrant and dynamic environment for space activities. This chapter delves into predictions for the future of space exploration, highlighting key areas of growth, emerging technologies, and potential challenges. By examining trends and anticipated developments, we aim to provide a comprehensive overview of what the next era of space exploration may entail.

3.1. Expanding Human Presence in Space

One of the most significant predictions for the future of space exploration is the expansion of human presence beyond Earth. This includes both short-term missions and long-term habitation.

- **Moon Missions:** NASA's Artemis program aims to return humans to the Moon by the mid-2020s, with the goal of establishing a sustainable human presence. This initiative not only involves crewed missions but also focuses on building lunar infrastructure. The Lunar Gateway, a planned space station in orbit around the Moon, will serve as a staging point for future missions to Mars and beyond.

- **Mars Exploration:** Following the Moon, Mars is the next target for human exploration. NASA plans to send astronauts to Mars in the 2030s. SpaceX's Starship is also being developed with the intention of transporting humans to Mars, potentially enabling the first permanent human settlement on the planet. Such missions will require advancements in life support systems, radiation protection, and sustainable living conditions.

3.2. Advancements in Technology and Infrastructure

Technological innovations will play a critical role in shaping the future of space exploration.

- **Reusable Launch Systems:** The development of reusable rockets, as demonstrated by SpaceX's Falcon 9 and Blue Origin's New Shepard, is revolutionizing space transportation. These advancements reduce the cost of access to space and increase the frequency of launches, making space more accessible to a wider range of organizations and countries.

- **In-Situ Resource Utilization (ISRU):** To support long-term missions on the Moon and Mars, ISRU technologies will be essential. This includes extracting water from lunar ice or Martian soil and producing oxygen and fuel from local resources. For instance, NASA's Perseverance rover is testing methods to extract oxygen from the Martian atmosphere, paving the way for future human missions.

- **Autonomous Systems and Robotics:** The use of autonomous systems and advanced robotics will be crucial for exploring distant planets and asteroids. Robotic missions, such as the Mars Sample Return mission and asteroid mining initiatives, will help gather valuable data and resources before human explorers arrive.

3.3. International Collaboration and Partnerships

The future of space exploration will likely be characterized by increased international collaboration and partnerships.

- **Global Space Governance:** As more nations and private entities participate in space activities, establishing a framework for cooperation will be essential. Collaborative efforts, such as the International Space Station (ISS) program, demonstrate the potential for joint missions that leverage diverse capabilities and resources.

- **Joint Missions:** Upcoming missions, such as the Lunar Gateway project, will involve multiple space agencies, including NASA, ESA, JAXA (Japan Aerospace Exploration Agency), and CSA (Canadian Space Agency). Such partnerships enable shared expertise, reduce costs, and enhance mission success.

- **Commercial Partnerships:** The rise of private space companies, such as SpaceX, Blue Origin, and Virgin Galactic, will lead to new business models and collaboration opportunities. These companies are not only providing launch services but are also developing technologies for lunar and Martian exploration.

3.4. Addressing Ethical and Environmental Concerns

As space exploration progresses, ethical and environmental considerations will become increasingly important.

- **Space Debris Management:** The proliferation of satellites and space missions raises concerns about space debris. Efforts to mitigate debris, such as developing technologies for active debris removal and enforcing responsible satellite design, will be crucial to ensure the sustainability of space activities.

- **Planetary Protection:** Ensuring that exploration missions do not contaminate other celestial bodies is essential for preserving their scientific integrity. Future missions must adhere to planetary protection protocols, which are designed to prevent biological contamination.

- **Equitable Access to Space:** The increasing commercialization of space raises questions about equitable access to resources and opportunities. Ensuring that all nations, especially developing countries, can benefit from space exploration will require proactive policies and international cooperation.

3.5. Educational and Societal Impact

The future of space exploration will have profound implications for education and society as a whole.

- **STEM Education and Workforce Development:** As the space industry grows, there will be an increasing demand for a skilled workforce in science, technology, engineering, and mathematics (STEM) fields. Educational programs focusing on space science and engineering will be vital for preparing the next generation of innovators and explorers.

- **Public Engagement and Inspiration:** Space exploration has the power to inspire and engage the public, fostering a sense of global unity. Initiatives that promote public understanding of space science, such as virtual reality experiences and live broadcasts of missions, will enhance public interest and support for space activities.

- **Cultural and Philosophical Implications:** As humanity ventures further into space, it will raise philosophical questions about our place in the universe. Concepts such as planetary stewardship, interplanetary ethics, and the potential for extraterrestrial life will shape our understanding of humanity's role beyond Earth.

Conclusion

The future of space exploration is rich with possibilities, driven by technological advancements, international collaboration, and a commitment to sustainability. As we set our sights on the Moon, Mars, and beyond, the challenges and opportunities that lie ahead will require innovative thinking, ethical considerations, and a collective effort from governments, private entities, and the global community. By embracing these trends, we can pave the way for a new era of exploration that not only expands our understanding of the cosmos but also enhances life on Earth.

4. The Impact of Artificial Intelligence in Space

Artificial Intelligence (AI) has emerged as a transformative technology across numerous sectors, and space exploration is no exception. The application of AI in space activities not only enhances the efficiency and capabilities of missions but also opens up new avenues for exploration and research. As we venture deeper into the cosmos, AI will play a pivotal role in data analysis, autonomous systems, mission planning, and even planetary exploration. This chapter examines the impact of AI in space, highlighting its current applications, potential future developments, and the challenges that lie ahead.

4.1. Enhancing Data Analysis

The vast amounts of data generated from space missions present both an opportunity and a challenge. AI offers powerful tools for data analysis that can significantly enhance our ability to interpret this information.

- **Image Recognition and Processing:** AI algorithms are being used to process images captured by satellites and space probes. For instance, the Mars Reconnaissance Orbiter utilizes machine learning techniques to identify geological features on Mars.

This enables scientists to focus on areas of interest more efficiently, expediting the analysis process.

- **Big Data Analytics:** With the advent of satellite constellations like Planet Labs' Doves, which capture daily images of the Earth, the volume of data has skyrocketed. AI tools can analyze these massive datasets to monitor environmental changes, assess urban development, and even predict natural disasters. For example, AI has been employed to analyze satellite imagery for deforestation tracking and disaster response.

- **Scientific Research:** AI assists in identifying patterns within complex datasets, leading to new scientific discoveries. The European Space Agency (ESA) has employed AI in astrophysical research, helping to classify celestial objects and interpret data from missions like the Gaia spacecraft.

4.2. Autonomous Systems and Robotics

AI is a driving force behind the development of autonomous systems and robotics in space exploration, enabling missions that are safer, more efficient, and capable of operating in environments hazardous to humans.

- **Autonomous Navigation:** AI-based navigation systems allow spacecraft to make real-time decisions, improving their ability to maneuver in space. The Mars 2020 Perseverance rover is equipped with AI algorithms that help it navigate the Martian terrain autonomously, allowing it to identify and avoid obstacles without human intervention.

- **Robotic Exploration:** AI-driven robots are essential for exploring environments that are difficult or dangerous for humans. For example, NASA's Artemis program will utilize autonomous lunar rovers to conduct scientific investigations and construct habitats on the Moon's surface.

- **Spacecraft Operations:** AI can optimize spacecraft operations, from managing onboard systems to scheduling scientific experiments. AI algorithms can predict equipment failures, enabling proactive maintenance that increases mission longevity and reliability.

4.3. Mission Planning and Optimization

AI contributes significantly to mission planning, enabling efficient resource allocation and strategic decision-making.

- **Optimizing Trajectories:** AI algorithms can analyze complex gravitational interactions and orbital mechanics to determine the most efficient trajectories for spacecraft. This capability can reduce fuel consumption and mission duration, resulting in cost savings. For instance, the Dawn spacecraft utilized AI to optimize its trajectory while exploring the asteroid belt.

- **Resource Management:** In long-duration missions, such as those planned for Mars, AI can assist in managing limited resources, including energy, water, and food. AI systems can analyze consumption patterns and suggest adjustments to ensure mission sustainability.

- **Simulation and Modeling:** AI-powered simulations allow mission planners to test various scenarios and outcomes. This predictive capability can enhance decision-making processes, reducing the risks associated with launching complex missions.

4.4. AI in Earth Observation

The application of AI in Earth observation has profound implications for monitoring our planet's health and addressing global challenges.

- **Environmental Monitoring:** AI enhances the capabilities of Earth observation satellites by enabling the analysis of environmental changes, such as climate change and deforestation. For example, Google Earth Engine employs AI to analyze satellite imagery for environmental monitoring, providing insights into land use changes and vegetation health.

- **Disaster Response:** AI systems can analyze satellite data to assess the impact of natural disasters, enabling quicker response efforts. During events like hurricanes or wildfires, AI can help identify affected areas and optimize resource allocation for relief efforts.

- **Urban Planning:** AI can support smart city initiatives by analyzing data from satellites and urban sensors. This information can help city planners make informed decisions regarding infrastructure development, traffic management, and sustainability.

4.5. Challenges and Considerations

Despite the many benefits of AI in space exploration, several challenges must be addressed to ensure its successful integration.

- **Data Quality and Bias:** AI algorithms are only as good as the data they are trained on. Ensuring high-quality, unbiased datasets is essential to avoid erroneous conclusions and decisions. This is particularly critical in sensitive applications such as disaster response and environmental monitoring.

- **Security and Privacy:** As AI systems become more integrated into space missions and Earth observation, issues of security and privacy arise. Protecting sensitive data from cyber threats and ensuring ethical use of AI in monitoring populations is a growing concern.

- **Reliability and Trust:** For autonomous systems, establishing trust in AI decisions is vital. Space agencies must ensure that AI algorithms are thoroughly tested and validated to mitigate risks associated with autonomous operations.

- **Regulatory and Ethical Considerations:** The rapid advancement of AI in space poses regulatory challenges. Developing guidelines and ethical standards for AI applications in space exploration is necessary to ensure responsible usage.

Conclusion

Artificial Intelligence is set to revolutionize space exploration, enhancing data analysis, enabling autonomous systems, and optimizing mission planning. As we look toward the future, the integration of AI will enable more efficient, safe, and sustainable space activities. However, addressing the challenges of data quality, security, and ethical considerations will be critical for maximizing the potential of AI in space. By leveraging AI's capabilities, humanity can unlock new frontiers in our quest to explore and understand the universe.

5. Space Colonization: Possibilities and Challenges

Space colonization represents one of the most ambitious and potentially transformative goals for humanity. As we look beyond our home planet, the prospect of establishing permanent settlements on other celestial bodies, particularly the Moon and Mars, becomes increasingly feasible. This chapter explores the possibilities and challenges associated with space colonization, examining the technological, social, economic, and ethical considerations involved. Through examples from current research and missions, we can better understand the potential pathways and obstacles that lie ahead in humanity's quest to become an interplanetary species.

5.1. The Vision of Space Colonization

The concept of space colonization involves creating self-sustaining human habitats on other planets or moons. This vision is driven by several factors:

- **Survival of Humanity:** One of the primary motivations for colonization is the long-term survival of humanity. Earth faces numerous challenges, including climate change, resource depletion, and potential catastrophic events (e.g., asteroid impacts). Establishing colonies on other celestial bodies could serve as a backup for human civilization.

- **Scientific Exploration:** Colonization would provide unique opportunities for scientific research and exploration. Settlements on the Moon or Mars could enable in-depth studies of planetary geology, astrobiology, and the potential for life beyond Earth.

- **Technological Advancement:** The challenges of colonization would drive technological innovation. Developing life support systems, sustainable energy sources, and advanced transportation methods would have far-reaching implications, not only for space exploration but also for improving life on Earth.

5.2. Potential Locations for Colonization

Several celestial bodies have been identified as potential candidates for human colonization:

- **The Moon:** The Moon is often viewed as the first step toward colonization due to its proximity to Earth. NASA's Artemis program aims to establish a sustainable human presence on the Moon by the end of the decade. The Moon's resources, including water ice at the poles, could support life and fuel further space exploration.

- **Mars:** Mars is considered the most viable candidate for colonization due to its similarities to Earth, such as a day length close to 24 hours and evidence of past water. Missions like SpaceX's Starship aim to send humans to Mars by the 2030s, with the long-term goal of establishing a permanent settlement.

- **Asteroids and Moons of Gas Giants:** While the Moon and Mars are the primary targets, asteroids and the moons of gas giants (like Europa and Titan) present intriguing possibilities for colonization and resource extraction. These bodies may harbor valuable materials and unique environments for scientific research.

5.3. Technological Challenges

The technological hurdles associated with space colonization are significant and multifaceted:

- **Life Support Systems:** Ensuring the survival of humans in hostile environments requires advanced life support systems. These systems must provide air, water, food, and waste management, all while being robust and sustainable.

- **Transportation:** Developing reliable transportation systems to ferry people and goods between Earth and colonies is crucial. Spacecraft must be capable of multiple missions, carrying both passengers and cargo safely.

- **Habitat Construction:** Building habitats that can withstand harsh conditions, such as radiation, extreme temperatures, and micrometeorite impacts, is a fundamental challenge. Innovations in materials science and construction techniques are essential for creating safe living environments.

- **Energy Generation:** Sustainable energy sources are vital for any colony. Solutions may include solar power, nuclear energy, or even innovative technologies like in-situ resource utilization (ISRU) to extract and utilize local materials.

5.4. Social and Economic Considerations

Successful space colonization requires addressing various social and economic factors:

- **Governance and Law:** Establishing governance structures for colonies is critical. International cooperation and the development of space law will be essential to prevent conflicts over resources and ensure peaceful coexistence.

- **Economic Viability:** For colonies to be sustainable, they must have economic models that support themselves. This could involve mining resources, scientific research, tourism, or manufacturing unique products.

- **Social Dynamics:** The social structure of a colony will need to be carefully considered. Issues of community, governance, and cultural identity will be central to creating a harmonious and productive environment.

5.5. Ethical Considerations

The ethics of space colonization raise important questions that must be addressed:

- **Planetary Protection:** As we explore other celestial bodies, we must consider the impact on existing ecosystems, if they exist. Ensuring that we do not contaminate other worlds or harm potential extraterrestrial life is a fundamental ethical concern.

- **Equity and Accessibility:** As space colonization becomes a possibility, it is essential to ensure that access to these new frontiers is equitable. The benefits of colonization should not be limited to a select few but should be shared with all of humanity.

- **Cultural Heritage:** The potential for colonization raises questions about the cultural implications of establishing human presence on other worlds. How will we preserve cultural identities in space, and how will new cultures form in extraterrestrial environments?

5.6. Current Initiatives and Future Outlook

Various organizations and space agencies are actively pursuing research and missions that lay the groundwork for space colonization:

- **NASA's Artemis Program:** This program aims to land humans on the Moon by 2024 and establish a sustainable presence by 2028. It serves as a stepping stone for future Mars missions.

- **SpaceX:** With its Starship program, SpaceX is developing the technology necessary for interplanetary travel. Elon Musk's vision of establishing a self-sustaining city on Mars has captured the imagination of the public and the scientific community alike.

- **International Collaboration:** Collaborative efforts among countries, such as the International Space

Station (ISS), provide valuable experience in living and working in space. These partnerships will be crucial for future colonization efforts.

Conclusion

Space colonization presents both remarkable possibilities and significant challenges. As we explore the Moon, Mars, and beyond, humanity stands on the brink of a new era of exploration and discovery. The technological innovations, social structures, and ethical considerations will shape our path forward. While the dream of establishing a human presence beyond Earth is ambitious, it is also a testament to our resilience and creativity as a species. By addressing the challenges head-on and fostering international cooperation, we can unlock the potential of space colonization and secure a future for humanity among the stars.

Conclusion

- Summary of Key Insights

- The Importance of Collaboration in Space Exploration

- Call to Action for Industry Stakeholders

Conclusion

The exploration of space has captivated humanity for decades, driving advancements in technology, science, and our understanding of the universe. In this book, "Exploring the Space Industry: Innovations, Challenges, and Future Trends," we have journeyed through the history, technology, applications, and current dynamics of the space industry, uncovering the remarkable achievements and hurdles that shape its future.

Summary of Key Insights

Throughout the chapters, we have highlighted several key insights into the space industry:

- **Historical Milestones:** The evolution of space exploration, from early developments in rocket technology to the pivotal moments of the Space Race, showcases humanity's relentless pursuit of knowledge and innovation. The establishment of governmental space agencies and the rise of commercial enterprises have transformed the landscape, leading to unprecedented collaborations and achievements.

- **Diverse Space Industries:** The space industry is multifaceted, encompassing government agencies, private enterprises, and a range of applications—from telecommunications to scientific research. Understanding the distinct roles of these entities is crucial for navigating the complexities of space exploration.

- **Technological Advancements:** Innovations in propulsion systems, satellite technology, and robotics are driving the industry forward. Emerging technologies such as space mining and habitat construction are opening new frontiers for exploration and exploitation of extraterrestrial resources.

- **Economic Impact:** The space sector contributes significantly to the global economy, with growth trends indicating an expanding market. However, economic barriers and funding challenges continue to pose risks to investment and development.

- **Regulatory and Ethical Considerations:** Navigating the legal and ethical landscape of space exploration is essential for sustainable and responsible practices. International treaties and national regulations must evolve to address the challenges posed by expanding human activity in space.

- **Challenges and Opportunities:** The technical, economic, and social challenges facing the space industry require innovative solutions and collaborative efforts. Public perception and support play a vital role in fostering an environment conducive to exploration and investment.

- **Future Trends:** Looking ahead, the potential for innovations, sustainable development, and the colonization of other celestial bodies presents exciting possibilities. The integration of artificial intelligence in space operations may revolutionize missions, making them more efficient and effective.

The Importance of Collaboration in Space Exploration

One of the most important themes emerging from this exploration is the significance of collaboration. The complexity of space missions necessitates cooperation between nations, agencies, and private companies. By pooling resources, expertise, and technologies, stakeholders can tackle challenges more effectively and accelerate progress. International partnerships, such as those exemplified by the International Space Station (ISS), demonstrate the power of collaborative efforts to advance scientific research and exploration.

Call to Action for Industry Stakeholders

As we stand on the brink of a new era in space exploration, it is essential for industry stakeholders— including government agencies, private companies, researchers, and policymakers—to come together to shape the future of the space industry.

- **Invest in Research and Development:** Increased investment in R&D is crucial for driving innovation and overcoming technological barriers. Funding initiatives that support emerging technologies will ensure that we remain at the forefront of space exploration.

- **Foster Public Engagement:** Building public interest and support for space initiatives is vital. Educational programs and outreach efforts can inspire the next generation of scientists, engineers, and explorers.

- **Establish Responsible Practices:** As we expand our presence in space, ethical considerations must guide our actions. Stakeholders should prioritize environmental sustainability, planetary protection, and equitable access to space resources.

- **Encourage International Cooperation:** The challenges of space exploration transcend national borders. By fostering international partnerships, we can share knowledge, resources, and expertise to achieve common goals and ensure that space remains a realm of discovery for all.

In conclusion, the future of the space industry is filled with promise and potential. By addressing the challenges and seizing the opportunities ahead, we can work together to explore the final frontier and expand the horizons of human knowledge. The journey is just beginning, and it is up to us to chart the course for generations to come.

References

References

1. Advanced Extremely High-Frequency (AEHF) Satellite Program, Lockheed Martin. https://www.lockheedmartin.com
2. Airbus - www.airbus.com
3. American Institute of Aeronautics and Astronautics (AIAA). (2022). *AIAA Workforce Development Programs*. Retrieved from AIAA
4. Arianespace - www.arianespace.com
5. Artemis Program - www.nasa.gov/artemisprogram
6. Astrobotic - www.astrobotic.com
7. Baird, J. (2019). "The Impact of Rocket Launches on the Environment." *Environmental Science and Technology*, 53(15), 8914-8920.
8. Berger, E. (2019). *Liftoff: Elon Musk and the Desperate Early Days That Launched SpaceX*. HarperCollins.
9. Black Girls Code. (2021). *Empowering Young Girls of Color in Technology*. Retrieved from Black Girls Code
10. Blue Origin - www.blueorigin.com
11. Blue Origin. (2021). "New Shepard: Suborbital Spaceflight." [Online] Available at: https://www.blueorigin.com/new-shepard
12. Blue Origin. (2021). *Our Mission*. Retrieved from https://www.blueorigin.com/
13. Blue Origin. (2021). *Our Story*. Link
14. Boeing - www.boeing.com
15. Brown, O. C. (2018). **CubeSat Handbook: From Mission Design to Operations**. Springer.
16. Canadian Space Agency. (2021). **Canadarm and Canadarm2**. Available at: https://www.asc-csa.gc.ca
17. CERN Space Research - home.cern/science/physics/space
18. Cernan, E. (2007). *The Last Man on the Moon: Astronaut Eugene Cernan and America's Race in Space*. HarperCollins.
19. **Chappell, M. (2021).** "Living in Space: Human Factors in Space Habitats." In *Human Factors in the Design and Evaluation of Medical Devices*. CRC Press.
20. China National Space Administration (CNSA) - www.cnsa.gov.cn
21. China National Space Administration (CNSA). (2021). *CNSA News Release*. Retrieved from Link

22. China Satellite Navigation Office. "BeiDou Navigation Satellite System." http://en.beidou.gov.cn/

23. Climate Change and Natural Disasters: Monitoring from Space. (2020). Journal of Earth Science, 15(3), 215-230.

24. CNSA. (2020). *China National Space Administration*. Retrieved from http://www.cnsa.gov.cn/

25. **Cohen, A., & Maggio, A. (2021).** "Building Space Habitats: Materials and Design Considerations." *Advances in Space Research*, 67(4), 1234-1242. doi:10.1016/j.asr.2020.12.001

26. ESA (2021). **Copernicus Programme**. Available at: https://www.esa.int/Applications/Observing_the_Earth/Copernicus

27. Euroconsult. (2020). *Satellite Communications and Broadcasting: Market Trends and Forecasts 2020-2025*. Retrieved from Link

28. European Space Agency (ESA) - www.esa.int

29. European Space Agency (ESA). "Galileo Overview." https://www.esa.int

30. European Space Agency (ESA). "Sentinel Satellites." https://www.esa.int/Applications/Observing_the_Earth/Copernicus/Sentinel-1

31. European Space Agency (ESA). (2020). "BepiColombo Mission." Retrieved from ESA.int.

32. European Space Agency (ESA). (2020). "ExoMars: Searching for Life on Mars." [Online] Available at: https://exploration.esa.int/web/mars

33. European Space Agency (ESA). (2020). *ESA Annual Report 2020*. Retrieved from Link

34. European Space Agency (ESA). (2021). "ExoMars: A Mission to Search for Life on Mars." https://www.esa.int

35. European Space Agency (ESA). (2021). "Lunar Gateway." Retrieved from ESA.int.

36. European Space Agency (ESA). (2021). "Sentinel-2: Satellite for Earth Monitoring." Retrieved from ESA.int.

37. European Space Agency (ESA). (2021). *ESA Annual Report 2020*. Retrieved from Link

38. European Space Agency (ESA). (2021). *Planetary Defence*. Retrieved from ESA Planetary Defence

39. **European Space Agency (ESA). (2022).** "Challenges of Living in Space: A Review of Current Research." ESA Technical Report. Retrieved from https://www.esa.int/

40. European Space Agency. (2019). *About ESA*. Retrieved from https://www.esa.int/

41. European Space Agency. (2020). "AI in Space: Harnessing the Power of Artificial Intelligence." Retrieved from ESA.int.

42. European Space Agency. (2020). *ESA Public Engagement Strategies*. Retrieved from ESA.

43. European Space Agency. (2020). *ESA Space Debris Mitigation Guidelines*. Retrieved from https://www.esa.int/Applications/Space_Safety/Space_Debris/Space_Debris_Mitigation_Guidelines

44. European Space Agency. (2020). *Space Debris Mitigation Guidelines*. Retrieved from https://www.esa.int/Applications/Space_Safety/Space_Debris/Space_Debris_Mitigation_Guidelines

45. European Space Agency. (2021). *Space Debris: A Threat to Space Operations*. Retrieved from https://www.esa.int/Space_Safety/Space_Debris

46. European Space Agency. (2021). *Voyager Missions Overview*. ESA. Retrieved from https://www.esa.int/voyager_missions

47. European Space Agency. (2022). *ESA Budget Overview 2022*. European Space Agency.

48. FAA. "Wide Area Augmentation System (WAAS)." https://www.faa.gov

49. FAA. (2022). "Commercial Space Transportation: Space Tourism Regulations." [Online] Available at: https://www.faa.gov

50. Federal Aviation Administration (FAA). (2020). *Commercial Space Transportation: Federal Aviation Administration*. Retrieved from Link

51. Federal Aviation Administration (FAA). (2021). *Commercial Space Transportation*. Retrieved from https://www.faa.gov/space/

52. Federal Aviation Administration. (2021). *Commercial Space Launch Competitiveness Act*. Retrieved from https://www.faa.gov/space/

53. FIRST Robotics. (2021). *About FIRST Robotics*. Retrieved from FIRST

54. Galaxy Zoo. (2021). *Participate in Science*. Retrieved from Galaxy Zoo

55. Genta, G. (2019). **Robotics in Space Exploration**. Springer.

56. Goddard, R. H. (1919). *A Method of Reaching Extreme Altitudes*. Smithsonian Miscellaneous Collections.

57. Goebel, D. M., & Katz, I. (2008). **Fundamentals of Electric Propulsion: Ion and Hall Thrusters**. JPL Space Science and Technology Series.

58. Google Earth Engine. (2021). "Earth Engine: Powering Global Change." Retrieved from EarthEngine.google.com.

59. Group on Earth Observations (GEO). (2021). "Global Earth Observation System of Systems." Retrieved from GEO-GEOSS.org.

60. Handberg, R. (2020). *International Space Commerce: Building from Scratch*. Routledge.

61. Heppenheimer, T. A. (2009). **Development of the Space Shuttle, 1972-1981**. Smithsonian Institution Press.

62. Hubble Space Telescope. (2021). "Hubble Space Telescope: Overview." [Online] Available at: https://hubblesite.org

63. Hubble Space Telescope. (2021). "Hubble's Legacy: 30 Years of Discovery." https://hubblesite.org

64. Hughes, S. (2018). "Ethical Dimensions of Space Exploration: The Case for Extraterrestrial Rights." *Astrobiology Journal*, 15(5), 467-482.

65. HughesNet. "Satellite Internet for Rural America." https://www.hughesnet.com/

66. Indian Space Research Organisation (ISRO) - www.isro.gov.in

67. Indian Space Research Organisation (ISRO). (2021). *ISRO News*. Retrieved from Link

68. **International Academy of Astronautics (IAA). (2019).** "Global Space Governance: Legal and Ethical Considerations." IAA. Retrieved from https://www.iaaweb.org/

69. International Space Station (ISS). (2021). *International Cooperation in the ISS Program*. Retrieved from ISS International Cooperation

70. International Space Station (ISS). (2021). *The ISS Program*. Retrieved from https://www.nasa.gov/mission_pages/station/main/index.html

71. International Space Station. (2021). "International Cooperation in Space." Retrieved from nasa.gov.

72. International Space Station. (2021). *The ISS Program*. Retrieved from https://www.nasa.gov/mission_pages/station/main/index.html

73. Iridium Communications. "Iridium's Role in Disaster Relief." https://www.iridium.com/

74. ISRO. (2019). *Annual Report 2018-2019*. Indian Space Research Organisation.

75. ISRO. (2021). *Indian Space Research Organisation*. Retrieved from https://www.isro.gov.in/

76. Japan Meteorological Agency. "Himawari-8: Monitoring Asia-Pacific Weather." https://www.jma.go.jp/jma/indexe.html

77. JAXA. (2010). **IKAROS Solar Sail Technology**. Japan Aerospace Exploration Agency.

78. Johnson, C. (2018). *The Impact of Social Media on Public Perception of NASA*. Journal of Space Policy, 45(2), 123-134.

79. **Kanas, N., & Manzey, D. (2003).** "Space Psychology and Human Factors." New York: Springer.

80. Kaplan, C. H., & Kruse, A. (2020). *Space Warfare in the 21st Century: Arming the Heavens*. Routledge.

81. Kaplan, E. D., & Hegarty, C. J. (2005). *Understanding GPS: Principles and Applications* (2nd ed.). Artech House.

82. Kaplan, M. H. (2020). *Spacecraft Structures and Mechanisms*. American Institute of Aeronautics and Astronautics.

83. **Kramer, B., & Lichtenstein, M. (2017).** "Engineering for Space: Sustainable Habitat Design." *Journal of Spacecraft and Rockets*, 54(1), 223-234. doi:10.2514/1.A34000

84. Launius, R. D. (2009). *NASA's Apollo Program: The Legacy of Public Support*. In *Space Policy and the Role of the American Public*.

85. Lewis, C.S. (1955). *Out of the Silent Planet*. New York: Scribner.

86. Lillesand, T., Kiefer, R. W., & Chipman, J. (2020). **Remote Sensing and Image Interpretation**. 7th ed. John Wiley & Sons.

87. Logsdon, J. M. (2010). *John F. Kennedy and the Race to the Moon*. Palgrave Macmillan.

88. Logsdon, J. M. (2015). *John F. Kennedy and the Race to the Moon*. Palgrave Macmillan.

89. Made In Space - www.madeinspace.us

90. Maral, G., & Bousquet, M. (2009). **Satellite Communications Systems: Systems, Techniques and Technology** (5th ed.). Wiley.

91. McDougall, W. A. (1985). *...The Heavens and the Earth: A Political History of the Space Age.* Basic Books.

92. McMillan, A. (2021). "The Ethics of Space Exploration: A Guide to the Debate." *Space Policy Review*, 12(3), 45-67.

93. Mettler, E. (2020). **Artificial Intelligence and Machine Learning in Space Missions**. Space Science Reviews, 216(5), 123-145.

94. **Miele, E., & Pellicciari, M. (2021).** "Isolation in Space: Effects on Psychological Well-Being." *Frontiers in Psychology*, 12, 1000. doi:10.3389/fpsyg.2021.1000

95. Moltz, J. C. (2019). *The Politics of Space Security: Strategic Restraint and the Pursuit of National Interests* (2nd ed.). Stanford University Press.

96. Mountrakis, G. & Im, J. (2019). **Recent Advances in Remote Sensing for Agriculture and Environmental Monitoring**. Remote Sensing, 11(23), 2786.

97. Musk, E. (2020). "Making Life Multiplanetary." Retrieved from SpaceX.com.

98. NASA (2020). **Landsat Missions**. Available at: https://landsat.gsfc.nasa.gov

99. NASA Commercial Crew Program - www.nasa.gov/commercialcrew

100. NASA Commercial Crew Program - www.nasa.gov/commercialcrew

101. NASA. "Aqua Satellite and Global Climate Monitoring." https://www.nasa.gov/

102. NASA. (2010). *NASA's Constellation Program: A Review of the Technical Challenges and Costs*. National Aeronautics and Space Administration.

103. **NASA. (2019).** "The Commercial Crew Program." NASA. Retrieved from https://www.nasa.gov/commercialcrew

104. NASA. (2020). "Commercial Crew Program." [Online] Available at: https://www.nasa.gov/commercialcrew

105. **NASA. (2020).** "Microgravity and Its Effects on Human Health." NASA Human Research Program. Retrieved from https://www.nasa.gov/

106. NASA. (2020). "The James Webb Space Telescope." [Online] Available at: https://www.jwst.nasa.gov

107. NASA. (2020). *Artemis Program.* Retrieved from https://www.nasa.gov/specials/artemis/

108. NASA. (2020). *Artemis: Return to the Moon.* National Aeronautics and Space Administration. Retrieved from NASA Artemis

109. NASA. (2020). *Mars 2020 Perseverance Rover.* Retrieved from Link

110. NASA. (2020). *NASA Budget Proposal for FY 2021.* Link

111. NASA. (2020). *NASA Budget Proposal for FY 2021.* Retrieved from Link

112. NASA. (2020). *NASA Workforce Report 2020.* Retrieved from Link

113. NASA. (2020). *Spacecraft Systems and Technology.* NASA Technical Reports.

114. NASA. (2021). "Artemis: A New Era of Moon Exploration." Retrieved from nasa.gov.

115. NASA. (2021). "Landsat: The Satellite That Changed the World." Retrieved from NASA.gov.

116. NASA. (2021). "NASA's Perseverance Rover: Mission Overview." [Online] Available at: https://mars.nasa.gov/perseverance

117. NASA. (2021). "Perseverance Rover: The First AI Rover on Mars." Retrieved from NASA.gov.

118. NASA. (2021). "Space Launch System (SLS)." [Online] Available at: https://www.nasa.gov/exploration/systems/sls/index.html

119. NASA. (2021). *Commercial Crew Program.* National Aeronautics and Space Administration. Retrieved from NASA Commercial Crew

120. NASA. (2021). *History of NASA.* Retrieved from https://www.nasa.gov/history

121. NASA. (2021). *Mars 2020 Mission Overview.* Retrieved from https://mars.nasa.gov/mars2020/

122. NASA. (2021). *NASA Education Programs.* National Aeronautics and Space Administration. Retrieved from NASA Education

123. NASA. (2021). *The Apollo Program*. NASA. Retrieved from
https://www.nasa.gov/apollo/

124. NASA. (2021). *The History of Space Exploration*. NASA.
Retrieved from https://www.nasa.gov/topics/history/

125. NASA. (2021). *The Journey to Mars: A New Era of
Exploration*. National Aeronautics and Space Administration.

126. NASA. (2022). "CubeSat Launch Initiative." [Online] Available
at: https://www.nasa.gov/content/cubesat-launch-initiative

127. NASA. (2022). **Mars Exploration Rovers: Spirit and
Opportunity**. Available at: https://mars.nasa.gov

128. NASA. (2023). **NASA's Advanced Propulsion Concepts**.
Available at: https://www.nasa.gov

129. National Aeronautics and Space Administration (NASA).
(2019). "Nuclear Thermal Propulsion." Retrieved from
NASA.gov.

130. National Aeronautics and Space Administration (NASA).
(2020). "The Apollo Program." [Online] Available at:
https://www.nasa.gov/mission_pages/apollo/index.html

131. National Aeronautics and Space Administration (NASA).
(2020). *Artemis Program Overview*. Retrieved from Link

132. National Aeronautics and Space Administration (NASA).
(2021). "Artemis: Our Moon to Mars Exploration Program."
Retrieved from NASA.gov.

133. National Aeronautics and Space Administration (NASA).
(2021). "Mars Missions." [Online] Available at:
https://mars.nasa.gov/mars-exploration/missions

134. National Aeronautics and Space Administration (NASA).
(2021). *Artemis Program Overview*. Retrieved from Link

135. National Aeronautics and Space Administration (NASA).
(2021). *NASA's Open Data*. Retrieved from NASA Open Data

136. National Aeronautics and Space Administration (NASA).
(2022). "The International Space Station: A New Era of Space
Exploration." https://www.nasa.gov

137. National Aeronautics and Space Administration. (2020).
Commercial Crew Program Overview. Retrieved from
https://www.nasa.gov/commercialcrew

138. National Aeronautics and Space Administration. (2020).
Planetary Protection Policy. Retrieved from

https://www.nasa.gov/sites/default/files/atoms/files/nasa_planetary_protection_policy.pdf

139. National Aeronautics and Space Administration. (2021). "AI and Robotics in Space Exploration." Retrieved from NASA.gov.

140. National Aeronautics and Space Administration. (2021). "The Moon: Gateway to the Universe." Retrieved from nasa.gov.

141. National Aeronautics and Space Administration. (2021). *NASA's Debris Mitigation Standard Practices*. Retrieved from https://www.nasa.gov/sites/default/files/atoms/files/nasa_debris_mitigation_standard_practices.pdf

142. National Oceanic and Atmospheric Administration (NOAA). "Geostationary Operational Environmental Satellites (GOES)." https://www.noaa.gov/

143. National Research Council. (2011). *Vision and Voyages for Planetary Science in the Decade 2013–2022*. The National Academies Press.

144. National Research Council. (2020). "Space Debris: A Challenge for Human Spaceflight." Retrieved from NationalAcademies.org.

145. National Science Foundation (NSF). (2019). "Microgravity Research: Advances in Scientific Discovery." https://www.nsf.gov

146. National Science Foundation. (2020). *Women, Minorities, and Persons with Disabilities in Science and Engineering*. NSF Report.

147. Neufeld, M. J. (2007). *Von Braun: Dreamer of Space, Engineer of War*. Vintage.

148. NOAA. (2021). **GOES-R Series: Advanced Weather Satellites**. Available at: https://www.noaa.gov

149. OECD. (2021). *The Space Economy in Figures: How Space Contributes to the Global Economy*. OECD Publishing.

150. OECD. (2021). *The Space Economy in Figures: How Space Contributes to the Global Economy*. OECD Publishing.

151. OneWeb - www.oneweb.world

152. OneWeb. (2021). "Bringing Connectivity to Everyone, Everywhere." Retrieved from OneWeb.net.

153. Peeters, W. (2010). *Space Tourism: The New Paradigm of Commercial Astronautics*. Space Policy.

154. Pelton, J. N. (2017). **Satellite Communications** (4th ed.). Springer.
155. Planet Labs - www.planet.com
156. Planet Labs. (2020). "PlanetScope Satellite Imagery." Retrieved from Planet.com.
157. Planet Labs. (2021). "Daily Satellite Imagery for Earth Observation." Retrieved from Planet.com.
158. Planet Labs. (2021). *About Planet*. Link
159. Planet Labs. (2021). *Company Overview*. Retrieved from Link
160. Planetary Resources. (n.d.). *Asteroid Mining: The Next Frontier*. Retrieved from https://www.planetaryresources.com/
161. Reichstein, M. et al. (2019). **Deep Learning and Satellite Imagery: Unlocking Potential in Environmental Science**. Nature Reviews Earth & Environment, 1(7), 356-368.
162. Relativity Space - www.relativityspace.com
163. Rocket Lab - www.rocketlabusa.com
164. Rocket Lab. (2021). "Photon: End-to-End Satellite Solutions." [Online] Available at: https://www.rocketlabusa.com/
165. Rocket Lab. (2021). *About Us*. Retrieved from Link
166. Roscosmos - www.roscosmos.ru
167. Roscosmos. (2020). *The Russian Space Agency*. Retrieved from https://www.roscosmos.ru/
168. Russian Federal Space Agency (Roscosmos). "GLONASS." https://www.glonass-iac.ru/en/
169. Seedhouse, E. (2008). *Tourism in Space: The Next Frontier*. Springer-Praxis.
170. SES. "O3b Network." https://www.ses.com/our-coverage/o3b
171. Siddiqi, A. (2000). *Challenge to Apollo: The Soviet Union and the Space Race, 1945–1974*. NASA History Division.
172. Siddiqi, A. A. (2000). *Challenge to Apollo: The Soviet Union and the Space Race, 1945-1974*. NASA History Series.
173. Siegler, M. A. (2018). **Autonomous Systems in Space Exploration**. IEEE Transactions on Aerospace and Electronic Systems.
174. Smith, R. (2018). *Space Debris: A Time for Action*. Space Policy Institute.
175. Smithsonian National Air and Space Museum. (2020). *The Space Race*. Retrieved from https://airandspace.si.edu/explore/stories/space-race

176. Society of Women Engineers (SWE). (2021). *SWE Mentorship Programs*. Retrieved from SWE
177. Space Data Association. (2020). *Space Debris Mitigation*. Retrieved from https://www.space-data.org/
178. Space Foundation. (2021). *The Space Report 2021: The Authoritative Guide to Global Space Activity*. Link
179. Space Foundation. (2022). The Space Report 2022. Retrieved from www.spacefoundation.org
180. **Space Policy Institute. (2020).** "Economic Analysis of Space Habitats: Funding and Sustainability." *Space Policy*, 52, 205-212. doi:10.1016/j.spacepol.2020.101282
181. Space-Based Infrared System (SBIRS), U.S. Air Force. https://www.af.mil
182. SpaceX and Google Cloud Collaboration - cloud.google.com/blog/topics/partners/spacex-partnership
183. SpaceX. "Starlink: Mission to Connect the World." https://www.spacex.com/starlink
184. SpaceX. (2020). *Crew Dragon Mission Highlights*. SpaceX. Retrieved from https://www.spacex.com/crew-dragon/
185. SpaceX. (2020). *SpaceX Missions*. Retrieved from https://www.spacex.com/missions/
186. SpaceX. (2021). "Dragon: NASA's Commercial Resupply Services." [Online] Available at: https://www.spacex.com/launches/dragon
187. SpaceX. (2021). "Falcon 9 Launch System." Retrieved from SpaceX.com.
188. SpaceX. (2021). "Starship." Retrieved from SpaceX.com.
189. SpaceX. (2021). "Starship: The Next Generation of Space Travel." Retrieved from spacex.com.
190. SpaceX. (2021). *Falcon 9*. Retrieved from Link
191. SpaceX. (2021). *SpaceX Missions*. Retrieved from https://www.spacex.com/missions/
192. SpaceX. (2023). *Falcon 9: Reusable Launch System*. Retrieved from SpaceX.
193. SpaceX. (2023). *Funding and Investment in Space Exploration*. Retrieved from SpaceX.
194. SpaceX. (2023). **Starlink Satellite Constellation**. Available at: https://www.spacex.com

195. Sutton, G. P., & Biblarz, O. (2017). **Rocket Propulsion Elements** (9th ed.). John Wiley & Sons.
196. Swarm Technologies - www.swarm.space
197. The International Space Station - www.nasa.gov/mission_pages/station/main/index.html
198. The Planetary Society. (2020). "LightSail 2: A New Era of Solar Sailing." Retrieved from PlanetarySociety.org.
199. The World Bank. (2021). *The Economic Impact of the Space Sector*. Retrieved from Link
200. Tsiolkovsky, K. E. (1903). *Exploration of Outer Space by Means of Rocket Devices*.
201. U.S. Commercial Space Launch Competitiveness Act of 2015. (2015). https://www.congress.gov/bill/114th-congress/house-bill/2262
202. U.S. Department of Defense. (2021). "Military Use of Space-Based Cybersecurity." https://www.defense.gov
203. U.S. Department of Defense. (2021). *Defense Space Strategy*. Retrieved from Link
204. United Nations Committee on the Peaceful Uses of Outer Space (COPUOS). (2020). *Long-term Sustainability of Outer Space Activities*. Retrieved from https://www.unoosa.org/oosa/en/ourwork/copuos/lts.html
205. United Nations Committee on the Peaceful Uses of Outer Space (COPUOS). (2020). *Draft Principles on Space Resource Activities*. Retrieved from https://www.unoosa.org/oosa/en/ourwork/copuos/space-resources.html
206. United Nations Office for Outer Space Affairs (UNOOSA). (2021). *Space Law*. Retrieved from https://www.unoosa.org/oosa/en/ourwork/spacelaw/index.html
207. United Nations Office for Outer Space Affairs. (1967). *Outer Space Treaty*. Retrieved from https://www.unoosa.org/oosa/en/ourwork/spacelaw/treaties/outerspacetreaty.html
208. United Nations Office for Outer Space Affairs. (1967). *Outer Space Treaty*. Retrieved from https://www.unoosa.org/oosa/en/ourwork/spacelaw/treaties/outerspacetreaty.html

209. United Nations Office for Outer Space Affairs. (1968). *Rescue Agreement.* https://www.unoosa.org/oosa/en/ourwork/spacelaw/treaties/rescueagreement.html

210. United Nations Office for Outer Space Affairs. (1972). *Convention on International Liability for Damage Caused by Space Objects.* Retrieved from https://www.unoosa.org/oosa/en/ourwork/spacelaw/treaties/liabilityconvention.html

211. United Nations Office for Outer Space Affairs. (1972). *Liability Convention.* https://www.unoosa.org/oosa/en/ourwork/spacelaw/treaties/liabilityconvention.html

212. United Nations Office for Outer Space Affairs. (1976). *Convention on Registration of Objects Launched into Outer Space.* Retrieved from https://www.unoosa.org/oosa/en/ourwork/spacelaw/treaties/registrationconvention.html

213. United Nations Office for Outer Space Affairs. (1984). *Moon Agreement.* https://www.unoosa.org/oosa/en/ourwork/spacelaw/treaties/moonagreement.html

214. United Nations Office for Outer Space Affairs. (2021). *The Long-term Sustainability of Outer Space Activities.* Retrieved from https://www.unoosa.org/oosa/en/ourwork/copuos/lts.html

215. United States Department of Defense. "Global Positioning System (GPS)." https://www.gps.gov

216. Viasat. "Delivering Connectivity to the Most Remote Regions." https://www.viasat.com/

217. Virgin Galactic - www.virgingalactic.com

218. Virgin Galactic. (2021). "The Future of Space Tourism." [Online] Available at: https://www.virgingalactic.com

219. Virgin Galactic. (2021). *About Virgin Galactic.* Retrieved from https://www.virgingalactic.com/

220. Wall, M. (2020). "SpaceX's Historic NASA Mission." *Space.com.* Available at: https://www.space.com/spacex-historic-nasa-crew-launch

221. Wertz, J. R., & Larson, W. J. (1999). **Space Mission Analysis and Design**. Microcosm Press.

222. Wertz, J. R., Everett, D. F., & Puschell, J. J. (2011). *Space Mission Engineering: The New SMAD*. Microcosm Press.

223. Wertz, J. R., Everett, D. F., & Puschell, J. J. (2011). **Space Mission Engineering: The New SMAD**. Microcosm Press.

224. XPRIZE Foundation. (2019). *Public Engagement in Space Exploration: A Study of Motivations and Attitudes*. Retrieved from XPRIZE.

225. XPRIZE Foundation. (2021). *The Role of Prizes in Space Exploration Funding*. Retrieved from XPRIZE.

226. Zubrin, R. (2013). *The Case for Mars: The Plan to Settle the Red Planet and Why We Must*. New York: Free Press.

www.ingramcontent.com/pod-product-compliance
Lightning Source LLC
LaVergne TN
LVHW051427050326
832903LV00030BD/2949